ALBANIA: FROM ANARCHY TO BALKAN IDENTITY

D0921985

MIRANDA VICKERS
JAMES PETTIFER

Albania

From Anarchy to
a Balkan Identity

NEW YORK UNIVERSITY PRESS
Washington Square, New York

First published in the U.S.A. by
NEW YORK UNIVERSITY PRESS
Washington Square
New York, NY 10003
Printed in England

Library of Congress Cataloging-in Publication Data

Vickers, Miranda.
    Albania: from anarchy to a Balkan identity / Miranda Vickers, James Pettifer.
      p. cm.
    Updated version of 1997 ed.
    Includes bibliographical references and index.
    ISBN 0-8147-8805-X
    I. Albania -- Politics and government -- 1990- I. Pettifer, James. II. Title.

DR978.3 .V53 2000
949.65--dc21

                                          99-054483

To Sir Reginald Hibbert
'Semper fidelis'

ACKNOWLEDGEMENTS

We would like first to note the division of labour between us in the writing of this book. Broadly, Chapters 1, 3, 12, 13 and 14 were the joint responsibility of both authors. Chapters 4, 5, 6, 7 and 8, were largely written by Miranda Vickers and Chapters 2, 9, 10 and 11 by James Pettifer.

There are many events we describe that require further detailed investigation in the future, but we hope we have provided at least a foundation for the study of what will be seen as a seminal period. In Albania the early days of opposition to the communist system have already begun to take on something of a mythical quality, and we hope our book will be a corrective to those tendencies. In the important matter of sources, it should be noted that at the time of our research some Albanian archives were not yet open to students and commentators; and, as far as we are aware, little documentation has survived from the early stages of the development of the opposition to the one-party state. We have cited sources exactly whenever these have been available.

We would like to record our thanks to those numerous people who were, or are, in leading positions in different spheres of Albanian life and found their way to talk to us and give their views about their country's past, present and future. Some of them, in current political conditions, felt the need for anonymity, and the book may therefore lack exact citations for certain events and views. The same applies to comments received from diplomats and officials of international organisations who have been kind enough to share their thoughts and recollections with us.

We wish to thank the following for their help with our work on the book: Dr James Gow, Alex Standish, Bob Churcher, Sir Reginald Hibbert, Shaip Latifi, Kyril Drezov, Michael Kaser and Arben Xhaferi – in particular, those who were kind enough to comment on parts of the draft text. We are indebted to the many friends and colleagues in Albania who took part in the dramatic events we have attempted to record and analyse, and who have been generous in discussing their experiences wit us. We owe particular thanks to Dr Shahin Kadare, Xervat Lloshi and Astrit Mulita for practical assistance in Albania. The publishers – C. Hurst & Co. in London and New York University Press – have played a substantial part in giving the book its final shape, and for this we are grateful.

All errors of fact and interpretation are our own responsibility.

London, January 1997   MIRANDA VICKERS
                                            JAMES PETTIFER

CONTENTS

PREFACE TO THE SECOND IMPRESSION

In the two years since the first edition of this book appeared, Albania has been the scene of many dramatic political events, and has received unprecedented world attention. That edition ended with a reference to the imminent collapse of the 'pyramid' investment schemes and to the beginnings of widespread social disorder. The scale and severity of the political and economic crisis could not have been anticipated, and the government of Sali Berisha was overthrown in the spring of 1997 in consequence. Albania entered a period of anarchy; hundreds of thousands of weapons were seized from military depots and law and order completely broke down in most parts of the country between March and June of that year. The savings of most of the population were wholly or partly lost, and the society was rocked to its foundations. The international community intervened to prevent a seemingly imminent civil war, and deployed a Greek-Italian-led military force known as 'Operation Alba', to try to restore public order. More than 2,000 people were killed and many more were wounded in the turmoil. Much public property and many physical and productive assets were also destroyed.

In general these events, and the nature of the collapse of the Berisha regime, have borne out the basic arguments we advanced in the first edition. These were that the process of transition from communism to a free market, pluralist economy was likely to be much more difficult and protracted in Albania than the international community realised, and that the Berisha regime was not a model for social and economic development in the Balkans as its supporters claimed. The ruling elite, or at least many sections of it, were seen to be corrupt and kleptocratic,[1] and it was widely understood in the 'international community' for the first time that secure democratic institutions had not been established in Albania. The rule of law meant little as the Democratic Party under Dr Berisha struggled to hold on to power by military means, and very large

[1] See James Pettifer, 'The Albanian Uprising', *Labour Focus on Eastern Europe*, London, no. 57, 1997, and reports by Antony Loyd and Richard Owen in *The Times* (London), March–April 1997.

sums of money embezzled by the 'pyramid scheme' operators were removed from Albania and have never been recovered.

In the second half of 1997 a coalition government dominated by the Socialist Party with its leader Fatos Nano as Prime Minister took power. Gradually law and order was restored over the southern and central part of the country, but the north of Albania has since remained outside the control of the Tirana authorities and intermittent violence between different armed groups has continued. The international military force 'Operation Alba' was withdrawn, although foreign military and police advisers have remained. The economy was not as severely affected by the period of anarchy as many experts feared, and a relatively high growth rate was maintained in 1997-8, particularly in construction. Emigré remittances were below their usual level, but high enough to enable the family support system to function normally. International aid was resumed from the World Bank, the European Bank for Reconstruction and Development, and the International Monetary Fund. An ex-physicist, Rexhep Meidani, established himself successfully as a moderate and well-respected President able to keep clear of some of the intense political partisanship of Tirana politics.

Throughout this period political tension in the Balkans remained high, with considerable diplomatic attention being given to the Kosova issue. During its early period the Nano government was under heavy Greek diplomatic influence, and Nano met the Serbian leader Slobodan Milošević at a high-profile Balkan conference in Crete, the first Albanian leader to meet the Yugoslavs at this level for fifty years. It was clear that although Nano wished to obtain a solution to the Kosova problem within Yugoslavia, his meeting with Milošević was seen as betrayal of the independence struggle in the eyes of the Kosovars. Meanwhile in Kosova itself the international community attempted to force through the implementation of the education agreement signed between Milošević and Ibrahim Rugova in September 1996, but little progress was made.

A critical development took place during 1997. It became clear to observers that a new military force, the *Ushtria Çlirimtare e Kosoves* (Kosova Liberation Army – KLA), had come into existence. It was led by a secretive, tightly-knit group of mostly young Kosovars based in Switzerland and Germany.[2] Attacks on the Serb

[2] For the origins of the Kosova Liberation Army see Miranda Vickers, *Between Serb and Albanian: A History of Kosovo*, London: Hurst, 1998, and *Ushtria Çlirimtare*

security apparatus by armed militants of this organisation became more frequent, so that by the autumn of and early winter of 1997 some areas of Kosova were becoming 'no-go areas' for Serbian forces.[3] The presence of the KLA as a new force was vigorously denied by the Democratic League of Kosova led by Ibrahim Rugova, who claimed that it was an invention of the Serbian secret police, designed to destabilise his own party and discredit Albanian nationalism. This viewpoint could not long be sustained after independent journalists were able to visit the central Kosova region of Drenica during the winter of 1997-8 and see that a KLA-controlled zone existed, and that the Serbs themselves had effectively declared war on the new Albanian military force. The following year, 1998, was dominated by the developing war and profound political crisis in Kosova which also cast a major shadow over the limited but real progress that had been made in re-establishing Albania as a functioning and re-stabilised state. It was also a year of political advance for the Albanians in Macedonia, with the end of the Social Democrat government of Branko Crvenovski in the autumn 1998 parliamentary elections, and the entry into the government coalition of the more radical of the two Albanian parties, the Party for Democratic Prosperity (PDP-sh), led by Arben Xhaferi.

The Kosova war generated much international diplomatic activity, with the gradually increasing involvement of the United States as the main mediator between the two sides, and the dominance of the negotiating process by the architect of the 1995 Dayton Accords, US diplomat Richard Holbrooke. The main military phase was the advance of the Kosova Liberation Army in the early spring of 1998 to the point where by late May the KLA controlled an estimated 30-35 per cent of Kosova. These KLA advances, however, were short-lived; a Serb offensive quickly followed, and in response NATO conducted an exercise in Albania in early June that was clearly designed to warn Milošević of the consequences of his aggressive anti-Albanian policy. Beginning in early June and continuing during the summer months, a vicious

---

e Kosovës. Dokumente dhe Artikuj, Aarau (Switzerland): Zeri i Kosoves, 1998.

[3] See report by James Pettifer 'Kosovo gunmen force Serb police to beat retreat' in *The Times*, London, 8 January 1998, and by Tom Walker, 'Serb forces shell Kosovo villages', *The Times*, 6 March 1998.

Serbian military clampdown began, with small-scale ethnic cleansing and burning of villages. This gathered pace by August, when tens of thousands of refugees had taken to the woods and hills to hide from Serb forces. It had now become evident that a major humanitarian disaster was in the making, and intensive diplomatic activity was begun to broker a deal with Slobodan Milošević. This concluded in the agreement of October 1998, when the Serbian President agreed to withdraw his extra army units and the special anti-terrorist police from Kosova.

At the same time the Kosova crisis was taking its toll on the Tirana political leadership. The Nano government had become more and more politically isolated from the mainstream of Albanian opinion on Kosova as the crisis deepened and the extent of Serbian violence and repression of the Kosovar national movement became clear. The favoured solution of a third, Kosova republic within Yugoslavia had its intellectual attractions for the political elite in Tirana, but was becoming increasingly remote from political and military reality in Kosova itself. The open and manipulative pressure from the 'international community' for a solution within Yugoslavia put major pressures on the Nano government. An early but key loss was that of the Interior Minister, Neritan Ceka, in May 1998. Ceka had played a key role in restoring public order in 1997, but was unhappy about the arbitary and inconsistent government policy towards the KLA. Nano, himself acting under international pressure, had ordered Ceka to make a major clampdown on the armed militants' supply lines in Albania.[4] Foreign diplomats still favoured a negotiated solution to the Kosova problem with Milosevic to restore a form of autonomy to what was described as 'the province of Serbia', with Ibrahim Rugova as its leader. Nano appears to have believed that a general reduction in international financial aid would be made if the KLA was not crushed. But events were to follow a very different course.

In September 1998, Albania was brought once again to the brink of civil strife by the murder of the popular opposition leader, Azem Hajdari, a colourful and attractive if unscrupulous northern politician from Sali Berisha's home town, Tropoja. The militants of the Democratic Party took to the streets, and supporters of different political factions fought pitched battles. A group of

---

[4] Interview by the authors with Neritan Ceka, Tirana, 24 May 1998.

armed men attacked the Prime Minister's office, and Nano was lucky to escape with his life. These events were the culmination of a year of political polarisation and a long-running campaign by the Democratic Party to undermine the government and block moves to introduce a new constitution. In the political aftermath Fatos Nano's resignation was forced on the party and the thirty-one-year-old Pandeli Majko, a hitherto largely unknown southern politician whose father had been one of Enver Hoxha's army generals, emerged as the new prime minister.[5]

Despite his youth and lack of ministerial experience, Majko was generally regarded as untainted by a Communist past and thus more acceptable to a population weary of older politicians burdened by a 'Communist mentality'. Majko had played a significant role in the student demonstrations that eventually brought down the Communist government in 1991, and thus represented a new generation of Albanian politicians intent on bringing a fresh approach to the country's political life. Throughout the year President Meidani had been demanding a more militant and realistic national policy on Kosova, and the overthrow of Nano was a strong vindication of the arguments he had put forward. The national question had become very urgent for all Albanians, and could not be pushed to the periphery of Tirana politics.

In the mean time, the situation in Kosova was going from bad to worse. During the winter of 1998-9 it had become clear that Milošević's summer and autumn offensive had not destroyed the KLA, and the force of international monitors – the Kosova Verification Mission – deployed under the October 1998 agreement was powerless to prevent much of the violence, however useful it may have been in restraining the Serbian security apparatus from excesses. Equally, the KLA began to realise that the military struggle for an independent Kosova could not be won without outside help, and that in order to receive it some compromise over independence might be needed for a transitional period.

Negotiations between the two sides were held in Febuary and March 1999 at Rambouillet, near Paris, where the Albanian negotiating team, now dominated by the Kosova Liberation Army

---

[5] For an analysis of the September coup attempt see Miranda Vickers, 'Albania Crisis Briefing', International Crisis Group, October 1998, Website: http://www.crisisweb.org.

under the leadership of Hasim Thaci, signed a draft agreement for a transitional period whereby Kosova would be under international military supervision by a NATO-controlled force.[6] This was unacceptable to Serbia, and NATO began bombing Serbia at the end of March after the expiry of a military ultimatum. Massive ethnic cleansing in Kosovo began immediately, and hundreds of thousands of terrifed refugees streamed out of Kosova into Macedonia and northern Albania in the largest forced population movement in Europe since the Second World War. Widespread intensification of violence against the remaining ethnic Albanian population continued, with the use of paramilitary death squads. The NATO bombing campaign built up slowly from its onset in late March and the hopes of the Holbrooke/Hill faction in the US State Department for Milošević's rapid return to the negotiating table in order to reach a 'Yugoslavist' solution to the crisis were disappointed. Instead a prolonged period of air war attrition followed, with major infrastructural damage being caused in Serbia by NATO's tactical bombing, but with a marked lack of success on NATO's past in disabling the body of the Serb security apparatus and military machine in Kosova itself. The Kosova Liberation Army was able to renew its local assaults against the Serbs and open up a vital corridor into Kosova from northern Albania that permitted the transfer of hundreds of new soldiers and military supplies to the interior of Kosova.

Yet in time the air campaign did achieve its objectives. In the first week of June, following the intervention of Russia in the diplomatic process, an agreed withdrawal of the Serbian forces was enforced and NATO forces entered the province from Macedonia. Thousands of refugees immediately began to return to their homes, and a free and independent Kosova now appears to be on the international political agenda for the first time in history. In Albania the NATO campaign was also a victory for the pro-Kosova Liberation Army policies followed by the Majko government. In contrast, the Democratic Party opposition led by Sali Berisha has yet to articulate a convincing policy for the long-delayed resolution of the Albanian national question in the Balkans.

In the time that has elapsed since the first edition of this book went to press, additional information has come to light in a number

---

[6] For a good analysis of the Rambouillet diplomacy, see Marc Weller, 'The Rambouillet conference on Kosovo', *International Affairs* (London), no. 75, 1999.

of areas and our observations on events may need some modification. The most important of these are concerned with the violence in Skanderbeg Square on 20 February 1991, when it is likely that about seventeen people died, and with the arms plot of November 1993 in Macedonia, where the role of the United States and its external agencies was more important than our earlier text suggested.

London, September 1999   MIRANDA VICKERS
                                                                JAMES PETTIFER

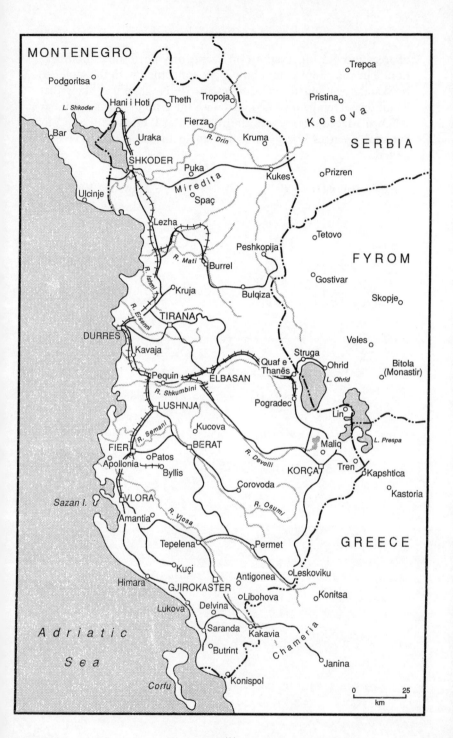

1

INTRODUCTION

In the perception of most Western observers of international affairs, Albania remained a curiosity during most of the communist period, a little known and isolated state, cut off from the outside would by political choice and geography. The dominant contemporary images of the country were those of the strictest Marxist-Leninist regime on earth – with the possible exception of North Korea – linked to a living medieval past of extreme backwardness. In its political culture it seemed to epitomise the most characteristically Balkan qualities, at a time when the Balkans were forgotten and largely irrelevant to the central issues of international relations.

But this obscurity in Western eyes is not new. Long before the isolation imposed by the communist state, the Albanians, as a small nationality struggling for recognition under Ottoman rule, failed to attract the support of larger non-Balkan powers. One reason for this was the successful integration of those Albanians who converted to Islam into the Ottoman state machine. Linked to this perception, the anti-Ottoman lobby in nineteenth-century Britain saw the essence of the Eastern Question as being the emancipation of oppressed Christian peoples from Islam; this could not apply to the Albanians with a majority of Muslims in their population. Ignorance also played a part: the commonest British view of Albania was exemplified by the historian Edward Gibbon who, on seeing the mountains of Albania as he sailed down the Adriatic, said that as little was known of the inhabitants as of the interior of America. The Albanians were perceived as primitive, tribal and fundamentally disunited, and therefore incapable of modern state organisation. No equivalent tradition existed in relation to Albania comparable to the Philhellenism of the political élites of Europe that provided constant support for Greek nationalism, or the pan-Slavist movement in Russia that did the

1

same for Serbian aspirations.

Although at the beginning of the twentieth century the writings of Edith Durham, Aubrey Herbert and others informed a wider public about Albanians, Gibbon's impression lingered on in much of northern Europe. The disastrous attempt to partition Albania under the 1914 Protocol of Corfu, when northern Epirus was given to Greece, highlighted the powers' disregard for Albanian national integrity. The Ambassadors' Conference held in Paris in 1921, faced with the chaos caused by the Corfu decision, sought to overcome it by setting up a still severely dismembered but centralised Albanian state, which it placed under Italian tutelage. This political psychology still exists today: during the crisis in Italy caused by the hijacking of ships from Durres by a mass of desperate refugees in August 1991, a leading article appeared in one of Britain's quality newspapers headed 'Europe's Albanian Problem'.[1] Albania has never really been seen by West European political establishments as a realistic candidate for full 'European statehood', whatever shape or form that has taken at different times. The Albanians of Montenegro, Macedonia and Kosova have been regarded as even more marginal in this neglected process of national unification and development.

Albania is by far the poorest country in Europe, with a *per capita* annual income of a few hundred US dollars, in the same league as many poorer Third World countries. Like every other former communist country in Eastern Europe, it has attempted the transition from communism to capitalism, with the restoration of a free market economy, widespread privatisation and new foreign, defence and internal security policies. However, the history of Albania does not offer a strong foundation on which to build democracy. Apart from a brief experiment in 1924, parliamentary government has never previously existed in the country. Thus, understanding of modern political parties and their role in a pluralist state is limited. Enver Hoxha's regime was haunted by fears of external intervention and internal subversion. Albania thus became a fortress state, its rulers determined to preserve the sovereignty and integrity not only of Albania but also of the communist system.

---

[1] *The Independent*, 10 August 1990.

Albania has therefore been largely regarded as no more than a Balkan 'Gulag', with little of value to contribute to world culture and certainly very far from being eligible, in the aftermath of communism, for membership of the European Union. This has affected Western policies towards Albanian national aspirations as an element in the Yugoslav crisis, reinforcing Serbian power in the region, albeit unintentionally. When Albania threw off a half-century of communist rule in 1992, it was faced with a Balkan peninsula torn by war and ethnic conflict and a particularly difficult aspect of what has become the New World Disorder; the situation is one in which it is both onlooker and participant. Albania avoided direct military involvement in the war affecting former Yugoslavia, but the Kosova crisis remains among the more serious and intractable causes of Balkan instability. The position of the ethnic Albanians in the Former Yugoslav Republic of Macedonia (FYROM) is becoming increasingly difficult. Albania's economy has been seriously affected by United Nations' economic sanctions, and its proximity to the war deterred almost all investment from multinational corporations.

The hardline communist regime under Enver Hoxha, which ruled Albania from 1944 to 1989, sought to create a united country under the socialist system, and to overcome the heritage of regional and religious differences that affected the development of the national independence movement during the time of the Ottoman empire. The dominant ethos of the regime was the desire to establish the 'new socialist man' who would be defined by his stable Albanian identity and communist consciousness. The extent to which that project failed can be seen in the overwhelming rejection of the communists after the years of anarchy and chaos between 1990 and 1992, and the victory of the opposition Democratic Party in the March 1992 general election. The latter heralded adoption of the radical free market economic and social programme of the current goverment. The long years of communism had none the less profoundly affected the people, particularly in their social and economic development. The post-communist governments have found great difficulty in breaking with many habits of the past, both personal and institutional. The communist administration depended on a small élite of qualified and intellectually sophisticated personnel in Tirana and other large towns, and the new government has been unable to distance

itself from the often élitist and undemocratic habits of thought
and political practice of many members of this social group. In
an interview in an Albanian newspaper published in May 1995,
the communist leader Ramiz Alia observed that his democratic
successors were 'provincial amateurs', a reference to the cohesive-
ness of the old Tirana political élite.[2] From him this was a supremely
damning charge.

The destruction of the institutions of the one-party state revived
many older elements of Albanian life. Religion was once again
a major factor in social identity, and elements of traditional Gheg-
Tosk, north-south rivalries re-emerged. There was major disorientation caused by the breakdown of the communists' rigid
system of social and moral values. During the winters of 1990-1
and 1991-2 Albanian society almost degenerated into general anarchy. In the West it was widely believed in 1990 that the Party
of Labour would never voluntarily surrender power, and civil
war was predicted. Nevertheless, after Enver Hoxha's death in
1985 there had been a process of reform of a very limited kind
under Ramiz Alia. The structure and functioning of the communist
party throughout society enabled the old system to collapse gradually
over an eighteen-month period; forcible removal through a popular
uprising along Romanian lines proved unnecessary. In these circumstances it is arguable how far some aspects of the new order
actually represented a genuine break with the old, given the origins
of the opposition Democratic Party among a particular section
of the Tirana élite which included many longstanding communists.

Within Albania the end of communism has also seen the re-
emergence of ethnic minority issues. These have been centred
on the status and rights of the large ethnic Greek minority living
mainly in the south of the country. These problems have been
linked to the wider issues of Albanian immigration into Greece,
by far the largest area of employment abroad for Albanian migrant
workers; however, many of those employed there are illegal immigrants and subject to penalties from the Greek authorities.
Bilateral relations with Greece have been strained for most of
the period covered by this book. It remains to be seen whether
the new Albania will be able to develop into a country with an
inner ethnic diversity, or whether it will follow the current Balkan

[2] *Kohe Jone,* 7 May, 1995.

trend by evolving into a nation–state without significant minorities or multicultural influences.

The collapse of communism marked the end of fifty years of uninterrupted dominance of the country and its institutions by close associates of Enver Hoxha – many of whom, such as Ramiz Alia and Mehmet Shehu, were wartime comrades in arms. The élite formed under communism came originally from Tirana and the Tosk south, where the communist-led Partisan movement had been strongest, an exception being Alia, who was born in the northern city of Shkoder. By contrast, the new leaders of pluralist Albania, including President Sali Berisha, are nearly all northerners. The Tirana professional and managerial élite formed under communism has been subject to great strains during this process. The shared communist and secular ethos dominated by southern Tosks has been threatened by the revival of regionalism in politics, and by the renewed importance of religion and ethnicity. A small but significant segment of the old élite under communism were partly or wholly of ethnic Greek backgound. This made them all of Orthodox background, whereas most Albanians are Muslims. Emigration opportunities have also deprived many areas of the economy of skilled and experienced personel.

Despite the transition to a free market economy, or perhaps partly because of it, the wages and salaries of the most skilled and professional strata have remained extremely low, whereas a new class of small entrepreneurs, mainly in the retail and agricultural sectors, have emerged as arbiters of economic power. This newly prosperous stratum provided solid support for the DP government's radical free market 'shock therapy' policies. Agricultural production increased in 1993-5, although cereal production is still a problem. It remains to be seen how far an agricultural surplus can form the basis for a broader reform of the economy, which still suffers from antiquated and obsolescent factories and equipment, and an almost total lack of indigenous capital for investment. Generally agricultural production (and thus the economy) contains a substantial subsistence element particularly in remote regions. Production itself consists largely of Mediterranean products that are already in chronic oversupply in adjacent markets and especially in the European Union, and it must be doubtful how much further the government can rely on this sector of the economy to produce further growth and social stability. In any event, there are few signs hitherto of the European Union being willing to make the reforms in the Common Agricultural Policy that would facilitate market access for these goods and transform the prospects of the Albanian and other East European economies in the process.

The vital extractive industries also remain depressed, with mineral output at very low levels. The most important commodity produced, chromite ore, of which Albania is the third largest producer after Russia and South Africa, has suffered from low world metal prices as a result of the international recession, and this affected national income. But in 1995 the metal price rose and the income available to Albania from chrome increased. Reduced demand caused by recession affected other important mineral exports such as copper and nickel, and extractive production was affected by the problem of antiquated equipment, as in the chrome mines and the manufacturing sector generally. The latter was completely protected against outside competition in the communist period, when it was able to produce poor quality goods by inefficent methods. After the end of communism and the opening up of the economy, most of these old enterprises ceased production. This was obviously an economic necessity, but it produced high unemployment in many towns, sometimes as high as 80 per cent of the working population. Education and training opportunities for young people suffered, and large sections of the youth have been deskilled, and are to be found working in semi-occupations in the retail sector, such as selling very small quantities of cigarettes in the street for a return which cannot even provide subsistence. Given the low average age-level of the population, with an estimated 40 per cent aged under twenty-five, this has clear political implications for the future, particularly if opportunites to work abroad are not always widely available.

The transition has affected many social institutions. The already deepseated problems in the provision of health care to the population have been exacerbated by the exodus of trained medical personnel to work abroad. In education a radical overhaul of the school and university curriculum has begun, made necessary by the end of compulsory military training and the teaching of Marxism-Leninism to university students. In local government and in many areas of central government, lack of finance has meant an inability to proceed with basic infrastructural development, such as urgently needed repair and rehabilitation of the road network. The telephone system is incapable of coping with modern business needs, although at the time of writing it is claimed that a major refurbishment programme will soon begin. Housing conditions and sanitary arrangements remain very poor in many towns and villages. It will be one of the main challeges of the next stage of the transition to ensure that these basic social investments are made to enable a new foundation of private sector investments to be made in the national economy. Although some help has been forthcoming from international institutions, it is wholly inadequate in scale to rebuild the deteriorating infrastructure inherited from the communists. The capital city of Tirana poses particular problems, with rapid population growth since 1992 arising from rural depopulation, especially from the north, and with widespread and serious electricity and water shortages contributing to a deteriorating quality of life for all the inhabitants.

In the institutional sphere the government has made considerable efforts to establish a new legal framework for landownership, a major key to economic development, but although privatisation has been by and large successfully completed in the countryside, progress has been much more limited in the cities, with disputes over property rights inhibiting progress on many construction projects, even in central Tirana. Another area of concern is the rapid growth of organised crime and Mafia-type activity, particularly in the coastal cities of Vlora and Durres, with their unfortunate proximity to parts of southern Italy where Mafia-like organisations have long been influential, and in Tirana itself. In Vlora serious Mafia activity increased in 1995 to the point where a whole drug industry has been developed (more than 30,000 cannabis plants were destroyed by police in a single operation). Although the problems of public order that affected Albania in the winters of 1990-1 and 1991-2 were largely surmounted, organised crime, with its associated corruption and peculation, has been an intractable problem for the government. Throughout this period, Albanian national security has been affected by the war in former Yugoslavia and the emergence of the Kosova problem as major factors in the politics of the region. A reform of the Albanian military apparatus was undertaken from the end of 1991, but it became a politically difficult and controversial issue for the new government. The security issues were complemented by the damage to the Albanian economy caused by the economic sanctions imposed on Serbia by the United Nations. Although accurate statistics on the effects are not available, there seems little doubt that they have been severe in many northern and eastern regions as well as more generally, deterring major international companies which may have contemplated investment in the country. At the time of writing, in 1996, only one major multinational, Coca Cola, had made direct manufacturing investment in Albania. Others, such as some oil companies, are beginning to invest on a small scale in product distribution. The UN sanctions have also caused a breakdown in legitimate economic life, whether under socialist or capitalist patterns of ownership, and encouraged the growth of organised crime and Mafia-type activities.

A social renewal movement is now under way, with the manifest goal of establishing a constitutional democracy. However, Albania's history, together with its inherited socio-economic status and political culture, presents obstacles to the emergence of a truly pluralistic society. Some of these could be seen during the debates that accompanied the failed campaign of the Berisha government in a referendum to gain popular support for a new constitution in the autumn of 1994. In such conditions of rapid social change, the status of many social groups has changed dramatically; established professionals, the elderly and those employed in the public sector have suffered serious falls in living standards, while a small business culture has grown with an equal rapidity in the main towns. The economic, political and cultural identity of the Albanian people is thus being redefined and it is the main object of this book to identify the elements in the transition that contribute to this redefinition.

Under communism, important events in recent Albanian history suffered from mythologisation. Historical reality was distorted and falsified, especially in relation to the Partisan struggle during the war against the Axis occupation and the process by which the Party of Labour took power.[3] There are signs that the the overthrow of communism is being subjected to similar patterns of distortion, at least in the minds of some participants, and this book attempts to record the most important elements in the process – notably during the critical winters of 1990-1 and 1991-2, when the

---

[3] See Appendix A, p. 291, for an account by Sir Reginald Hibbert, a British veteran of the Partisan war in 1943-4, of the fiftieth anniversary of the Liberation. His document illustrates the ideological problems the Second World War caused the Berisha government.

Democratic Party emerged as the dominant opposition force – and to attempt at least a preliminary analysis of their significance. The historical account that has appeared in Albania, in the school textbook *Historia e Popullit Shqiptar*, has disturbing parallels with some of the socialist historiography it was meant to supplant; it is subjective and focuses almost exclusively on the alleged role of Dr Sali Berisha in the dramatic events which led to the DP's victory in March 1992. The process of national renewal is rooted in this period, and the definition and interpretation of the events of 1990-2 are likely to remain of key importance in Albanian political life and in the formation of the new national identity for a long time. It therefore seems important to explore what happened as fully as the available sources allow.

The book is based on research in Britain and in Albania, where a large number of participants in the political struggle have been interviewed, and also on the authors' personal experiences in reporting on, and taking part in, some of these momentous events as they evolved. It is the writers' belief that the future stability and prosperity of Albania are inseparable from the future stability of the Balkans as a whole, and they hope that the book will contribute to the understanding of what Albanian people have had to face and the difficult choices they have had to make since the demise of communism. About half the text is devoted to narrating events as they happened, and half to the study of particular topics, such as religion and the Kosova problem, which have had an important influence on Albanian identity and national external relationships during the process of transition.

2

THE CRISIS OF THE ONE-PARTY STATE AFTER ENVER HOXHA'S DEATH, 1985-90

Western observers have often seen Albanian politics and society in terms of mystery, conspiracy and ruthless violence. In neighbouring Balkan countries, with a somewhat greater knowledge of how Albanian society functions, a single phrase has sufficed to sum up the political system: 'the Albanian pyramid'. This expresses the role of the clan, or extended family, in rural Albanian society, and appositely describes a hierarchical structure in which the oldest and most distinguished man effectively makes the law. In the Albanian Party of Labour (PLA) Enver Hoxha played just such a role. He had never left the communist leadership group after the party was formed in 1941 or the Tirana government after it took power in 1944. Although many of his closest collaborators were well aware of his faults and limitations, he remained at the apex of the pyramid; for many Albanians he was a little revered and often hated father figure, whose ideology was of little or no appeal, especially to the young. Yet it was he who had put Albania on the map as a modern industrial country in contrast to the near-medieval conditions prevailing at the time of the Axis occupation.

The death of Hoxha had been anticipated, particularly among the Tirana élite, who knew for some years that he was suffering from a degenerative illness. In Albanian life it is very difficult to avoid the figure of the father, symbolising the power of the past (Ismail Kadare's novel *Doruntine* shows this clearly).[1] Hoxha's funeral was a great event in itself, but more significant than the official ceremonies were the pilgrimages of whole villages from

---

[1] *Doruntine,* London, 1988. This remarkable novel investigates the nature of patriarchy in Albania, and the difficulty in challenging traditional values.

the Partisan south to Tirana to attend. From 12 to 15 April 1985, hi⌐ body lay in state in the hall of the Presidium of the People's Assembly, where hundreds of thousands of people filed past. Many people who were not PLA members broke down weeping by the coffin. On 15 April, in gentle rain, Hoxha was buried. Crowds forty-deep lined the route of the funeral cortège to the national heroes' plot. This is in the cemetery on a high wooded hill opposite the presidential palace which he occupied for so long. Handfuls of soil brought from his birthplace in Gjirokaster were cast on to the coffin. Resting in the company of rows of honoured Partisans under neat white memorial stones, he seemed secure in the nearest thing to immortality that a communist society could offer. But he occupied his official grave for a much shorter time than he occupied his spartan office in the palace over the road. Only eight years later his body was exhumed and buried in obscurity, and on the tenth anniversary of his death in 1995 his few remaining admirers laid their bunches of red roses in a local cemetery in downtown Tirana.

As later events showed, his death in 1985 was the beginning of the end of an epoch. The Hoxhaist legacy was a poisoned chalice for the PLA, but emotions at the time bore out the old Albanian proverb 'When the father beats his son, the child cries but still clings to him as the only protector he knows'. The rule of the PLA could only be justified by a legitimacy derived from the Hoxha years, but if it was to stand any chance of continuing in power, many aspects of that inheritance would have to be repudiated. The dilemma was never solved, even when the survival of the one-party state depended upon it in the critical months of 1990. Two days after Hoxha's death Ramiz Alia was elected First Secretary of the PLA. Born in Shkoder on 18 October 1921 of Muslim parents from Kosova, he flirted briefly with the occupying powers, but joined the communist party in 1943 and played a minor part in the Partisan resistance. In 1948 he was elected to the Central Committee and in 1956, after study in the Soviet Union, became a candidate Politburo member and subsequently a full member. He was a small man of modest appearance and pleasant manners, who had none of the cheap but real charisma of Hoxha, whose expensive overcoats, jaunty hats and patent leather 'co-respondent' shoes mimicked matinée-idol fashions of the 1930s. He spent much of his career in administrative posts, and survived the purges in the Party by learning to keep a low profile on controversial issues, exhibiting total loyalty to Hoxha (although that had not saved others from disgrace) and enjoying the patronage of Hoxha's wife Nexhmije, from the time of the war onwards. In the 1950s he began his rise to prominence as an important administrator and technical expert on the early industrialisation programmes, a quiet presence outside Hoxha's inner circle.

During the years immediately after Hoxha's death, the central choice between modernisation and conservatism was never faced. That it could have been postponed at all is explained by the unique isolation of Albania in these years. After the breaks with the Soviet Union and China, it was an island of increasing poverty and demoralisation, with a rapidly disintegrating infrastructure, crumbling buildings, malnourished and poorly clad workers and peasants using primitive agricultural equipment, all surrounded by slogans reminding them that '*Partia mbi te gjitha*' (The Party is above everything). The economy and society in general depended on extreme, spartan egalitarianism. The ratio between the highest and lowest incomes was 1:2 so that in the mid-1980s a factory director would take home approximately 900 leks a month, an assembly worker 750 and a roadsweeper 600. The communist party, the Albanian Party of Labour, had about 120,000 members out of a population of 3 million. Daily life proceeded in slow motion, and the atmosphere was one of extreme tedium. The PLA controlled every organisation in the country without exception; there was no independent civil society whatsoever. Churches and mosques remained closed after the anti-religious campaigns of the 1960s, which were followed by the Party leadership asserting that Albania was the world's first atheist state. Even the family was not sacrosanct, with the huge networks of informers run by the *Sigurimi*, the secret police, reaching into every living-room.

It has been conventional wisdom that Ramiz Alia took over from Hoxha only during the last two years of his life when he was increasingly incapacitated by diabetes and other serious illnesses. In reality, the transfer of power had begun much earlier. In 1983, at an important PLA economic conference called to discuss the next (1986-91) Five-Year Plan, Hoxha played no part and Alia conducted all the business. Alia had been head of state over the same period, and increasingly shared the ceremonial and public duties of leadership with Hoxha. He had, for instance, spent a good deal of time sending the numerous and fulsome Albanian greetings on national days, and other anniversaries, often concerning very small countries, which had once been done by Hoxha only. Alia's background as a technocrat and industrial manager fitted him for the attempt to revitalise the flagging economy and plan the increases in productivity and output that were supposed to underpin the projected growth in living standards in the late 1980s. It was also clear, at least to members of the Tirana élite, that the continued regular appearance of volumes of Hoxha's *Collected Works* (they eventually totalled seventy-one volumes), had to mean that others were writing them, because in the final years of his life the old leader suffered from dementia and was barely capable of writing his name, let alone a book.

When the PLA's five-year Party Congress opened at the beginning of 1986, Ramiz Alia's tentative and modest proposals for reforms faced their first serious test. The proposals were of a minor, technocratic nature, and in reality permitted slightly wider income differentials. This was Alia's first decisive test of political strength and skill after coming to power the previous year. Industrial and agricultural development was given top priority for discussion at the Congress – 1985 had been a very poor one for production. But while many delegates clearly recognised that all was not well, it was soon equally clear that there was little appetite for reform, and in practice few changes of any kind took place during these years. Life in the countryside continued much as it had been since collectivisation began, with the peasants putting in the minimum amount of work necessary to keep out of trouble on the large *latifundia*-type fields. Meanwhile they devoted their real energies to vegetable gardening on their small private plots and tending illegally-held pigs and chickens. In the towns the workers and their families endured increasingly erratic meat and cheese supplies, and would spend whole days scouring the streets for someone selling produce on the black market. The PLA was forced to resort to increased food imports throughout these years, and a common sight was the surprise arrival at the urban markets of lorry-loads of rice or flour. This would occur very early in the morning, the deliveries being timed to dissipate local discontent. Bread was virtually free and, with maize, was the main component of the popular diet in the countryside, augmented by vegetables in the summer and pickles in winter. Cheese was the main protein source (Albanians have never been great fishermen, and supplies of fish were sparse).

The same problems of poor food supplies, low industrial and agricultural productivity, crippling shortages of spare parts and other technical problems continued to afflict the economy throughout this period, and Alia and other Party leaders spent much time trying to remedy them. However, until the crisis of communism overwhelmed Eastern Europe in 1989, there was little sign in these years of internal change. In November 1986 at the regional Party congress in Tirana, an effort was made to provide incentive payments for efficient workers, but with little result; few of the delegates seemed to understand what an incentive scheme was. Stagnation in all fields continued, and one of the so-called achievements of the Hoxha era, the absence of foreign debt, was now a millstone around the necks of the leadership. All Albanian industry urgently needed modernisation, but the necessary remedies would inevitably incur debts to foreign banks, something that could not be contemplated for ideological reasons. The achievement was anyway a confidence trick; it arose not from economic progress but from the repudiation of large debts to previous superpower partners when the regime broke with them politically. These debts were vast: some hundreds of millions of dollars were owed to China for just one industrial installation, the Elbasan ferro-chrome concentration plant. The Soviet Union was owed even larger sums on the Drin valley hydroelectric schemes and other projects. The total sums subject to re-negotiation in 1995 appeared to be in the region of US $3 billion.

Thus Hoxhaist fundamentalism had a high price. In 1988, three years after Hoxha's death, the PLA produced a memorial volume, *Our Enver*, supposedly written by Alia and published under his name. It reaffirmed the Hoxhaist legacy in uncompromising terms, but sometimes with an underlying note of concern about the future:

> When reaction and the revisionists are trying to cause ideological chaos, Enver Hoxha showed that the road of the revolutionary forces and the prospects of the liberation struggle have not been closed, that the changes which have occurred and the present-day developments in the world do not negate Marxism-Leninism, or the class struggle as the universal law of development

of class society. Enver Hoxha has proved that, despite the temporary zigzags, the cause of revolution remains on the agenda, not only as an aspiration of the peoples and the world proletariat, but as a question put forward for solution.[2]

In practice Albania opened out a little to the outside world in the Alia years, even if there was little internal change other than an ossification of the PLA, and those changes that did occur were often not publicised within Albania itself. In a speech to the People's Assembly in late 1987, Alia distinguished between what he described as the 'primary' tenets of the system, which 'must be preserved and developed', and the 'secondary' which must undergo constant 'change and refinement'. The 'Primary tenets' to which Alia referred were the basic principles of Hoxhaism, which in theory combined the centralised management of the state from above with the initiative of the masses from below. Because the former included Stalinist organisational principles, such as democratic centralism, the road to internal reform was largely blocked. Nevertheless, foreign policy after 1987 showed some signs of departure from the fortress mentality, with an improvement in trade relations with a number of East European countries and in relations generally with traditionally hostile Balkan neighbours. There was also an opening to secular Islamic countries such as Egypt and Libya. Albania's participation in the Balkan Co-operation Conference in February 1988 was a notable landmark, and the appearance in Belgrade of its delegation, headed by Foreign Minister Reis Malile, heralded a significant improvement in Albanian–Yugoslav relations. It was the first time Albania had participated in such a gathering and the country's new international diplomacy was much in evidence. The mature and calm stance it took on most issues astonished observers who expected to be confronted by the conventional Marxist-Leninist declamations and inflammatory rhetoric which had characterised Albania's contribution in the few international gatherings in which it participated. Gone were the dry, ideological, denunciatory speeches of the past, compared to which the new approach was conciliatory and pragmatic. The congress concentrated on generally

---

[2] *Our Enver*, Tirana, 1988. It is not known whether Alia actually wrote this book, just as it seems certain that some of the final volumes of Hoxha's 71-volume *Vepra* (Collected Works) could not have been written by Hoxha owing to his long final illness.

uncontroversial issues, such as Balkan sports and cultural activities, tourism, educational exchanges, scientific co-operation, customs affairs, and provision for small-scale cross-border trade. In a move clearly designed to convince the domestic audience that genuine changes were taking place, a large Albanian television crew was present to film the event.

Thus, in a limited way, Albania began to re-enter the European political arena. To keep up the momentum, another Albanian delegation returned to Belgrade two weeks later for follow-up talks on the various issues raised and to sign a protocol on cultural co-operation. In a slightly more liberal internal atmosphere, leading intellectuals, such as the writer Ismail Kadare, began to call for artistic freedom along Western lines. In a key development, television sets capable of picking up transmissions from Yugoslavia, Italy and Greece began to appear in Albania in these years, and at the beginning of 1988 criticisms of the dogmatism of the PLA were appearing in the domestic media. A degree of intellectual liberalisation appeared in the literary field, with the innovative novels of Ismail Kadare receiving official approval. However, only a tiny fraction of the population was involved in these intellectual developments; the vast majority were still either subsistence farmers in isolated communities or workers under heavy Party and *Sigurimi* control, and neither were able to mount an effective challenge to the regime in Tirana. Tolerated dissident groups such as those that ultimately overthrew communism in Hungary, Poland and other East European countries did not exist in Albania. The intelligensia were almost entirely located in Tirana, and had only started to become a force in society when the University opened in 1957. They were thus an immature intelligensia and closely integrated with the PLA. Their style was paternalistic and authoritarian, frequently combining intellectual mediocrity with a blind loyalty to even the most absurd elements of Hoxhaist dogma.

The *Sigurimi*, which closely monitored any opposition to the government, operated a reign of terror by covering the whole country with a network of informers, including children who were taught to spy on their parents. The *Sigurimi* web was so tight that organised dissent was impossible. The shadow of Enver Hoxha was everywhere, on huge billboards by the side of the road, with endless slogans painted on buildings and even on the dramatic and beautiful mountains, where Young Pioneers had to carry stones to make ENVER patterns in 30-foot letters thousands of feet above sea-level on the grassy slopes. Even senior managers and army officers were supposed to study Hoxha's works daily. The only recreation allowed to forced labour prisoners was to sit and listen to Hoxha's works read aloud in lunch-hours.

But by the spring of 1988 open criticism of the regime's dogmatic policies had begun to appear in the Albanian press. One report stated:

> In the past the Albanian Communist leaders have claimed to be equally opposed to 'sectarianism' as to 'opportunism'. By the former term they mean 'leftist' behaviour, which it is claimed, leads to dogmatic and conservative positions; the latter term is usually associated with 'rightist' thinking, which in Albania implies revisionism. Throughout its history the Communist Party has concentrated its attacks on 'rightist' and 'revisionist' forces, while paying only lip service to its alleged struggle against the 'Leftists'. The deep-seated mistrust of the people both within and outside the Party that led to repeated purges was, in fact, largely caused by the 'leftist orientation of the Hoxha leadership'. It is therefore of some significance that the post-Hoxha communists directed their attacks on 'sectarianism' or 'leftism', a process that was launched by Ramiz Alia himself at the 9th Party Congress. In fact, the current Albanian leadership's attack on sectarianism should be seen as a manifestation of the new attitude in the country to outdated and conservative ways of thinking.[3]

The international context of Albanian isolation was also changing. However complete it seemed, in reality the Albanian position depended for its stability on the existence of a world socialist presence, if not a unified system as in the past. However despised, the position of the Soviet Union and its satellites was still important to the viability of Albanian 'socialism'. But times were changing in Eastern Europe. It appears that in the summer of 1988 the Albanian leadership realised that *perestroika* would bring fundamental changes to Soviet society, and a whole orchestrated series of attacks on the concept and its originator, Mikhail Gorbachev, appeared

---

[3] Radio Free Europe, Background Report/14, 5 February 1988.

in the Tirana press. The most extensive analysis was published in the Party newspaper *Zeri-i-Popullit* just before the 19th Congress of the CPSU opened at the end of June. It claimed that Gorbachev was 'following in the footsteps of his spiritual father, Nikita Krushchev', and that the Albanian party would 'continue resolutely to fight Soviet revisionism, the most perfect and dangerous revisionism'.[4] In late 1988 and early 1989, Albanian politics and life were characterised essentially by stagnation and inertia, although it was clear to all informed observers that the country could not remain isolated for ever from the dramatic events that were transforming the East European political landscape. Nevertheless, for a while the old system carried on. Foreign correspondents, who were beginning to visit the country more regularly under cover of tourist visas, noted in their reports the timeless world of Hoxhaist dogma, often linked to a sense, among the public, of innocence and isolation from the political and cultural currents developing elsewhere. However, this detachment and unrealistic atmosphere could not last much longer. The mass population movements from East to West Germany through Hungary, which eventually led to the dismantling of the Berlin Wall in November 1989 and the bloody end of the Ceauşescu regime in Romania in December, reverberated throughout Eastern Europe. The old system could not endure, even in Albania, and new oppositional voices were beginning to be heard.

One of the first works to mark an increase in intellectual dissent in Albania was a novel published in late 1989 criticising human rights violations by the Ministry of the Interior. The author, Neshat Tozai, carefully did not attack the PLA itself, but it could easily be inferred that he placed the ultimate responsibility for the repression on the country's communist leaders. Other intellectuals took advantage of what appeared to be a mild relaxation of controls in the cultural sector to express views that till then the PLA had anathematised.[5] Also in 1989 the author Ismail Kadare

---

[4] *Zeri-i-Popullit*, Tirana, 21 June 1988.

[5] E. Biberaj, 'Albania at the Crossroads', *Problems of Communism*, September/October 1991, p.4. In view of the ideological atmosphere at the time, it is hard to see what this 'fight' would have consisted of, or how it could have been conducted, given the ideological bankruptcy of the PLA. It should be noted that for many years in Tirana it had been difficult to buy many of the basic texts of Marx, Lenin and many other classic Marxist theorists, although Hoxha's works were available in vast quantities, the 71-volume *Vepra* (Collected Works) being published as late as 1990.

vigorously criticised at a literary conference the government's interference in literature, arguing that no government could either grant or deny a writer's freedom to create.[6] By the end of the decade, the problem for the PLA leadership was how to manage change in such a way as to maintain, as far as possible, the monopoly of power it had enjoyed for fifty years, and to avoid major disorder and bloodshed. In its jaundiced view of the Gorbachev reforms in the Soviet Union, fear of disorder and anarchy was a paramount factor; this had been evident in all the Party leadership's statements on the subject in the preceding four years. At the time it seemed in the West as though this was special pleading by Alia and the Party. The hidden agenda was that fear of disorder would possibly deter the Albanian people from risking the necessary changes towards a pluralist system and would lead to the PLA remaining in power.

In retrospect, given the anarchy that ensued in 1990-1, as well as many subsequent problems, the fears of the PLA leadership may appear to have more practical substance, if no less self-interest. Ramiz Alia neatly expressed the central dilemma of those in power in Tirana in his speech to the United Nations General Assembly as late as September 1990:

> The changes that are taking place at present in Central and Eastern Europe, the complex and still ill-defined situations that are being created in this wide region, and the new and varied differences that are emerging, of which one does not know what forms they will assume and what consequences they will bring about, call for serious and wise reflection and actions on the part of all and everybody. Exaltation of democracy and human rights alone cannot be the magic key to the solution of the major, indeed we would say dramatic, problems of those countries. It is an evident fact that in some countries this exaltation is leading to anarchy, decline and the degradation of political, social and economic life, and conflicts and clashes with characteristics of a civil war.[7]

It is perhaps worth reflecting on the language of this key international policy statement following the East European revolutions.

---

[6] *Drita*, 11 November 1989, p. 5.
[7] Albanian Telegraphic Agency, no. 81, 28 September 1990.

It is clear that, while stating a truism that formal democracy does not in itself prevent international or ethnic conflict, Alia did not appear to understand the extent or finality of the victory of capitalism represented by the changes in Eastern Europe. To the PLA leadership at this time, the notion of a 'return' to capitalist economies throughout the world seemed foreign. In practical terms, this ideological blockage had clear implications for Albania's domestic policy of keeping the existing patterns of property ownership and the socialist economic system, but with a pattern of 'human face' reforms, increased international contacts and, in the economic sphere, greater emphasis on joint ventures with foreign multinational companies to provide essential investment and technological assistance. If this was the view of the leadership almost a year after the fall of the Berlin Wall, the reactions, both practical and ideological, which the revolutions of 1989 engendered can only be guessed at, and will only become known when the PLA archives are opened.

Like the years preceding it, 1989 was a year of protracted economic problems for Albania, particularly in agricultural production, and the new regimes in Eastern Europe had reneged on many of the trade and barter agreements for industrial goods which it had negotiated previously. The chronic problems in manufacturing and the extractive industries caused by increasingly aged Chinese machinery and shortages of spare parts grew still worse, and the crisis was exacerbated by a second year of serious drought, which affected most of the Balkans. Nevertheless, in its own thinking and political language the Party remained ossified. It was as if there were different languages for public and private use. The continuation of Stalinist and Hoxhaist habits of thought and political organisation till the end of 1989 can be illustrated by the decisions of the 9th Plenum of the PLA Central Committee, held in the third week of January 1990.

It should be noted that only a week before, on January 11, troops had been brought from Tirana into the northern regional capital of Shkoder to suppress an opposition demonstration in the main square against food shortages and in favour of democratic reform. Information is scanty on other street-level protests during this month, but there seems little doubt that given the appalling economic conditions of mid-winter and the sense among the people that political change might at last be possible, some events did take place. Against this background the Central Committee remained under the control of hardliners, who at this stage probably included Alia himself. The fact that the protest took place in Shkoder, a traditional northern centre of opposition to communism, may have helped the PLA hardliners, who would have been able to characterise the protesters in traditional ways. In any event, the Central Committee concentrated on the alarming political changes taking place in Poland, Hungary, East Germany, Bulgaria and the Soviet Union. It analysed the situation as one.

.... where rightist forces have taken power. The bourgeoisie and international reaction are seeking and working so that anything which might recall socialism is destroyed there. In the bourgeois propaganda the socialist ideal has been proclaimed as anachronistic. Reaction is presenting communism as a spectre which is a threat not only for the bourgeoisie but also for the people.[...] The counter-revolutionary process has been supported also by the masses of the working people who have become disillusioned by revisionist rule, by its bureaucracy and violence and the economic stagnation.[8]

In these terms, Alia's diagnosis was essentially Hoxhaist, with a call from the Party leadership for its activists to strengthen their internal political and economic efforts by more discipline and self-reliance. In a key passage on political work, Party cadres were required to

.... extend their links with the working masses of town and countryside...rejecting any manifestation of formalism, officiousness and bureaucracy. In particular, the organisations of the masses, the Democratic Front (DF), the Albanian League of Youth (LYUA), the trade unions (TUA) and the women's organisations (WUA), as well as other organisations, must be better activised. The press, radio and television must radically improve their work, so that the word of the Party reaches the masses more quickly and is not transmitted through general slogans and phraseology but through convincing, understandable arguments.[9]

[8] *The Deepening of the Revolutionisation of the Life of the Party and of the Country*, Tirana, 1990.

[9] Ibid.

It was clear that the leadership were well aware that the PLA was exhausted as a political force: this can be explained by the theory advanced by some younger PLA members that Albanian communism had essentially worn itself out during the Maoist-inspired Cultural Revolution in the late 1960s and early 1970s, and that after the break with China many Party cells and organisations were only shadows of their former selves, going through the motions of Party work for the sake of appearance, while in practice they had largely abandoned Hoxhaist ideals and ideology. The ghost of the National Liberation War in the 1940s still clearly haunted Alia on the issue of pluralism, which the Central Committee saw as 'a call for the revival of Balli Kombetar and Legaliteti...and the creation of new anti-popular, anti-democratic and anti-national organisations'.[10] But it is in the economic sphere that the Central Committee report was most alarmist. It states

> Attention must be paid to export plans which must be fulfilled on time and with quality.[...] Reductions of cost and increases of productivity must be the example everywhere. The plans which are linked to the food and clothing of the people must be fulfilled. Nothing can justify the shortages of vegetables, milk and even meat on the market of any city. The decisions which have been taken about the collective garden, about increasing meat production etc. must be applied creatively and with persistence.[11]

But although the document reveals something of the political and economic problems faced by the PLA at that time, the specific measures to improve the situation are largely rhetorical and timid in practice. In his keynote speech to the Plenum, Ramiz Alia claimed credit, on behalf of the deceased Hoxha, for predicting the dramatic changes in Eastern Europe and the return to capitalism which the revisionist forces would bring. His response, however, was one of a number of familiar ritual invocations to strengthen the Party's leading role, coupled with an attack on Gorbachev for 'filling a revisionist vacuum'. The Party would open its meetings to the public, take greater care in selecting experts and cadres for key posts, and make the state planning system more flexible;

[10] Ibid.
[11] Ibid.

workers would now approve the appointment of factory managers. In the vital sphere of livestock production, peasants would be allowed to keep animals themselves, and be encouraged to sell their produce in the food-starved urban markets. However, none of these steps remotely measured up to the extent of the crisis the Party and government would face in the coming twelve months. Much of the psychology of the leadership's policy rested on the assumption that, in some unspecified way, Albania would be able to follow its own path and insulate itself from international developments. After all, the leadership had been following this policy in relation to the international communist movement for some years – with success, if seen from a Tirana perspective and measured only in terms of the leadership's survival rather than the welfare and prosperity of the country. Even to the more intelligent among them, like Central Committee secretary Spiro Dede, it did not seem impossible that the policy could succeed against the background of the new conditions in Eastern Europe.

A considerable change began to affect the thinking of the Party leadership in the next three months. Formal Party control over the Democratic Front, the mass organisation to which nearly all Albanians were expected to belong, started to disintegrate when journalists from the DF newspaper *Bashkimi* demanded the right of independent editorial control; the majority of the journalists and publicists who founded the Democratic Party newspaper the following year took part in this movement. It served as a catalyst, as did the effort by leading Party intellectuals like the historian Arben Puto, most of whom had been Hoxhaist acolytes, to distance themselves from the Party by setting up human rights groups. A wave of open discussion of the future swept through Tirana and the larger towns, with the students of Tirana University in the forefront. Some restrictions on foreign travellers were lifted, and after February 1990 the number of visas issued to Western journalists greatly increased. The decisions of the Plenum were obviously irrelevant in the new international context, and in the late winter and early spring of 1990 Ramiz Alia himself assumed a Gorbachev-type reforming role, and there was a new focus on the Party leader as the standard-bearer of reform. Openness was the keyword during those months. Even the official photographs of Alia were changed to a new pose very similar to one adopted by the Russian leader. In practice this 'openness', or Albanian *glasnost*, meant the virtual restoration of genuine free speech in private and in public, but every effort was still being made to contain the pace of institutional change within the structure of the one-party state.

However, events moved too fast for the PLA. After an unprecedently short period, a 10th Plenum of the Central Committee was held on 16 and 17 April. Although evidence on the subject is largely anecdotal, this seems to have been forced on the leadership by dissatisfaction in the Party's lower ranks with the slow pace of reform, and through warnings from localities that the general situation was passing out of Party control. At the meeting, Ramiz Alia's auspiciously titled keynote speech to the plenum – 'Democratisation of socio-economic life strengthens the thinking and action of the people' – was a strange mixture of new and old thinking. Boasting that 'the 9th Plenum clearly reflected the militant and anti-bureaucratic spirit of our Party', it outlined the 'achievement' of an allegedly substantial purge of inefficient managers of enterprises, and made new proposals for enterprises to become self-financing and be allowed to distribute profits made in excess of the plan. The speech also echoed some traditional Hoxhaist themes, repeating the view that Albania would follow its own path and remain 'socialist'. However, reality was acknowledged far more than three months earlier, when Alia mentioned the international context of Albania's crisis: state socialism had collapsed over a large part of the world, and Yugoslavia was entering a period of crisis with the possibility of war in Kosova. It is not difficult to read this speech as using the problems of Yugoslavia to divert attention from those at home, but perhaps Alia, more than most of his contemporaries in government in Albania and in Western Europe, saw clearly how great the crisis about to overtake the Balkans would be. As a northern Albanian with real personal experience of the region – he had been active in Kosova during the war – Alia was unlike almost every other member of the Tirana leadership, which at this time was still dominated by southern Tosks. Most of these former associates of Hoxha had had little personal contact with the Yugoslav Partisans during the war.

In general, Alia's speech and the Plenum as a whole did little to tackle the Party's central problem during these months, most notably the revolution of rising expectations which was beginning to grip the whole country. In classic revolutionary mode, every minor reform whetted the popular appetite for more fundamental structural changes. The minor changes in the draconian penal code and the lifting of certain restrictions on peasant agriculture with the allocation of 1 or 2 *stremmas* of land per peasant family for private plots meant little to the young in the towns, who were now more than ever aware of the potential for radical change. Absenteeism at work soared, and in some rural areas state farms began to collapse as peasants stole livestock from the common herds. In districts where communism was traditionally weak, especially in the north, centrally-imposed regional and local leaderships came under threat – a bad omen for the future of the one-party system. Alia commented on this problem in the key Tropoja region of the far north, where recommended candidates had failed to be elected to regional committees. In Tirana individual centres of dissidence on the East European model were beginning to appear, although there had not so far been any public demonstrations against the government. Industrial production continued to decline with a contemporary report estimating that output was only about 50-60 per cent of full capacity due to breakdowns, absenteeism and shortages of fuel and spare parts.

But most important was the beginning of the social process that was fatally to undermine the one-party state. It came from an entirely unexpected direction. For many years the Western embassies in Tirana had existed in an area largely closed to the public and under heavy surveillance by the *Sigurimi*. With the decline in the Alia government's credibility and the growing inefficiency of the internal security apparatus, it had become possible for individual Albanians to walk right up to the foreign embassy buildings. Although the Alia reforms were welcomed by all sections of the population, they did not touch what was seen by most Albanians, particularly the young, as a fundamental oppression: their inability to travel or work abroad, or to own passports. But direct action in Tirana itself provided an answer at a time when attempting to cross the external borders of Albania was still highly dangerous. A shoot-to-kill policy was still carried out by the internal security troops posted there. Tirana now offered possibilities for a new type of popular struggle without such risks. In February 1990 a Korca family called Popa, consisting of six people, climbed into the garden of the Italian embassy and lived there in a shed for several weeks. The unwillingness of the Italian authorities to hand them over to the Albanian police proved a catalyst in the turbulent street life of Tirana, and, unknown to foreign diplomats, the buildings of the various embassies became the focus of attention among Tirana's dissatisfied young. Scarcely any of them believed the PLA to be capable of reform, and the decisions of the April Plenum fell largely deaf ears. In desperation, in a key decision that proved a fulcrum for later dramatic events, the People's Assembly on 10 May gave Albanians the right to own passports and to travel abroad, and further relaxations were made in the penal code. The number of offences carrying the death penalty was reduced from thirty-four to eleven, and capital punishment for women was abolished. The offence of 'religious propaganda' was struck off the penal code, and the power of local authorities to deport whole families for internal exile to other parts of the country was scrapped. These announcements were linked to the decision of the government in March to apply to join the Conference on Security and Co-operation in Europe (CSCE) and to act as host to the UN Secretary-General, Javier Pérez de Cuéllar, on the first-ever visit to Albania by a holder of that office.

As the hot summer months of June and July came, the normally crowded streets of the capital became a ferment of discussion and opposition activity, though still without the formal framework of the East German and Czech demonstrations. The political atmosphere became more tense. Passports for the population still did not materialise, and the young became bitterly angry at what they saw as the government's broken promises. Fear of the *Sigurimi* was still rife, and it was widely believed that the army would be summoned to fire on demonstrators. Nevertheless, on 2 July the patience of the people finally ran out and a crowd of about 400, mostly unemployed young men, stormed the main diplomatic quarter and occupied a number of Western embassy buildings. Their numbers soon swelled to about 4,500. It has never been established clearly who were the leaders of this movement and to what extent the occupation had been planned. Because most of those concerned were subsequently given asylum in Italy and have not since been interviewed by journalists or historians, these questions remain unanswered.

At the time of these dramatic events in Tirana, hundreds of people began to trek from all over the country towards the Adriatic port of Durres, where would-be refugees seized a ship and attempted to sail it to Italy. In terms of popular feeling the situation in July 1990 can be compared to the time of the 'Great Fear' before the French Revolution and to many similar, essentially peasant movements in other parts of the world and other epochs, when a hitherto suppressed and cowed rural population has realised spontaneously that it had the power to overthrow a hated urban political and economic system and form a new government. However, there was still a long way to go before the PLA would surrender power. Soldiers did fire on the Tirana demonstrators who attempted to seize the embassies. The government declared a partial state of emergency, and ordered the security forces into Durres, where they fought pitched battles on the beaches with the demonstrators. *Sigurimi* agents were visibly posted at almost every street-corner in Tirana, and the only foreign tourists in the country at the time, two busloads from Britain and another from the Netherlands, were forced to visit Apollonia and Butrint not once but twice because both sites were in the south, far from any major towns and the tensions of Tirana and Durres. Speaking to an emergency Party Plenum on 6 July, Alia claimed that the embassy invasions were not a spontaneous outbreak of discontent but organised by forces abroad which wanted to see the end of socialism in Albania and the subordination of the country to foreign powers: 'The danger comes not from these disoriented persons, but from those who lurk behind them, at home and abroad.[...] These destructive, anti-democratic, anti-Albanian forces...aim to deprive the people of state power and the country of its freedom and independence. Nobody should forget this. Destructive acts like those of 2 July in Tirana have a pronounced anti-national goal, in which instigation from abroad is evident.'[12]

No evidence has been produced to support these claims. Although Western governments and intelligence agencies were no doubt interested in the future of Albania and wished to see the end of communism there, there is every sign that the embassy occupations were an indigenous response to a local situation, rather than something organised in Bonn or Washington. Also, given the developing crisis in Yugoslavia, it is possible that at this stage some Western governments, particularly the French,

[12] 'The Continuation of the Process of Democratisation is Vital For Progress in the Country', Tirana, 1990.

saw the Alia regime as contributing to Balkan stability, fearing civil war and a Romanian-style upheaval if the PLA were forced from power by street demonstrations. Tension was also high in Kosova in July 1990, with what existed of Albanian democracy there being suppressed by the ascendant Milosević regime, and Alia may have feared that the Yugoslav crisis would spread into Albania. The embassy seizures and associated turmoil in the Tirana streets caused a major crisis within the Party leadership. The ultra-conservative group around Hoxha's widow Nexhmije lost influence when Alia sacked the hardline Interior Minister and head of the *Sigurimi*, Simon Stefani, on 7 July, along with three Political Bureau members, Manush Myftiu, Prokop Murra and Vito Kapo. A fellow hardliner, Lenka Cuko, was sacked as Central Committee secretary and replaced by a reformist, Spiro Dede. Hardliners subsequently claimed that the demonstrations were encouraged by reformists in the leadership in order to undermine them, but whatever the details, the July events in a certain sense marked the end of Hoxha's legacy: despite the widespread deployment of troops and paramilitary forces on the streets, the coercive powers of the one-party state were not used to any effect against the demonstrators. The government was forced to grant an amnesty to those who took part, most of whom anyway had been safely evacuated to Western countries. The people had won the first battle where it mattered – in the streets of the capital city; for the next six months an increasingly radical, violent and confrontational street culture began to dominate almost all Albanian towns and cities, culminating in the 'Winter of Anarchy' of 1991-2.

With hindsight, it is notable that the current Democratic Party government had as much difficulty as its predecessor in providing reasonable explanations for these great popular movements. A recurrent theme in all comment on the disorder has been that it was organised consciously by the *Sigurimi* secret police to discredit the country and so prevent the Democratic Party government from inheriting useful means of production, such as the many factories that were destroyed in the transition, as well as schools, transport equipment and other infrastructure. There is no evidence in the public domain to support these allegations, any more than there was to support Alia's seemingly paranoid views about foreign intelligence agencies. In both cases the allegations perhaps reveal more about the mentality of the Tirana governing élite than about the causes of the events themselves. The people were taking revenge – in a country noted for it – on a hated and disintegrating social and political system, as the reports of foreign correspondents at the time make clear.

The capacity of the principal Western governments to influence events in this period was limited. Although talks with the British and American governments on the question of the Albanian gold reserves impounded after the Corfu Channel incident forty-four years before had begun in February 1990, neither government was represented by diplomats in Tirana during this time.[13] The German embassy, which was completely gutted during the July riots, remained virtually inoperative while being repaired. Other Western embassies, including the traditionally influential French one, remained closed and under armed guard. The only fully functioning missions were those of communist countries like China and North Korea, which by now had little or no political influence over the Alia administration outside the ranks of the traditionally Chinese-oriented diplomatic corps. As a result, the government had nowhere to turn for support or advice – this at a time when the rapidly developing crisis in Yugoslavia was beginning to preoc-cupy Western governments. There was nothing to prevent street politics becoming dominant, as the coercive *apparat* of the one-party state was removed, and the government suffered both domestic and international isolation. The roots of some of the later highly uncritical Western support for the Berisha government are to be found in this period; any government with which it was possible to have dealings, however undemocratic, was preferable to the vacuum of 1990.

The PLA's initial response to the increasing disorder was to legislate. Within three weeks of the embassy sieges, on 31 July, a further revision of the penal code was announced, with a key concession to popular pressure for travel rights, in that 'the flight of a person outside Albania is no longer considered treason, but only illegal border trespassing'. However, the code contained a

---

[13] On 15 May 1946, Albanian guns fired on British minesweepers trying to clear the Corfu channel of mines, because Tirana claimed than the British ships were in Albanian territorial waters. The British then sent four destroyers into the channel, and on 22 October two of them struck mines and sank with the loss of forty-four men. For a full account of these events see Eric Leggett, *The Corfu Incident*, London, 1974, and Leslie Gardner, *The Eagle Spreads his Claws*, London, 1966.

restatement of the draconian Article 78 of the Constitution whereby district chief of police were given blanket rights to ban political meetings or public gatherings that might 'violate public order', 'insult the national feeling' or 'damage relations with other states'. Thus, despite the sackings of the ultra-hardliners earlier in the month, the PLA leadership was still able to stifle political opposition and prevent the formation of illegal political movements. As before, fear of public disorder was used as a pretext for these restrictions. The violence and adverse international publicity generated by the embassy occupations had obviously shocked the government and PLA. The next nine months would be dominated by tensions between two impulses: the removal of the coercive power of the state and, in the absence of any functioning and respected state or civil society, the trend towards anarchy.

The same contradictions continued in the economic and diplomatic spheres. Relationships developed in the Hoxha period continued as if no political change had been taking place: a major contract was signed in September with the Chinese government agency Machinepex for the rebuilding of the sulphuric acid plant at Lac. However, in the same month there was a significant break with the past when, amid considerable publicity, Ramiz Alia visited the United States and, as well as addressing the UN General Assembly, met Albanian émigrés in New York and Boston, nearly all of whom were Ballist and Legaliteti anti-communist exiles from the conflicts during and after the 1944 Liberation. Such a meeting would have been unthinkable only twelve months earlier, when all émigrés were characterised as working with the CIA and MI6 for the overthrow of socialism. In the same spirit of openness to the outside world, Albania began to participate in CSCE gatherings, and diplomatic contacts developed with the United Nations with the visit of the Secretary-General mentioned earlier. Pérez de Cuéllar showed particular interest in the human rights situation, and made it a condition of his visit that he could see the inside of an internment camp. He was shown Burrel gaol in the Mati, an important centre of the forced labour system, which processed 'criminals' for the nearby Spaç pyrites mines. Pérez de Cuéllar was deeply shocked by what he saw, even though food rations had been improved just before his arrival. It was made clear to Alia that Albania could not receive any international aid or join any international organisations until the Hoxhaist system of repression had been finally dismantled.

However, desirable as such normalisation of international contacts might be, and encouraging to the process of internal reform, it is difficult to avoid the impression that by focusing on foreign affairs during this period, Alia fatally neglected the deteriorating economic situation and social conditions, and his genuine struggle for reforms within the PLA itself faltered accordingly. The supply of food to the cities as winter approached was inadequate, and increasing numbers of peasants were stealing animals from the collective farm herds, either to make up their own herds or simply to slaughter them for their own winter food. Urban markets were empty. Power breakdowns became more frequent, and almost any kind of public property became a target for popular revenge against communism. Many individual Albanians were interpreting democratisation as the right to appropriate common property regardless of its origins or purpose, and there was vandalism against schools, hospitals and, more understandably, PLA and government offices.

As autumn came, the political ironies and contradictions became ever more pronounced, to the point of absurdity. In October, the draft law for the new elections to the People's Assembly was introduced. This was important in so far as it marked the end of direct Party control of candidates through the PLA recommended list system; it allowed organisations such as trade unions and military veterans' associations to put forward candidates, and introduced the principle of voting by secret ballot. However, at exactly the same time the Party held the 'Week of Enver', devoted to the memory of the dead dictator. According to the Albanian Telegraphic Agency report, in that week the coal-miners at Valais overfulfilled their targets by 200 tons of coal a shift, the workers of the garment industry overfulfilled production targets, and so on. On the one hand, Alia and the PLA leadership sought to introduce reforms which, if fully implemented, would soon have ended their power and, on the other, they continued to act as though the Hoxhaist framework and a rigid communist society could be maintained indefinitely.

This schizophrenic approach was maintained when, for an unprecedented fourth time in one year, the 12th Plenum of the Central Committee met on 6 November. The title of the Plenum document, 'The Strengthening of the People's State Power and the Improvement of the Political System reinforce Democratic Developments', was itself revealing of the crisis in the Party. Clearly Alia believed that renewal of the one-party state was somehow compatible with increased formal democracy. In his keynote speech, he dwelt at length on the July events, and public order issues, showing that the possibility of a Romanian-style mass uprising against PLA rule and widespread bloodshed haunted him. He said 'Democracy means order – order at work, discipline and production', and called on communists to give increased attention to these objectives. Most of the rest of his remarks were addressed to two main issues, the problems of economic reform and the elections to the People's Assembly, due in February 1991. It is clear from his speech that the PLA did not expect, or want, the emergence of an organised political opposition, and was prepared to do everything in its power to prevent it. The optimism that briefly prevailed in Tirana during the early autumn, with the renewal of international contacts, Alia's American visit and the new draft electoral law, were dashed, particularly in the minds of young Tirana radicals. The PLA would clearly do everything in its power to maintain the structure of the one-party state and minimise economic reforms. Thus it was inevitable that the political centre of gravity would soon return to the streets. Albanians of the older generation reacted with bemused incomprehension to the development of the popular struggle, and predictions of a coup were common. Although no coup occurred, such apprehension was only to be expected among people who had grown up under the communist regime and had no doubts about the inherent ruthlessness and extremism of its leaders. But what was not widely realised was how far the internal life of the one-party state had been corrupted, and how difficult it would be for the small leadership group to agree on policies for its own survival.

3

THE TIME OF DARK FORCES, NOVEMBER 1990-MARCH 1991

The 12th Plenum of the PLA Central Committee in November 1990 was the last occasion when the Party attempted to articulate a coherent programme for the future of Albania. For the political system in which the Party had enjoyed a monopoly of power for so long it was a watershed. Three months later an organised opposition had been formed, troops had been used to quell unrest in the streets, and the one-party state was in its final, painful stages of disintegration. The hopes raised by the prospect of free elections had evaporated with the realisation that the only opposition candidates that could be put forward were obliged to operate within the framework of the Democratic Front. This was still controlled by Hoxha's widow Nexhmije, who in turn had her own hardline group on the Politburo – the 'Group of the Widow' – which acted as the guardian of tradition and Enverist orthodoxy. In the towns, as winter began and material conditions worsened with real hunger and food and power shortages, the increasingly desperate youth began, as already mentioned, to attack PLA and other government buildings as symbols of communism. In late November troops were moved from outlying bases to many large cities, and tension rose throughout the country. In Albania these months have been known ever since as *Forcat e Errëta*, 'the time of dark forces'.

The street politics of Tirana were to play the decisive role in the next series of events, being themselves increasingly dominated by the city's large student community At this stage the Tirana workers were not much involved in the movement, but disorder and protest were spreading ever wider. In provincial towns such as Elbasan, serious unrest had been endemic since the attempts to seize ships during the summer. It has been condemned on television by Gramoz Pashko and other leaders of the present opposition, as well as the government. Troops were guarding public buildings, and there were frequent minor clashes between police and demonstrators. The same patterns of protest developed in other towns such as Kavaja and Shkoder, which were becoming strongholds of opposition. However, it was possible for the authorities in these centres to arrange a media blackout on the disturbances, and security forces were present in sufficient numbers to intimidate demonstrators. At this stage in the winter the *Sigurimi* were still intact and generally feared, but in Tirana this was not the case. Although there were several military bases in and near the city, they did not contain enough soldiers for the authorities to control the centre of the city when faced with tens of thousands of demonstrators, without a major civil-military confrontation involving tanks. The opposition movement had broadened since the days of the embassy sieges the previous summer, when a significant proportion of the young men involved were from a semi-criminal and alienated subculture. It now included most of the respectable young intelligensia and increasing numbers of older professional people, who were now aware of the growing weakness of the state apparatus.

In any case the nature of the protests themselves did not easily lend themselves at this stage to a military form of security control. The PLA faced an important problem in securing the loyalty of the army leadership in any confrontation that might prove explosive. An attack on a public building at night by a few people who would then rapidly disappear into the darkness was a much more typical expression of the public mood than the kind of large-scale organised meeting and street demonstration that had developed elsewhere in Eastern Europe. Tirana could not draw on the long-established dissident culture of cities like Prague and Budapest, with their networks of opposition intellectuals capable of organising large formal political meetings or practical action. Thus protest in Albania had a random, anarchic character. Increasingly, for inhabitants and foreign visitors alike, Tirana at night became a place of terror, with sleep interrupted by the sound of pistol shots and the crash of broken glass, all in total darkness as power cuts became endemic. The city was full of narrow winding alleyways without street lights or street names. There was no adequate civil police force. In the communist period, thanks to draconian penalties for the most minor offences, there had been very little crime, but now the city had become a free-for-all, appearing relatively normal by day but reverting to chaos at night. Hospitals were lit by smoking rolls of newspapers, – and hotel corridors in the city centre became sinister dark tunnels patrolled by violent thugs. Only young men could consider risking travel at night in the city and then only with a group of companions.

Alia could see that in these circumstances the old method of rule could not continue; after an outbreak of violent rioting in Shkoder in early December, he made the critical decision to send Dr Sali Berisha, the country's leading cardiologist, to act as the PLA's mediator with the radical and increasingly restive student body in Tirana University. It is clear that by this stage Alia was the only member of the leadership capable of making decisions – for which the Central Committee, despite its frequent meetings acted largely as a rubber stamp. Berisha, who was to become President himself only two years later, was a northerner from Tropoja and had been a member of the PLA for twelve years. He had a reputation as a serious, rather hardline communist who took Hoxhaist ideology seriously, and was not at that time thought to be one of the many Tirana professionals who joined the PLA only for careerist reasons. But in fact he had been acting in association with a group of senior opposition intellectuals who were to be the founding fathers of the Democratic Party. In the chaos of the time, Berisha's emergence as a mediator attracted no particular attention, since many new political leaders were emerging on the back of the popular movement. In reality it was a seminal event.

A former law professor commented on the situation in an interview with one of the present authors just before the formation of the Democratic Party:

'In general, before August 1990 the intellectuals were not so satisfied with the situation. Then Alia organised a meeting of fifty intellectuals in Tirana including Berisha, myself, Kadare, Pashko and others, and they discussed the problem of ideological pluralism. The intellectuals were very passive during this period – their courage failed, only the students had courage. Intellectuals were afraid of violent revolution, they were with Gorbachev. Berisha was sent by the Tirana Party Committee in 1990 to work with the students who were on strike. A Committee member telephoned and told me that some comrades had been sent to talk to the students, to ask them to be moderate and not to revolt. When the new parties were legalised in December 1990, Berisha became a leader of the students. They formed a new party called the 'Party of the Youth and Intellectuals', and a few days later chose the name 'Democratic Party'. Azem Hajdari was chosen President. When he returned from the United States, he lived in the prestigious Hotel Dajti. Neritan Ceka was not a member of the DP at the time, but Preç Zogaj, Albert Carici and Edmond Drako were. The Communist Party was disintegrating fast, especially after the statue of Hoxha was pulled down. It was not in a position to do anything'.[1]

The original DP founders have always claimed that a new political movement appeared to be emerging and they simply put themselves at the head of it. This is indeed what appeared to happen in that the PLA allowed a new party to be formed as a first concession to a multi-party system, believing that it would be led by trusted ex-communists such as Berisha, Gramoz Pashko (son of Hoxha's close henchman Josif Pashko), and leading independent intellectuals such as Dr Shahin Kadare, a cancer specialist and brother of the famous novelist, and Dr Neritan Ceka, director of the national archaeological institute. It perhaps flatters this group to say that they put themselves at the head of a movement, because in retrospect there seems little doubt that at least some of them of them were put there by Alia. In an interview in prison in 1995 Alia goes into detail about his instructions to Berisha:

'On the evening of 10 December 1990 I learned that at the Party Committee in Tirana they were holding a meeting with a group of lecturers about the events which had happened on the university campus. The aim was to send them to talk to the students and try to calm them down. Among the professors and lecturers at that meeting was Sali Berisha. The truth is that I did not know much about him except that he was a cardiologist and had been to France on a specialisation course, also that he was a communist. [...] I was interested that Berisha was from Tropoja because the student leaders were also from the north. I instructed Berisha to tell the student leaders that

---

[1] Interview by Miranda Vickers with Professor Luan Omari, 23 September 1993.

I would go and meet them if they respected the agreement reached with the previous government to attend classes as normal.'[2]

It seems clear that Alia was once again using the fear of disorder to try and shape the character of the emerging opposition. But, as in the preceding year, events were moving too quickly for him. Even at this stage, Alia still seems to have had some hope that something of the old system would survive. In his speech to the National Party Conference of the PLA on 22 December, he spoke of the 'psychosis of demobilisation' that was affecting the whole of life in Albania, with plummeting production, the beginnings of mass emigration and 'mistakes' in the work of the Party. In this speech, however, he also spoke of the Party's 'historic achievements', and of the future work of Albanian communists who have 'the confidence and will to master the most advanced contemporary ideological and political thought, just as they are able to translate it into life'. The outline programme agreed at the Congress for the coming election campaign proposed economic reforms, the de-bureaucratisation of the Party, a reduction in the size of the Central Committee and various other cosmetic reforms, but it did not face up to the loss of its leading role in Albanian life. During this month it seems that Alia imagined the Party might keep its traditional position while co-existing with an opposition, whose views would be made known to him and the PLA leadership by the trusted professionals he had placed in charge of it. Apart from its inherent impracticability, this scheme shows how far the political culture in Tirana was from any notion of political parties in the Western sense; this was a phenomenon that did not occur in the same way anywhere else in Eastern Europe. Even under the very difficult political conditions of war-time it has been possible for political parties to function in Serbia, Croatia and other Balkan states; but this was not true of Albania, and it may account, at least in part, for the victory of the PLA in the first democratic elections, held the following spring.

Linked to the disintegration of the PLA was the movement of leading PLA intellectuals and apologists into the human rights field, again taking energy and talent from the opposition party-building process. At the end of 1990 the Forum for the Defence of Human Rights and Fundamental Freedoms was established,

---

[2] Published in *Koha Jone*, 7 May 1995.

following the introduction of political pluralism, which in turn evolved from the student movement. Its founder was Arben Puto, a noted historian who had close links to the ruling circle under the communist regime. In an interview Puto stated that the initial aim of the Human Rights Forum was to secure the release of all political prisoners; so far about 500 had been released, leaving about 215 still detained. He was asked for the size of the total prison population, and replied:

'Well, we are a young organisation with no office, no full-time staff and no real facilities to speak of, so I have to rely on the official figures given me by the Ministry of the Interior. These give a total of 3,141 prisoners, of whom 2,800 are classed as common criminals. As for their conditions, we think they are changing for the better, but till recently they were truly horrific. Even if they are improving, you have to take into consideration the general living standard in our country; as a judge of the High Court suggested to me, when a foreign delegation comes here it should first visit the flat of an average family before going to see a prison.'

Puto was finally asked the intriguing question why, after being such a loyal PLA member for so many years, he had suddenly decided to become part of an independent human rights organisation. He replied:

'I'm glad you've asked me this question because for foreigners it is very difficult to imagine the system we lived under. The only way I can answer it is by giving you a brief personal history. I joined the Communist Party in 1944 when it offered two clear ideals – independence and social justice. Like many others I was not happy with the way things developed after the Liberation, and especially after the death of Stalin and the revelations at the 20th Party Congress. I was among many members who asked for our own history to be re-examined at this time. Because of this 'error of judgement' I have always been a second-rank member of the Party. Indeed, I have been involved in several political scandals, including the Mehmet Shehu business, where despite family connections (my two sisters were married to top Politburo figures), I was accused of hiding material I had gathered in the archives in London in order to protect Shehu. This was in 1982, ten years after

I had been there! [Shehu, a leading figure in the Partisan movement, had been Prime Minister, and was regarded as Hoxha's likely successor until his mysterious 'suicide' in 1981.] I was tried in a five-hour hearing presided over by a prosecutor and Xhelil Gjoni, and was close to being expelled. You have to understand that many scholars and intellectuals were against the excesses of the system but were afraid to speak. Today it is different.'[3]

In considering the effect Puto and similar intellectuals had on the student movement, it is necessary to form some judgement on how far they had really rejected the PLA and the political culture it represented. Some would claim that they were so imbued with its values and mentality as to be all but incapable of reinventing themselves politically, and that most of these new 'pluralist' activities had more to do with the urge to survive than with any genuine commitment to pluralism. On the other hand, it was far from clear at this stage whether the opposition would triumph, and if there had been a coup or a hardline take-over (likely to have led to civil war), association with the opposition leadership could well have been literally fatal for men such as Puto.

The same questions applied to Sali Berisha himself are much more damaging. Much of his political appeal, particularly to his foreign supporters, was based on the assumption that he represented a clean break with communism. The truth may well lie between the two extremes, in that many of the founding fathers may have sincerely wanted to break with the political past, but were incapable of doing so. The political culture of the Tirana élite under communism was of a peculiar narrowness, extremely provincial, often extraordinarily self-satisfied in view of how modest Albania's achievements were in many fields, and full of internal contradictions. It has been difficult for those, like Berisha, who had any standing in the political, cultural and intellectual life of Tirana under communism to escape from the psychology and attitudes of being part of a Marxist-Leninist élite, and this has been a major difficulty for the country in developing an independent, efficient ruling élite in the post-communist transition.

This culture was also unlikely to throw up effective leaders for the new popular movements, given its intellectual formation.

---

[3] *East European Reporter*, spring/summer 1991, pp. 115-16.

In the view of the students, simple solutions such as basic university reforms were needed as a first step, rather than the Byzantine procrastination and slow thought-processes of Ramiz Alia and his circle. Faced with these evasions, extraparliamentary agitation set the pace, with a crowd of 15,000 people demonstrating in Tirana on 23 December in support of the DP in the forthcoming elections. The national federation of trade unions announced a week later that it was breaking away from Party control and setting itself up as an independent organisation. For the first time opposition activity was reported in the official press and on television. On 5 January 1991 the inaugural issue of the DP newspaper, *Rilindja Demokratike,* appeared, the first opposition publication in post-war Albania. However, it was only permitted a print-run of 60,000 copies twice weekly, compared with 100,000 six times a week for *Zeri-i-Popullit,* and its distribution, especially in rural areas, was sporadic. On 6 January more than seventy Albanians fled at night to the Montenegrin town of Ulcinj, using the inner tubes of tyres and makeshift rafts to cross the Bojana river which marks the frontier.

At the same time, far away from Tirana in the snow and ice of the remote Buret mountains bordering Greece, equally momentous events were unfolding. Small groups of refugees had begun to assemble, many of them members of the ethnic Greek minority in the south, and they walked through the frozen limestone passes and waded across icy rivers into Greek territory. When it became clear that they could do so safely if they could survive the weather, more and more refugees followed. The border control mechanisms of the one-party state had collapsed, and Albania's physical isolation had ended. Within days, thousands of people had arrived in northern Greece, penniless, hungry and desperate; small towns near the border, like Filiates, were overwhelmed. They had established a pattern for Albanian economic migration that was to persist for the future, eventually with serious consequences for Greek-Albanian relations. Some even reached Athens, arriving in the well-to-do districts of Kolonaki and Glyfada like visitors from outer space. Their clothes were tattered and outdated. Bellbottom trousers were common and in their broken shoes they wandered around in a world they had glimpsed only in films but thought they could never reach. It was noticeable that the Albanians would stand and stare at urban Greece, often for minutes at a time in silence, as if they were seeking reassurance that a prosperous modern society actually existed. They discovered that it did exist, and that they were able to work within it. Very soon Omonia Square became (and has remained) an informal Albanian meeting point and labour market, a hiring fair of a type Thomas Hardy would have recognised.

The Greek embassy in Tirana was unwilling to issue many visas to would-be migrants, fearing that they would settle in the north-west of Greece and become the nucleus of a Muslim minority there. Most migrants had planned to enter Greece legally and spent about 300 leks each to buy a passport, but with hundreds queueing for visas that might never materialise, many took the law into their own hands and marched south. Thousands more people gathered in villages near the border and planned to cross when the opportunity arose. At this stage the response of the people of northern Greece was very positive, especially in towns like Ioannina where many Greeks were partly of Albanian descent. Collections of money were organised by well-wishers to provide decent clothes and shoes for the migrants, soup kitchens were set up, as at Filiates, and hospitals gave free treatment to those who were ill or suffering from exposure. But these simple and generous acts were not always reciprocated. Some penniless Albanians committed thefts, and soon the Greek popular mood began to change. It was equally difficult for the government in Athens to come to terms with what was happening and to evolve a sensible policy. Few senior figures in the Greek Foreign Ministry or the political establishment had any first-hand knowledge of Albania, and Cold War stereotypes still prevailed. Just as the reaction in Athens to the demise of Yugoslavia was full of factual illusions and wishful thinking, and officials clung to the old political reality long after it had ceased to have any substance, so the same process affected policy on Albania. In defence of the Greek political establishment, it should be said that the border had been closed since the time before some officials were born, and that planning on border issues had been exclusively in the military domain (for instance, the Greek junta persuaded NATO to pay for large road improvement schemes in the border area).

In these difficult circumstances, the Greek Prime Minister Constantine Mitsotakis went to Albania for talks on 15 January. It was the first official visit by a Greek leader since the Second

World War. The main objective was to impose some sort of stability on the situation, and Mitsotakis pressed the Albanian government to control its own population, and promised in exchange various forms of economic assistance. Mostly these were schemes which had already been discussed in previous years, like the Vjoses hydro-electric proposals, rather than the commitment of immediate economic aid and work permits which had been anticipated. The Albanians wanted to ensure that old Greek irredentist claims connected with Vorio (Northern) Epirus and the minority in Albania would not be revived in the future. Mitsotakis refused to comment directly on this issue. Some Albanians have always believed that the Greeks never accepted the 1913 Protocol of Florence on the delineation of the Greek-Albanian border. Most Albanian politicians and commentators were irritated by Mitsotakis and found him arrogant, and the visit was not a success, either in Tirana or in the main minority areas. When the Greek leader addressed a public meeting in the Greek minority village of Dervican, in the Drinos valley, he was pelted with eggs and rotten cabbages by villagers who believed that he had sold out their interests to the Tirana communist leaders – symbolising the difficulty the minority issue and Vorio Epirus would bring to bilateral relations in the next three years. The border crossing at Kakavia was to become a place of misery, with desperate people waiting in the freezing winter winds and snow for any form of transport to and from Greece, and often subject to arbitrary police violence and bureaucratic humiliation. It often seemed as if the days of the postwar displaced persons camps had returned, high in the Balkan mountains rather than in Central Europe. On 29 January more than 5,000 refugees were returned from Greece, after an Athens spokesman announced that all Albanian illegals would be automatically returned. This process has been endlessly repeated ever since. The economic projects which Greece, in its own interests, was anxious to pursue with Albania soon fell by the wayside as the brief period of good relations gave way to enmity and misunderstanding.

In a gesture aimed at stemming support for the nascent opposition DP, as well as retaining the political initiative, the government announced the release of more than 200 political prisoners. This was a largely cosmetic gesture since the forced labour system had almost broken down, and political prisoners had begun to escape from confinement. Their gaolers, seeing the writing on the wall, sometimes released them without central authorisation, and often wanted to escape from Albania themselves to avoid retribution. Families who had been condemned to internal exile for political offences were beginning to return home. President Alia said on state radio that the government was considering freeing all remaining political prisoners; this move was made in a bid to dilute the influence of the DP, specifically by co-opting many of its policies and so conveying to the population the government's commitment to the reform process. Following threats from the nascent opposition to boycott the coming elections unless they were postponed, the government reluctantly announced that they would now take place on 31 March, and not on 10 February as originally planned. Alia showed considerable diplomacy in his statement explaining the about-turn over the election date: 'There may be many arguments for and against. However, the important thing in such situations is finding the best solutions, those that lead to understanding and not division, to unity and not rifts among the people. Stubbornness and egotism of whatever nature are bad counsellors in such matters.'[4] Apologists for the actions of Alia and his leadership during this period claim that he was leading the PLA on a skillful course by introducing reforms at a pace which the hardliners could tolerate, and holding to his own personal agenda by introducing democracy at a speed he felt the whole country could adapt to. Evidence for this view is lacking, and in his own memoirs Alia consistently justifies his position by exaggerating the possibility of civil war. Analysis of the events during the critical November-December period strongly suggests that, on the contrary, he tried continually to maintain the one-party state despite a rising tide of popular protest.

These were vital interlinked questions for the opposition in the next three months. It had to try and establish viable party organisations nationally, and at the same time prevent hardliners in the PLA from staging a coup or military take over and so abort the whole reform process and parliamentary elections. They were more successful with the second task than the first. Albania, unlike the former communist countries of Central Europe, has no tradition of political parties to draw upon, and at first there

---

[4] *Report on Eastern Europe*, 1 March 1991, p. 6.

were no funds for essential back-up such as motor vehicles or office equipment. The communists held a monopoly in this area, and the Tirana intellectuals who formed the nucleus of the DP leadership were not all temperamentally inclined, or professionally able, to work hard in remote localities to build up the new organisation. In practice, as with many other processes in this period, the new party grew on the basis of traditional loyalties, with the communists soon facing disintegration in northern areas such as Shkoder, with its long history of right-wing support, while in communist strongholds in the south, such as Fier and Berat, the DP only developed slowly. In Tirana other new political forces were appearing: the Ecology Party, founded on 7 January 1991 was one. At the same time population movements were not confined to the Greek border. Demonstrators fought a pitched battle in Shkoder with police, with shots being fired by both sides, after it was rumoured that the Yugoslav border was going to be opened at Hani-i-Hoti; four people were wounded.

In an atmosphere of increasing desperation, the meeting of the People's Assembly on 8 January passed measures allowing the establishment of foreign banks in Albania, and granted pardons to a further 202 people who were doing forced labour for political offences, and a week later Ramiz Alia met a major opposition delegation, led by the DP Organisation Commission chairman Azem Hajdari, one of the new personalities thrown up by the students' movement, a burly dark-haired Muslim in his thirties. Like Berisha, he came from Tropoja in the far north, where his father was an active communist. A fiery populist orator, he played a crucial role in mobilising the Tirana student community against the government in this period. He also played an important part in the development of fellow Tropojan Sali Berisha's leadership role, in that he could say what Berisha knew needed to be said, often in terms that approached crude mob oratory, and spared Berisha the need to say it himself. This has been seen as a key political skill of Berisha's, since he later used the DP Party Chairman Eduard Selami in a similarly manipulative role. The meeting worked out certain guidelines for the conduct of the spring elections.

The increasingly critical state of the economy preoccupied Alia in this month, and a long special meeting of the Council of Ministers was held on the subject against the background of an important official visit by the Turkish Minister of State, Isin Celebi.

The Council noted: 'The economic situation is deteriorating as a result of the continuous manifestation of wrecking indiscipline and the violation of legal rules in many enterprises and sectors of vital importance for the normal functioning of the economy.[...] The Council of Ministers calls for all parties and other political, social and economic organisations to render their contributions for the stabilisation of the economic and social situation.'[5] The ostensible reason for the meeting was to agree a strategy for the government to confront the turmoil at the important Valias lignite mine, near Tirana, where the striking miners had started to wreck the administrative offices and machinery. However, the Valias problem was only a microcosm of wider processes taking place generally as the revolutionary mood spread from the Tirana streets throughout the country. Many basic foods were in very short supply by this stage of the winter, with long bread queues, and milk was almost unobtainable in the cities. As government property was attacked, the government's own administrative processes were breaking down. Desperate to regularise the situation, the Council met again on 25 January, and passed decrees legitimising the right to strike after secret ballot, and putting forward safeguards for historic monuments. The latter was necessary because, in Tirana especially, the street opposition was focusing its attacks on the symbols associated with Hoxha, and the numerous Partisan monuments built over the last fifty years. The decree stated that as well as acknowledged national heroes such as Skenderbeg and the Frasheri brothers, 'Enver Hoxha and other prominent activists in the centuries-old life of our people are untouchable and legally defended by the state.' In a conciliatory gesture, the last remaining busts of Stalin were hastily removed from public buildings, following the demolition of his bronze statue in Tirana's main park. A massive Stalin bust in the entrance hall of the National Bank had been removed a few weeks before.

The passing of such a decree at this time suggests that Alia may have been receiving intelligence reports about the intentions of the opposition, as the attack on Hoxha's colossal gold-leaf-covered statue in Skenderbeg Square a few weeks later may already have been planned. The role of the remaining parts of the *Sigurimi*

---

[5] See James Pettifer, *The Greeks: Land and People since the War*, London: Viking, 1993, pp. 177ff.

in these events is of great interest, and it is to be hoped that its archives will eventually be opened. The relationship of the Democratic Party to the street campaigns during January and February is uncertain. It seems that Berisha sought to put himself above the endemic disorder and violence, and in response to the pitched battle fought on the beaches at Durres on 9 February claimed in a press conference that the DP stood for national reconciliation and calm, and condemned the violence. He did not express sympathy for the cause of the demonstrators. Here he seems to have played the role envisaged for him by Alia, who three months earlier singled him out as a suitable opposition leader. Without the forward movement at popular level, it was still possible that the PLA might hang on to power. Berisha and the other DP leaders relied on the students and the street activists to bring change, but could not risk a coup by offering to give them open support. In this complex process Hajdari played a vital role. Others who had been close to the communists, or leading Hoxhaists themselves, also condemned the Durres demonstrators. In this Alia still had an important card to play in that he could mobilise traditional close links among the Tirana élite who had been corrupted by communism and were afraid of the changes the popular movement might bring.

By the end of January it was at last apparent in the hitherto complacent Western capitals that Albania was facing a major crisis, and that the long-awaited final upheaval against the communists had begun. Voice of America reported on 7 February that Berisha had predicted a coup on the basis of reports of major military movements in Albania, with tanks being brought to bases near the cities. The Defence Minister, Kico Mustaqi, claimed that these movements were the result of the Gulf War, then at its height,[6] but this seems implausible. In retrospect, the reports seem to have been a product of the frenetic political atmosphere of the time, and it is uncertain whether the troop movements had any reality. Most Albanian tanks were old Soviet and Chinese models, and many could not run normally because of engineering problems and spare part shortages. Their only military use was to be dug in as fixed artillery pieces in the event of an invasion from Serbia or Greece, and the usual method of moving them

[6] Albanian Telegraphic Agency, 12 January 1991.

was on the backs of transporters because their engines were mostly in such poor condition that they produced poisonous fumes that endangered the crews. They would also have completely lacked the necessary operational mobility to be of any value in controlling urban disorder. None the less, the scare had an impact abroad. A week later invitations were issued to Albanian representatives to discuss the possibility of joining the International Monetary Fund, and discussions of US diplomatic representation in Tirana were accelerated. Turkey and Italy offered Albania new economic aid packages, and Western governments hurried to assist Alia and the reform programme. In the view of some outside observers, the real prospect dawned of the PLA completely losing control of political life under pluralism, and of a collapse of the social order and a military take-over. Others saw the crisis as spilling over into Kosova and thus precipitating war with Serbia.

The popular campaign accelerated at the beginning of February. The student organisation of Tirana University organised a strike, and its demands became more ambitious. Seven hundred students and lecturers went on hunger-strike and demanded an end to compulsory military training and the compulsory study of Marxist-Leninist theory. They also called for Enver Hoxha's name to be removed from the University. This stage of the campaign marked the appearance of the DP deputy leader Gramoz Pashko in a key role, as the effective liaison between the old Tirana élite in the DP leadership and the new young radicals. Pashko is a complex and contradictory man, an academic economist of high calibre who later took university teaching posts in the West, but he is also vain and, his enemies would say, unstable, Orthodox in religion and with closer links to Greece than any other leading Albanian politician, something which at this stage in the transition was still an asset. These negotiations gained him a high national profile, and he retained his credibility with the students as a respected economist. It may be that Pashko's influence at this stage led to the students making increasingly radical demands: later in the month they called for the resignation of the Foreign, Interior and Justice Ministers. In response, and as an attempt to rally communists behind the party, Alia went to the southern port town of Vlora on 12 February and made a militant speech defending PLA policy. Vlora, centre of the depressed and culturally backward Liab region, had always been a centre of PLA support, going back to wartime days, and was notorious as a recruiting ground for the *Sigurimi*. Alia admitted that there had been 'shortcomings and mistakes', but called for order, discipline and an end to 'indiscipline, hooliganism and vagrancy'.[7] But it was to little avail.

Tension rose to intolerable levels in Tirana during the next week, and it was clear that a confrontation with the government was approaching. On 20 February, a crowd estimated by Liam McDowall, the Associated Press correspondent present, to number more than 100,000 people assembled in Skenderbeg Square after a student march from the University. It seems clear that the students were by now fully confident in the strength of their own movement and no longer prepared to heed calls for restraint, whether from the government or from leaders around Berisha and Pashko, who at this stage operated very much as a dual leadership. The student core of the movement was boosted for the first time by a mass infusion of workers and the older 're-spectable' elements in the population, an inauspicious sign for the survival of the Alia government. As February ended, the PLA's control of events was manifestly slipping away when several thousand people marched to the centre of Tirana and pulled down the giant 10-metres-high gold-leaf-covered statue of Enver Hoxha in Skenderbeg Square. There was some violence, and security forces fired blanks in their attempt to disperse the protesters. An estimated twenty people were injured, but witnesses reported that many of the police fraternised openly with the demonstrators. Within hours statues of Hoxha were brought down in Durres and Korça. In Vlora the statue of the communist hero and ex-Foreign Minister Hysni Kapo, who died in 1979, was also toppled. Later on 20 February, in response to the growing unrest, Alia declared presidential rule.

In a nationwide television and radio broadcast, Alia said that a Presidential Council would take over the country's government 'because things are getting out of control'. This move was in-terpreted by some as an attempt by Alia to contain the power of the PLA's conservative factions led by the unpopular hardliner Adil Çarcani, and of the *Sigurimi*. Xhelil Gjoni, brother-in-law of Hysni Kapo, was widely tipped to become Alia's successor as

[7] Albanian Telegraphic Agency, 9 February 1991.

First Secretary of the PLA. Undeterred, the demonstrators continued the next day publicly burning the works of Enver Hoxha. Their pages littered the streets surrounding Skenderbeg Square and in one corner a huge bonfire engulfed a seemingly unending supply of the dictator's portraits and writings. While unequivocally accusing the opposition and students of behaving undemocratically and seeking to destabilise the country, Alia had also conceded almost all their demands.

The atmosphere remained tense as armoured patrols moved around the city and helicopters hovered overhead. Demonstrators continued to loot and burn, creating destruction in the city centre on a scale that had not been seen since the Liberation in 1944. The 'Flora' bookshop near the Hotel Tirana, where Hoxha had worked as an underground communist organiser before the war, was reduced to ashes. In an unforgettable scene, a small boy rode round the square on a donkey carrying a portrait of Enver Hoxha in front of him. But hardliners would not surrender easily, and the next day a group of officers loyal to Hoxha established a 'Commission for the Defence of the Homeland' and demanded that the statue of their hero be re-erected. In traditional Hoxhaist centres such as Berat, groups of 'Enverist Volunteers' took oaths of loyalty before the national flag and fired shots into the air. In streets throughout the country communists and their opponents clashed during this week.

A frequent cause of such conflict was the demolition by students and radical workers of the hundreds of communist monuments that stood everywhere by roadsides. In the early evening of 22 February a crowd of demonstrators gathered in front of the Enver Hoxha officers' club, and had started to vandalise the building when internal security troops guarding it opened fire. In the shooting that resulted one civil policeman was killed, and according to the authorities two others were wounded and various demonstrators were injured, whereas oppositionists claimed that police and army killed thirty people and caused injuries to seventy. The details of this incident have never been clarified, but it could undoubtedly have developed into the catalyst for a bloody confrontation between the government and the people had the government felt willing and able to use the troops stationed in and around Tirana to try to disperse the demonstrators. That they did not may be partly because the clashes involved different factions in the armed forces, and would have emphasised to Alia and the leading group in the PLA the insecure loyalties of many officers and conscripts.[8] What matters was that the final symbolic confrontation with Hoxha and his legacy had taken place, and the coercive power of the one-party state had been shown to be only a façade. The streets belonged to the people and, by implication to the new government they would elect.

Although the Ministry of Defence had mobilised infantry and tanks between 20 and 23 February, they had done little to prevent the demonstrators achieving their objectives. Politically the week's events finally affirmed the bankruptcy of the old system and the inability of the last hardliners to prevent the elections. It is not clear how far the demonstrators' activities were planned and how far spontaneous. At the time they appeared largely spontaneous, with the key inner core of students based in the University in regular touch with the DP leadership, but certainly not controlled by it. The street confrontation fitted perfectly into a pattern of events in which the DP and other opposition forces needed to test the strength of the old order in the weeks before the election and show that popular street power was irresistible. When the memoir by Gramoz Pashko of events at this time is published, it may clarify this question. However, in view of their caution over open street conflict with the state apparatus, it seems unlikely that the DP leadership planned the mass demonstrations to any great extent; more probably the people felt a need to avenge themselves symbolically on the memorials of the dictator and the system he created, and quickly took the opportunity offered.

The PLA Central Committee issue an appeal for calm, with a heavy stress on patriotism, and appealed to the students to end the hunger strike which they had begun a few days before. This calmed the political atmosphere, at least temporarily, but Alia's assumption of presidential rule was an additional burden for him in that he was now directly and personally responsible for every government decision of any importance. Retrospectively, this phase of the crisis could be seen as having reintroduced into Albanian politics the notion of a single strong leader at the top who would lead the country forward, something that subsequently helped

---

[8] In July 1996 ex-communist Defence Minister, Kico Mustaqi, was convicted of inciting military cadets to open fire on demonstrators at the academy, and sentenced to five years' imprisonment.

Sali Berisha in his drive to take control of the DP and remove the existing joint leadership of Pashko and others. After Alia met the leaders of the DP and the Republican Party, the acute tension in Tirana eased, and negotiations with Ministry of Education representatives brought the hunger strike to an end. By this stage it was clear that the student leadership was working closely with Pashko and Berisha, and moderate counsels were prevailing, at least for a time. However, this moderating alliance was not present in the countryside. The leadership of the DP and of the smaller opposition groupings was almost exclusively Tirana-based, and therefore could not restrain the increasingly turbulent countryside and the small provincial towns.

A week or so later, on 7 March, thousands of desperate people converged on the ports of Durres, Shenglin and Vlora, where they seized ships and sailed them across the Adriatic to Brindisi. After violent clashes with the security police and troops, who had fired into the crowded ships, other would-be migrants were prevented from leaving, and the government immediately put the port of Durres under martial law. Police were also instructed to prevent large gatherings of people throughout the country. On the Italian side, the navy was ordered to block the coast against further migrant ships. The Italian public were shocked by the sight on television of thousands of ragged, destitute Albanians suffering in the midsummer heat, and considerable medical and other help for them was mobilised among individuals. But the government did little, and sympathy quickly ran out as the refugees rioted in their squalid enclosures and many fled into the countryside. Running battles broke out between police and Albanians as the system at reception centres collapsed, and it was decided to deport all the refugees back to Albania. In the north the 2,000-strong Serbian minority living around Vraka, north of Shkoder, attempted to leave the country on 6 March and were turned back by the border police, but Belgrade later offered them asylum and most left later in 1992. Some returned to Albania, after finding living conditions in Serbia difficult after the outbreak of war and the imposition of UN sanctions. Many of the Vraka people were initially offered land in Kosova, but they refused it for the ironic reason that they had not left Albania to live among people 90 per cent of whom were ethnic Albanians.

In Tirana the period of relative calm brought by the Alia-opposition meeting did not last long as it was rumoured that the foreign embassies, which had been closed since the riots the previous July, were to reopen, thousands of people immediately assembled near the diplomatic quarter, believing that all who wanted to go and work abroad would be able to obtain visas. These were predominantly young men, often hungry and living rough in Tirana after being displaced from their villages. In many areas the collective farm system was breaking down, and local people were beginning to stake out claims to the land their families had owned before 1944. This resulted in the displacement of families who had been moved into new localities during the collectivisation process. The crowd that had converged on the embassies was forcibly dispersed by the security police. As the ship *Tirana* returned to Durres from Italy on 11 March carrying about 2,000 people who had fled there by ship-seizures and other means, disorder flared up in the city. Most of the railway rolling stock at the main station was burnt out.

During this month Fatos Nano, a prominent young economist who was a leader of the reformist group in the PLA, began to achieve greater prominence. He had been chosen to be a member of Alia's presidential advisory group, and in a sign that he was becoming an important force in his own right, he dealt with the high-level Italian delegation that visited Tirana in March. He later became a leader of the National Unity government and was closely involved in the Italian food aid programme later in the year. This is the period when, because of its scale, the turmoil in Albania began to be a European problem and to demand a European response.

During the last two weeks before the 31 March elections, the PLA concentrated on presenting itself as the only organised force that could save the country from further chaos. It made important gains in these weeks on the diplomatic front, with the visit of a delegation from the IMF and the signing of an agreement with the United States on reopening diplomatic relations. The election campaign was conducted very differently, with irregular patterns of activity in different parts of the country. The DP had only six cars allocated to it from the central government pool, and its leaders were thus unable to campaign effectively in many places. The state television concentrated heavily on Alia and PLA activities, and was criticised on these grounds in the reports of international election observers. The opposition leaders were little known to the public, and many meetings were held merely to familiarise people with the candidates rather than as serious campaign efforts. Also DP policy on a number of important issues, particularly land reform and land privatisation was far from clear. This lacuna cost the DP dear as many peasants voted for the PLA through fear of losing their land if the election were won by the DP, who even then were seen as likely to restore the land to the pre-war owners.

Fatos Nano played a prominent role in the PLA campaign, presenting a package of Gorbachev-type economic reforms, and trying to generate an image of experience and competence. The PLA image as the party that could actually achieve results was assisted on 19 March when the first major delivery (1,004 tons) of Italian food and medicine docked at Durres. This always rankled with the DP leadership, who claimed that the Italian Socialist government of Benedetto Craxi was trying to keep the PLA in power. Later there were accusations that the actual process of the food shipment had been subject to Mafia influence, and that much of what was supposed to be delivered never reached its Albanian destination; the thefts were linked to a similar fraud in aid destined for Ethiopia. The last week of March was dominated by the election itself, a total novelty for all but the oldest Albanians. A seemingly endless stream of foreign experts, journalists, election observers and television crews was arriving in the country. Often unintentionally, the visitors played into the hands of the surprisingly sophisticated PLA election machine by supplying a stream of important foreigners who could be shown on television to advantage in the company of PLA leaders. Ramiz Alia, probably aware of being fatally compromised by his past, kept clear of most of the campaign, leaving Fatos Nano to present the PLA's new moderate and reformist face to the people in a series of meetings in major urban centres. In the election address he gave to voters in his own Tirana constituency, he claimed: 'The Party of Labour conceived the platform of Albanian democracy. It is its standard bearer and applies it.'

The Democratic Party concluded its campaign with a rally in Skenderbeg Square, organised in defiance of an Interior Ministry ban on rallies there. Berisha promised a European future for Albania and a special relationship with the United States if the DP were elected. As events proved over the next two years, the second objective was to be much easier to achieve than the first. The central fact in the situation was that the election took place at all, in reasonably fair conditions and in full view of international observers. The only obvious negative factor was the strong pro-Alia influence in the television coverage. However, the result was to leave Albania with as many questions as answers, and to contribute little to social or economic stability, despite the generally favourable response of the international observers to the way the poll was conducted.[9]

[9] See report available from the office of the Organisation for Security and Cooperation in Europe, Prague office, May 1991.

4

1991 – POPULAR MOVEMENTS AND THE END OF COMMUNISM

By the last week of March 1991, Albania was gripped by election fever. The world's media and 260 international observers had descended upon Tirana and then, after an exhausting sojourn of a few days, they left as quickly as they had come. This was the first time that the nascent democracy in Albania was reported by the world press as a whole – a process that, more often than not, reproduced longstanding stereotypes. The capital's few relatively good hotels were soon full to capacity. Albanians eagerly invited foreign journalists to sleep on the floors of their already cramped apartments. Nearly every report in the Western press included the phrase 'The last bastion of Stalinism set to fall', and used words like 'backward', 'primitive' and 'time-warp' to describe the European country which had given the journalists a greater 'culture shock' than they would have received from most Third World countries. By concentrating on externals, the reports did little to elucidate the residual strength of the PLA and the organisational weakness of the opposition outside the major cities.

Following emergency talks between the government and opposition parties, it was agreed that there would be a 'no-strike policy' till 1 May in exchange for delaying the elections until 31 March, which gave the opposition more time to organise before the polls. Other smaller parties registered for the elections, including the Republican Party, the Agrarian Party, the Ecology Party and the Democratic Union of the Greek Minority (Omonia). The PLA and its affiliated organisations such as the Democratic Front, the Union of Working Youth of Albania, the War Veterans' Committee and the Women's Union nominated 644 of the 1,074 registered candidates. With wages as low as $20 a month, and unemployment at around 40 per cent, the DP campaign promised to bring about a transformation of living standards – to be achieved by European Community (EC) membership, Western financial aid and *Gastarbeiter* jobs in Italian and German factories. When Gramoz Pashko returned from a visit to the United States he was told that if the DP won the elections it would receive a blank cheque from the Americans for humanitarian aid.' Later he explained the nature of this 'blank cheque': admission to the IMF, CSCE, the World Bank and the European Bank for Reconstruction and Development, and two years' supply of food and other aid. In an atmosphere of heightened optimism, many Albanians began planning which family members would go abroad and how much money they would be able to send home. Walls in Tirana were soon covered with DP campaign posters echoing European Community symbols – one even showed Albania as an extra star on the EC flag. The projection of 'Europe' as the instant answer to the country's many problems indicates the immaturity of Albanian politics at this time. In some senses the EC was seen in the popular mind as a psychological and practical substitute for the communist superpower patrons of the past, and as a source of jobs, investment funds and a new national identity. In practice, none of these objectives was to be realised over the next five years on anything like the scale expected. In defence of the DP publicists, it should be remembered that this period saw the high tide of optimism in the whole of Europe about the Maastricht process and political unification, and the election campaign in Albania only reflected the wider currents of contemporary ideas.

Of the smaller parties the most important was the Republican Party (leader Sabri Godo), founded in January 1991 with a manifesto similar to that of the DP but further to the right. It promised a programme of gradual land privatisation, relying on new foreign investment, in contrast to the DP's advocacy of rapid privatisation and immediate transition to a free enterprise system. The Ecology Party, with its very small membership, campaigned for social harmony and environmental protection rather than on mainstream political or economic issues. Omonia, while supporting democratic changes, campaigned on issues specific to the Greek minority. The Agrarian Party promised to raise the living standards of the country's predominantly rural population, comprising almost 60 per cent of the total. The PLA for its part understood that its efforts had to be concentrated on winning over the peasantry.

In what appeared to be a direct response to the opposition's stance on agricultural policy, Ramiz Alia wrote in a *Zeri-i-Popullit* article: 'Nothing comes from words and fantasies. In these very difficult times, the peasants are not deceived by impossible utopias. I am writing to you at a time when many poisoned arrows are being aimed at both the co-operatives and the policy that has been pursued in the countryside since the Liberation [in 1944]. These are efforts to sully the past and exaggerate mistakes'.[1] However, the ruling communists went beyond mere rhetoric in their struggle to win over the peasantry; they also invested money to capture the agricultural sector. Alia noted that 1,000 new tractors had been distributed to the districts and that the recently completed urea chemical plant would increase its production of fertilisers. (The tractors were imported from China and the Chinese also helped construct the plant, where the machinery alone cost $32 million.[2] The fact that these links remained testifies to the strength of the old pro-China lobby within the Albanian Foreign Ministry and, to a less extent, other government ministries.)

Despite the preceding unrest, Albania's first multi-party elections for six decades were peaceful. There was almost a 97 per cent turnout among the 1.9 million people eligible to vote, the highest level in any multi-party election in Eastern Europe. In the first round, the PLA won 162 of the 250 seats in the Assembly. The DP won sixty-five including seventeen of the nineteen for Tirana, and some 40 percent of the votes cast. Further rounds of voting took place on 7 and 14 April in the electoral districts where no candidate had won an absolute majority in the first round. In these rounds the DP won ten seats, the PLA seven, and Omonia two. Overall, the PLA won a total of 169 of the 250 seats in the People's Assembly, just over the two-thirds majority (167 seats) required to adopt a new Constitution; the DP won seventy- -five seats and Omonia five. 'We consider this a major victory for the Party of Labour', said Xhelil Gjoni, secretary of the Central Committee of the PLA. 'It reflects the vitality of the Party and its connections with the masses.' Gjoni went on to explain the ruling party's wish to form a coalition with the opposition: 'Our Party, with Ramiz Alia at the head, expresses its will to co-operate

[1] *Zeri-i-Popullit*, 18 January 1991.
[2] Ibid.

and collaborate with the opposition for the freedom and independence of the country.' However, the DP stated that under
no circumstances was it prepared to enter a coalition with the
next government. Their offer of a coalition showed how little
the communist leaders grasped the notion of real political opposition
within a democracy. According to a DP spokesman, Genc Pollo,
a son of one of the old *nomenklatura* who later became Berisha's
key spokesman: 'Albania would be without an effective opposition
if the DP entered into a coalition, while our own reputation
would suffer as we were forced to share responsibility for an
economic mess not of our making.'[3]

The opposition had won almost all the urban constituencies,
while the rural population, who were wary of change and anxious
for their security, voted predominantly for the PLA. A crucial
factor in the defeat of the DP was the widespread belief that it
would privatise and redistribute the land to the pre-war landowning
class, whereas the PLA had promised to protect the peasantry
from privatisation. The PLA fared best in the Tosk-inhabited
south where communist sympathies remained strongest. The fact
that the communists hardly bothered to stage any campaign at
all in the urban centres suggests that they were confident of strong
support there. The most surprising result therefore was the failure
of Alia to win a seat for himself in the People's Assembly; he
won only 36 per cent of the votes cast in his Tirana constituency
and became another victim of the urban electorate's determination
to rid themselves of the communists. This humiliating defeat shocked the population, and a report in the Austrian daily *Die Presse*
described it as hitting Tirana like a bomb, adding that people
had cried, including some of his critics, and there had been 'no
overwhelming joy'.[4] In complete contrast, the charismatic Sali
Berisha won a resounding victory in Kavaja, an anti-communist
bastion south of Durres, which now called itself 'Albania's capital
of democracy'. In November 1989 Kavaja had been the scene
of one of the first open pluralist political assemblies, and the
'Pluralism Committee' subsequently established there was a model
for transitional political organisation in other cities. These committees were a forum for a wide variety of opportunists to develop

[3] *East European Reporter*, spring/summer 1991, p. 109.
[4] *Report on Eastern Europe*, 26 April 1991, p. 4.

activity against the one-party state. Many were later transformed into the local Democratic Party leaderships. Berisha said to reporters: 'Morally, we are the winners. This is the real end of communism in Albania.' His colleague Gramoz Pashko, who won around 80 per cent of the vote in the city of Vlora, told a crowd of sad and bemused DP supporters to be patient: 'The Communists who sucked our blood for forty-six years are finished, and in two months they will be in pieces.'

Apart from the land issue, the opposition suffered mainly because it was so recently formed, and with the poor infrastructure throughout the country and state control of television, it had lacked the mobility and access to the media necessary to disseminate its views widely and quickly. The DP complained of its lack of media representation and of the psychological pressure so widely felt to vote for the PLA. They also claimed that the elections had been conducted amid a 'climate of fear'. However, the consensus among independent Western observers was that the elections had been generally fair, and that fraud and manipulation were minimal. They admitted the PLA's control of election scrutineers in some rural areas and its domination of the media, particularly television, but concluded that its victory was largely the result of an undeveloped and uninformed political culture. Genc Pollo, when asked by a foreign journalist whether the DP made mistakes in its campaign, replied:

'Perhaps our biggest mistake was not to oppose more strongly the first-past-the-post electoral system. The problem was that first we had to concentrate on having the elections postponed, and then there were all kinds of other questions to face such as the depoliticisation of the army and release of political prisoners; at the time we just didn't know which issue would turn out to be the most crucial. With a more proportional system we would have definitely won more seats, but what was more important ultimately was that we lacked all the things necessary to fight an effective campaign: cars, equipment, staff, everything. This wasn't our fault.'

Asked whether the DP had received any help for its campaign from abroad, Pollo replied: 'Yes; financial aid was forbidden, but we received some small material assistance – posters for instance.'[5] Whether this is the whole truth must be doubted. Large funds had certainly been raised among Albanian émigrés in the United States to aid the opposition campaign, and the powerful Kosovar diaspora in Germany and Switzerland strongly supported the DP. Although this did not happen on the same scale as in the election the following year, when the money raised by the Albanian-American Civic League was a major force in the campaign, it is difficult to believe that at least some money and equipment did not reach the DP. The issue also marks the entry of the émigré factor into Albanian politics, something that became important over the next two years when returning Balli Kombetar and Legalitete supporters from the United States and elsewhere played a major part in the formation of the Berisha government's policy on some issues.[6]

The election results were in some ways similar to those in other former one-party Balkan states undergoing the transition from communism, where many rural voters were wary of change, while the better educated and informed urban population were impatient for swift and fundamental reforms. Here the press may have been a major factor: rural voters tended to depend for information on state-controlled television, and opposition newspapers found distribution difficult outside the main towns. The landslide communist victory was, in one sense, detrimental for Alia since it propelled the opposition into extra-parliamentary agitation, and strengthened the hands of the hardliners within the PLA who were determined not to relax their hold on power. A more evenly balanced outcome might have suited him better, enabling him to marginalise hardliners with a strong parliamentary opposition.

There was an immediate reaction to the PLA's victory in Shkoder, where hundreds of young people rioted on 2 April, alleging that there had been incidents of fraud and intimidation during the elections. In marked contrast to the pre-election restraint, the government moved quickly and ruthlessly to quell the unrest. The security forces dispersing the crowd shot four people dead and injured many others. A statement by the Minister of Internal

[5] *East European Reporter*, spring/summer 1991 p. 109.

[6] For an interesting if rather speculative survey of the émigré movements, see Gus Xhudo, 'Albania's émigrés: helpful or hurtful?', *Jane's Intelligence Review*, March 1996. Also, generally, *Illyria* newspaper in the United States.

Affairs, Gramoz Ruci, called the demonstrators 'terrorists' and said that the Presidium had authorised the security forces to maintain order and 'act with all legal means', adding that everyone, without exception, 'must bow to the will of the people and the actions of the law'.[7] Sporadic violence continued, with shooting incidents around the town and in the vicinity of Rozafat castle and the historic Leaden Mosque. According to Gramoz Pashko, the home of an opposition official in the southern town of Saranda and the DP headquarters in the industrial city of Elbasan were both bombed on the same day, 3 April. Peasants coming into Shkoder to sell their produce were beaten by town-dwellers angry with them for making the communist victory possible. There were reports of cars with the number plates of the southern city of Fier being vandalised because of the town's support for the communists. In Kavaja the police and security forces stayed well out of sight, whereas in Fier, where the communists won all nineteen parliamentary seats, they were everywhere and communist banners flew over several buildings. One visitor, perceiving the alienation of the people from the state as more severe than in any other ex-communist country, wrote:

> The most dramatic form this alienation takes is the wholesale destruction of public property. The country's entire rail system has been closed down, after mobs stripped the trains at the Tirana railway station of all their seats and fittings, and smashed all their windows. School classrooms lack even seats, window panes and everything else that can be carried away, prised off, or simply broken. The buses in Tirana have empty sockets where their headlights once were. A student later put the point more simply: 'The state has been stealing from us for 45 years. Now it's our turn to steal it all back from the state.' Others see more sinister causes at work. Dr Berisha and his party's spokesmen have complained repeatedly about 'dark forces in society' (meaning the *Sigurimi*, the former secret police) pursuing a 'scorched earth' policy to discredit the move to a market economy and make people yearn for the good old days.[8]

With the elections over and won, it seemed possible that con-

[7] Albanian Telegraphic Agency, 3 April 1991.

[8] Noel Malcolm, *Spectator*, 28 March 1992.

servative elements in the PLA, including the military, might now try to halt the process of reform. Indeed, to placate the professional members of the armed forces, it was decided to reintroduce ranks, which had been abolished in the 1960s. After the violence in Shkoder, Alia appealed once more to the DP for a 'national salvation coalition government' to diffuse 'unnecessary political antagonisms'. However, the opposition again rejected his proposal, insisting that those responsible for the shootings in Shkoder be brought to trial. Alia had been seen by many as a strong politician who favoured dialogue and as the motivating force behind the reforms, which were strongly opposed by conservatives in all the state security organisations. Even non-communists credited him with resisting the pressure from conservatives within the PLA to halt the reform process, and for this reason the DP was reluctant to stage an open confrontation with him. He was also credited with avoiding bloodshed by making repeated concessions to reformists. Although Alia and his followers had certain obvious privileges (villas, cars, private beaches, hunting reserves and foreign travel), there was little evidence of the blatant and large-scale corruption revealed elsewhere in Eastern Europe. Nevertheless, in July 1991 Hekuran Isai, Minister of Internal Affairs at the time of the February disturbances in Tirana, claimed that he had refused to carry out orders issued by Alia to shoot at demonstrators. Alia strongly denied these allegations, arguing that he had managed to prevent another Tiananmen massacre. On the evidence available to date, particularly interviews with senior military officers who were in almost daily touch with Alia at this time, Isai's statement must be doubted. There seems to be considerable evidence that Alia was trying to avoid bloodshed at this time albeit for reasons of self-interest.[9] However, he seems to have remained severely compromised by his former close relationship with Hoxha.

The new People's Assembly first convened on 10 April, but opposition deputies refused to attend. At this first session, a representative of the DP, the archaeologist Neritan Ceka, announced that opposition deputies would not participate in the legislature until those responsible for the deaths in Shkoder were identified. The Assembly reconvened a week later, after the DP ended its boycott and a parliamentary commission was established to in-

[9] This subject is discussed in more detail in the chapter on defence.

vestigate the Shkoder shootings. It reported, within a week, that the police were to blame for provoking initially peaceful demonstrators to violence. Although no final draft of a new Constitution had yet been accepted, the communists and the opposition did agree to adopt a transitional law as a stop-gap until the full and final draft of the Constitution could be completed. The new, incomplete draft with only forty-six articles nevertheless contained many structural changes, which included establishing political pluralism and renaming the country from 'the People's Republic of Socialist Albania' to 'the Republic of Albania'. The Constitution made no reference to Marxism-Leninism as an ideology or to the 'leading role of the PLA'. The state was defined rather vaguely as 'democratic and juridical, based on social equality, the defence of freedom, and the rights of man'. It endorsed the right to own private property, to strike, to demonstrate and to emigrate. Instead of a Presidium of the People's Assembly, there was to be an executive President of the country, elected by two-thirds of the votes cast in the People's Assembly. When Ramiz Alia was elected to this new post by an overwhelming majority, all the opposition deputies abstained. Despite its limitations, the provisional Constitution signalled a significant break from the country's inflexible Stalinist past. One of the most important features of the new law was in Article 7, which stated that the 'state observes the freedom of religious belief and creates conditions in which to exercise it'. Nevertheless, despite their election success, the communists were now on their knees; the victory they had won was totally hollow. The DP, a party barely three months old, was now in the ascendant since clearly, unlike the PLA, it belonged to the future.

The government of Fatos Nano and the general strike

Following his election as President, Alia resigned as First Secretary of the PLA. This was in accordance with a new constitutional amendment which prevented the President from holding office in a political party. He also resigned from the Politburo and the PLA's Central Committee. In early May, the People's Assembly, trying to strengthen its shattered morale, approved a new government headed by the thirty-nine-year-old economist Fatos Nano. Asked by a Western journalist whether he was a communist, Nano said: 'I'm not a Stalinist, I'm not a Maoist, I'm not a Pol

Potist. I'm a true Albanian, interested in the integration of Albania in Europe.'[10] All the new ministers were PLA members, and the DP strongly opposed the appointment of the former Internal Affairs Minister, Gramoz Ruci, as the new chairman of the National Security Committee, because it was under his command that the four demonstrators had been killed in Shkoder on 2 April. A fresh investigation into the Shkoder killings was immediately announced.

Never before had an Albanian political leader presented such a bleak picture of the economy as Nano did when he outlined his government's programme to parliament. The opposition deputies refused to approve the new programme, arguing that the government failed to accept responsibility for the country's grave economic and social situation and that it had provided no time-frame for implementing its programme. In an interview on 17 May during a visit to Czechoslovakia, Gramoz Pashko reiterated that the DP would not serve with the communists in a coalition government; the 'only point' on which the Democrats agreed with the communists, he said, was the Kosova issue. The DP was pressing for another election.[11]

The programme which Nano presented to the Assembly envisaged fundamental reforms, including extensive privatisation and a rapid shift to a market-based economy. However, the new government was faced with a rapidly disintegrating economy; inflation was running at around 260 per cent per month, and over 70 per cent of the workforce were idle. It did not have the large-scale support from the international financial community which had been promised to the DP opposition. In mid-May the 'no-strike policy' expired, and the country was immediately plunged into political uncertainty as the newly-established independent trade unions organised a general strike. Around 300,000 workers from all sectors demanded unrealistic pay rises of up to 100 per cent, pension increases, a six-hour working day, and a further investigation into the April shootings in Shkoder. Later in the month, as the government continued to reject the unions' demands, the miners began a hunger-strike. Alia appealed on national radio for an end to the stoppages. Realising that he was

---

[10] *The Independent,* 16 May 1991.

[11] *Report on Eastern Europe,* 7 June 1991, p. 3.

treading on very thin ice, he admitted that the country was paralysed: 'I appeal to all to return to work as the sole possibility to save the country and ourselves from the fatality of failure. The situation is extremely grave. Economic and political life are almost at a standstill.' However, his plea fell on deaf ears. The miners' leader, Sami Kariqi, said: 'We do not want to destroy the country, we just want to get rid of the communists.' The strike showed, according to the crowds in Tirana, that 'the government may have the parliament, but we have the country'. Given the lack of resources of the strike committees and the total political in-experience of their youthful leaders, the strike was surprisingly successful and apart from one or two of the big factories in PLA centres like the Berat textile mills, most of the country was soon at a standstill.

As the general strike reached its fourth week, with the opposition in control of most urban centres, the government bowed to the inevitable. It appealed yet again for an interim coalition 'caretaker' government until fresh elections could be held the following year. With so little experience of multi-party politics, it was no surprise that the DP at first refused to enter a coalition with the communists for fear of being discredited in the eyes of their staunchly anti-communist supporters, and were swept along by the militancy of the poorer classes in society. The general strike was the first large-scale anti-government action ever taken by independently organised labour in Albania, and it contributed to an atmosphere of intransigence at street level over many different issues throughout the whole summer. This posed a serious dilemma for some of the DP leadership, who did not want to be seen as putting them-selves at the head of a revolutionary syndicalist uprising against the results of the first democratic elections. To moderates such as Ceka and Kadare it was more important to protect the democratic process itself than immediately to win power, although this honourable and understandable position opened them to criticism from the power-hungry Berisha and his group. The DP eventually agreed to join the coalition, seemingly in response to the country's critical socio-economic situation, and on condition that the new government would act merely as an interim administration until there could be another general election.

The serious effects of the strike were not immediately apparent, even to those most closely involved within Albania, and certainly not in the West. On the whole the workers' conduct was orderly and attracted little attention in Western news media now accustomed to a diet of turmoil and violent conflict from Albania. The strike was played out in pleasant spring weather, and the atmosphere in the Tirana streets was relaxed compared to the savage tensions of the recent winter months. On the surface the stoppage was concerned with political reform as much as with economic and social issues, but the reality was that it marked a major breakdown in labour force organisation and discipline. The beginning of the end of most Albanian manufacturing capacity can be traced to this period, as people totally lost faith in the old command economy, and voted with their feet over their jobs and prospects. The PLA leadership now reluctantly had to accept that communism was in terminal retreat. Under psychological pressure, paralysed and confused, they realised that the Party's last chance to enforce its authority had passed and it was clearly unable to use its two-thirds majority in parliament. The Party itself was disintegrating and, more important, it had lost the psychological will to hold on to power.

This collapse of power and authority was closely linked to the fact that the PLA had hardly any urban representation outside traditional communist centres such as Berat, Fier and Permet. In retrospect the strike in its implication was as much a general uprising of the towns against the country as against a particular government. The trade union leaders sensed that the urban workers were ready to deal a final and decisive blow to the PLA, and it was a final irony that a party which had so idealised the image and ethos of industrial workers was ultimately brought down by that very social group; the workers were saying that the interests of the peasants should not determine the future social development of Albania. The strike also threw up new opposition leaders, people who had had no connections with the old system and were from a much lower social stratum than the DP's founding fathers, most of whom came from the Tirana élite.

The strike headquarters was in a tiny Ottoman back street of the city with trailing vines covering the posters on the walls and hundreds of people crowded outside, all waiting for news of developments in other parts of the country and cheering the strike leaders as they came and went. Sympathetic peasants rushed along the narrow street on horsedrawn carts loaded with food for the urban strikers. Ismail Kadare, while on a visit to the United States, claimed in an interview that communism in Albania was dead.[12] The workers of Tirana and other towns and in the remote mines far away near the Yugoslav border had killed it. But they were also helping to sign the death warrant of some of their own industries in a tragic process of disintegration and collapse. When the strike ended, so many workers and managers had emigrated or moved to Tirana that some enterprises never resumed production.

Ylli Bufi and the Government of National Stability

The general strike succeeded in its primary objective of bringing down the government. On 4 June Nano, who reluctantly admitted the obvious fact that his government no longer enjoyed popular support, resigned and thus brought to an end forty-seven years of communist rule in Albania. Apparently Alia had great difficulty finding a new head of government. Several people, all communists as foreseen by an all-party agreement, wisely turned down the offer, but within a few days Ylli Bufi (*bufi* means 'dunce' in Albanian), who had been Minister for Food under Nano, was appointed Chairman of the Council of Ministers to lead a new 'Government of National Stability' approved by the legislature. Twelve of the new ministers were non-communist. The PLA itself held twelve portfolios, while the DP gained seven and the Republican Party, the Social Democratic Party and the Agrarian Party shared the other five between them. The most pressing task was to heal the bitter rifts between young and old, rural and urban, opposition and communist. Ylli Bufi, outlining his programme for stalling the country's decline told parliament: 'We need to calm down the people, bring stability, restore order and hope, and carry on the democratisation.' He added with an air of pleading desperation: 'The only way out of this crisis is to get credit and help from abroad.' The new government's chances of survival depended on the co-operation of the trade unions, who agreed to a no-strike deal until elections the following year.

The 10th Congress of the PLA was convened on 10 June. The very survival of the Party was now at stake, and the delegates

[12] *New York Times*, 23 May 1991.

had to decide what measures to take next as the country slid ever deeper into economic and social despair. The motions agreed upon at this historic Congress marked the beginning of an official re-evaluation of Albania's post-war history. The Party was organisationally and ideologically a shadow of its former self, but in order to revitalise its image, it hastily approved fundamental changes to its structure and ideology. The PLA was renamed the Socialist Party of Albania (hereafter referred to as the SP) and Fatos Nano was elected president of a new Managing Committee, replacing the Central Committee. In a wide-ranging purge of the Party leadership nine former members of the Politburo were expelled from the SP and others were demoted. The Party's ideology was also reformed; its new manifesto stated that the SP would be modern and progressive, and committed to democracy, social justice and economic reform. Thus it was hoped to recast the Party along the lines of a democratic socialist party following the tradition of the West European Left. It was generally acknowledged that the present reality of the situation in Albania called for alternatives – namely a new political system and a market economy. This provoked clashes between reformers and conservatives; the latter responded by standing in groups in the congress hall, raising clenched fists and chanting the traditional Albanian communist slogan, 'Enver's Party – Always Ready'. The hardliner Xhelil Gjoni, one of three party secretaries who led the PLA after Alia's resignation as First Party Secretary in early May, delivered the keynote address to the Congress. He engaged in unprecedented public criticism of certain aspects of Hoxha's rule, referring to Hoxha's supposed 'infallibility' and the 'cult' which surrounded him, from which, he said, his fellow party and state leaders had profited 'in terms of authority and privileges'.

However, the concluding remarks of Gjoni's re-evaluation demonstrated how difficult it was for the PLA to reassess Hoxha's place in post-war Albanian history on any rational basis. He appealed for the avoidance of divisive issues: 'There is one thing that can definitely be said: Enver Hoxha was not mistaken in his stand on freedom and independence. He was a popular leader who knew how to unite the people and how to rouse them. Let the historians deal with the mistakes, and let him remain the inheritance of our party and of his country. It is for the common good to avoid discussions that would divide us. Enver Hoxha should be accepted for what he was. It is our duty, knowing the values [he stood for], not to confuse them with [his] mistakes.[...]But, in isolating the mistakes, we should demand of Enver that which he could and should have done, and not what we would have had him do.' Moreover, hundreds of delegates to the Congress responded angrily to the scathing attack on the Hoxha era by the writer Dritero Agolli, chairman of the Albanian Union of Writers and Artists. In reply to Agolli's assertion that Hoxha's rule had given rise 'to the cult of the ugly', the Party conservatives chanted old slogans. However, they were in a minority in the Congress and unable to prevent Agolli from being elected to the fifteen-member Party Presidium, which consisted mainly of known reformers.[13] Despite this, the walls of official buildings throughout the country were bare, with just a tell-tale hook to remind the onlooker of where the portrait of Comrade Enver had so recently hung. There was also a noticeable absence of portraits of Alia. Everywhere bookshops were empty, their communist literature hurriedly packed away in boxes. Works that had enjoyed the status of quasi-religious texts were now widely used as toilet paper.

In July the hated *Sigurimi* was 'officially' dissolved and replaced by a new institution called the National Information Service (NIS). This 'major step towards democratisation' impressed few – so the state informers had a new name – but it seemed to even the casual observer that there was an increase in the number of furtive-looking types lurking in bushes and alleyways in the major towns. Under the new decree, the NIS – previously controlled by the Council of Ministers – was to operate independently of any political organisation. Under its shadowy chairman, Irakli Kocollari, the NIS would have as its main function the enforcement of the country's constitution and laws. Kocollari had been a rising star in the *Sigurimi*, and for a time held one of its key foreign appointments as intelligence officer in the Athens embassy. Problems automatically arose over who should be employed in the new service: those former *Sigurimi* personnel with 'unblemished' characters and service records who had not abused the system, or newly-trained government officials. A former *Sigurimi* official, Veip Proda, argued in the daily *Bashkimi* that an important reason for the agency's peaceful

[13] *Report on Eastern Europe*, 19 July 1991, p.2

transformation was the 'adequate educational level of the staff' (almost 90 per cent with higher professional or state education). He seemed to believe that this enabled many in the *Sigurimi* to recognise that a peaceful transition was the only way to make progress and implement reforms. As for the 'mistakes' made by this agency, which was infamous for the brutality and random violence of its dealings with the people, and for its vast register of files on individuals, he blamed the 'mediocre and arrogant bosses some of whom, whatever the cost, made a habit of ordering or coercing people'. Proda concluded that because the 'honourable' members of the *Sigurimi* had accepted the process of 'democratisation', the NIS should keep them in its ranks and accept them warmly as brethren: 'Then we shall discover what a great human and humanitarian outlook they have'.[14]

By the summer the economic situation showed no signs of improvement, and in the first week of August a further 10,000 people attempted to emigrate *en masse* to Italy. Like those involved in the previous attempts, most were unemployed and complained of lack of food in their home areas and administrative chaos throughout the country. There were violent clashes in and around the port of Durres, as police tried to prevent them from seizing moored ships. In the pitched battles a large number of dockside warehouses were burnt out, and the government estimated the resulting damage was at about 300 million lek (about 29m). In a further blow to industry, nearly all imports of badly-needed industrial spares and pharmaceutical products were destroyed. The European Union immediately agreed to double its emergency aid but everywhere the country had returned to the anarchy of the previous winter and late spring. In Tirana at this time, groups of youths made random attacks on public buildings in broad daylight. In Italy the alarmed authorities, who were still trying to cope with previous batches of destitute Albanians, now ordered the forcible repatriation of all the refugees. Thousands of pathetic people arrived a few days later in burning heat in Durres harbour and Tirana airport. At the same time, on 8 August, the colossal statue of Enver Hoxha overlooking his birthplace in Gjirokaster was torn down. The security police attempted to defend it and fired into the air, but soon yielded to the angry crowds, many of whom belonged to the large local Greek minority. The head was removed from the statue – the nose and eyes battered with sledgehammers and smeared thickly with donkey droppings – and driven in triumph round the steep streets of the town on the back of a lorry. The last statue of Hoxha still standing, at Korça, was demolished the next day in more orderly circumstances, although diehard Hoxhaists tried to re-erect it before it was removed under cover of darkness by town-council workmen and thrown into a river. In the north and north-east, army discipline broke down and there was general looting in Kukes. With tension rising in Yugoslavia, Alia held an emergency meeting with defence chiefs to find ways to restore 'order and discipline' in the army.[15]

The continuing turmoil was causing major changes in settlement patterns. Small places such as Lac, which had been largely established under communism and linked to a single factory, which was now stripped and partly burnt to the ground, resembled ghost-towns as the young left in order to emigrate and the old returned to traditional landholdings in the hope of surviving on subsistence agriculture. There was also a dramatic shift of other sections of the rural population to the bigger towns: the absence of appropriate legislation had left many peasants, especially in the mountainous areas, with little or no land. Many were ejected from old collective farms as 'newcomers' if they had come to prosperous lowland areas during collectivisation. Injuries and sometimes deaths were common in this process as terrorised families, afraid for their lives, fled back to their highland villages, or tried to emigrate to Italy or Greece. Thousands of peasants began to settle in and around Tirana, which by July 1992 had a population approaching 400,000; as many as 30,000 had arrived during 1991.[16] The new arrivals built their houses on co-operative land on the outskirts of the capital and other large towns. By doing so they exacerbated the chronic food shortages, taking away land formerly used to grow vegetables for the townspeople, who had to queue in the middle of the night for meagre and erratic supplies of milk and other essentials. Those peasants who remained in the countryside were hoarding any food they produced, thus contributing to the overall food shortage. By July the country was importing £47 million

[15] Albanian Telegraphic Agency, 27 August 1991.
[16] Radio Tirana in English, 1430 gmt, 1 July 1992.

worth of bread grain and having a difficult time paying for it. The foreign debt was by now scheduled at £238m., together with the loan of around £150m, which the communists had borrowed from the World Bank in February. In September the Deputy Prime Minister, Gramoz Pashko, appealed at a meeting in Brussels of the Group of Twenty-Four industrialised states (G-24) for emergency food aid. He made a strong case and convinced the delegates that mass starvation in the coming winter was a realistic prospect. The G-24 responded by providing more than $150,000,000 in emergency aid, and some 500 Italian soldiers were sent to Albania to help with the aid distribution. This was the beginning of 'Operation Pelican'.

In a belated attempt to prevent further chaos in the countryside, the National Stability Government introduced long-awaited legislation on the privatisation of land and the replacement of People's Councils (local administrative organs) by multi-party bodies. The decision to grant peasant families the private use of up to one acre of co-operative land only unleashed a free-for-all. Some collective farm members were reportedly seizing land on the basis of pre-collectivisation boundaries, while others were left with no land to cultivate. The rural chaos came after four successive years of drought, and the land-grab coincided with what should have been a time of peak activity in the fields. At the end of the year the state of the country could hardly have been worse.

In Tirana around 20,000 people rallied on 8 December. They did so not only to celebrate the first anniversary of the pro-democracy protests, but also to protest against the dire shortages of essential foods and fuel. It was a particularly severe winter and everywhere people were desperately chopping down trees for fuel; these included the stately elms and poplars planted in King Zog's time along all the country's main roads, providing much-needed shade during the intense summer heat. To try and cope with the chronic fuel shortages, the army was mobilised to transport wood to the remote zones. Soldiers and police had to restore order in the northern Kruja district after hungry crowds stormed food banks. The panic set in after the Prime Minister, Ylli Bufi, announced that current food supplies would only last one week longer; this led to frenzied rioting in the town of Lac, where mobs ransacked a food-processing plant as well as bakeries, restaurants and other food stores. During this riot two people were killed, including a policeman. There were also serious disturbances in other parts of the country.

In December the DP Party chairman, Sali Berisha, charged the Socialists with deliberately obstructing the reform process in the countryside and instigating the current vicious crime wave and refugee crisis. This was to be a constant Berisha theme in the coming years. The crisis marked the entry of the future President on to centre stage in the political drama. The DP newspaper, *Rilindja Demokratike,* often reported that the Socialists were encouraging hooliganism in order to implant the idea that democracy implied lawlessness, anarchy and instability. Berisha called for DP members to resign from the coalition government; seven ministers promptly pulled out of the twenty-one-member Cabinet. This occurred while Gramoz Pashko was having talks in London with the IMF. Pashko was furious, cut short his trip, and returned to Tirana. It was then that he acknowledged a split among the DP leadership, and criticised Berisha for breaking up the government and thus, he claimed, leading the country even further into anarchy and economic catastrophe. However, Pashko declared later that it had been necessary to withdraw. In an interview a few months later, he was asked why he had entered a coalition with the Socialists in June 1991, and then pulled out in December. He replied:

'We entered the coalition to avoid bloodshed in Albania. The Socialists were planning an equivalent to the Reichstag fire, they called on mercenaries from the south of Albania to come to Tirana and demonstrate with weapons. We wanted to free Albania from its isolation and to introduce a new open-door policy. We also wanted to ensure bread for our people and prevent hunger. We pulled out because the communists were extremely intolerant. They did not respect the laws passed in parliament, they were inflexible, they abused our presence in the government, they used us as a political shield and left us with the responsibility of governing but kept political power for themselves. For these reasons we left the government and I consider it totally correct.'[17]

In the same week Nexhmije Hoxha, now aged seventy-one, who had been expelled from the Party in June, was arrested and,

[17] *East European Reporter,* March/April 1992, p. 55.

together with others from the former hardline group in the leadership, charged with corruption. Thus began the series of witch-hunts,
mixing corruption with politics, that would so preoccupy the
country's leaders over the next few years. The full history of the
split in the DP cannot yet be written since many participants are
still active in Tirana politics, and those in government are unwilling
to discuss their role in what occurred. Much remains to be discovered, especially about the role of the United States in the
events, which by December marked the emergence of Dr Sali
Berisha as the future leader of the country. It was a departure
from the previous pattern of collective opposition leadership, and
the conflict heralded the formal birth of the Democratic Alliance
Party nine months later. This ritual period, in its way, also highlighted the failure of the Tirana élite to evolve a model of working
party politics, leaving the field open for Berisha to establish a
highly centralised presidential system once he had the necessary
domestic and foreign support in place. It may be said, of course,
that after the political damage of the communist years it was too
much to expect of any élite, but the failure was to prove important
in the next stage of the transition.

5

THE DEMOCRATIC PARTY VICTORY

At the dawn of 1992, Albania's immediate prospects could not have appeared more bleak. Living conditions in the cities were appalling, the government was on the point of collapse, and a hardline minority of communists still threatened to fight for their political lives. As the crisis deepened, Prime Minister Bufi resigned. Alia hoped to restore some measure of stability to the government by appointing as the new Prime Minister of the caretaker government Vilson Ahmeti, another former Food Minister and a more respected figure. He then signed a decree for fresh elections on 22 March. For the people the onset of winter brought a repetition of the nightmare of the previous year, though without the same levels of random violence and disorder. Severe electricity shortages deprived large parts of the country of power for days at a time. Water supplies only functioned for a few hours, mostly at night, so that people had to get up to store water in any available container. There was no paper to print newspapers from the end of December until February.

There were riots, causing several deaths, in the southern mining town of Pogradec on 22 January, when crowds of peasants entered the town on donkeys and burnt down the central food warehouses. Although taking place in a relatively remote town near the Greek border, these riots had much wider political significance. Pogradec was an important industrial centre and the site of the giant Guri i Kuq iron and nickel mine, one of the largest in Eastern Europe. It had been developed in the 1970s, under the supervision of Chinese technologists, into a mainstay of the extractive sector of the economy, and was connected by rail to the port of Durres and the metal concentration plant at Elbasan. It was also one of the last bastions of communist support in the region: the miners were relatively favoured under communism, and the area generally

75

had a strong Partisan tradition dating back to the war. The town had a large garrison and was the centre for the border-control troops in the region. But the peasants in the surrounding area were no longer prepared to tolerate these privileges, and showed it by attacking the food warehouses. Before the war some of the surrounding highland villages were strong centres of support for King Zog, like many ethnic Albanian villages near the Greek border, and the riots marked the reawakening of these political forces in Albanian life.

In all the lowland regions trees in the streets and parks were being felled for fuel. Racketeers brought logs into the towns to sell for large sums. Many basic government services had ceased to exist and nobody was sure who, if anyone, was in charge. International understanding of the depth of the crisis was hampered by the parallel disintegration of ex-Yugoslavia, with its accompanying violence. Media coverage of Albania in the West concentrated on stereotypes based on the mass emigration attempts, and the local turmoil and severe hardship were not considered news. In some ways this has been the case ever since. In a wider ideological context the 'New World Order' was beginning to appear hollow and as a result media perceptions of countries like Albania changed; they were no longer potential candidates for modernity and 'Europe', but part of a Balkan peninsula rent by war and bloodshed and likely to remain so for the foreseeable future. As a result, few stories from Albania found their way into the international press in this period or in the following years, and the recurrent horrors of urban life in winter were unknown to all but a small circle who followed Albanian developments and lived in Albania, sharing the life of the people. They will never be forgotten by those who experienced them.

The March 1992 elections

On 20 March in Skenderbeg Square the DP held a huge rally as the climax of its election campaign. Berisha and other DP leaders spoke to a crowd estimated at 100,000, urging them to unite for real democracy. Asked in an interview whether the DP was confident of succeeding in the countryside this time, Berisha replied: 'We are much better organised than before. We are present everywhere and the role of the communists is diminishing day by day. We have destroyed the traditional power troika consisting of the chairman of the agricultural cooperative, together with the village mayor and the secretary of the regional party organisation, which was closely related to the state security apparatus.' Berisha showed naivety in his reply to a further question on controlled and stable borders to stem another haemmorrhage of refugees: 'Democracy means stable borders but democracy also means the free movement of people. Europe should accept a greater ratio of emigration from Albania ... I will insist upon this.'[1]

European Community policy was beginning to concentrate on the containment of migration from countries such as Albania, and the issue of refugee movements from the Balkans was inevitably seen in the very lurid light cast by the Yugoslav conflict. In 1992 only a few thousand visas were granted to Albanians, mainly to learn catering skills in Germany. This was a great disappointment for the government, which approached Turkey for similar rights but without success. The Socialists also campaigned on the issue of gradual integration into Europe and, as in the previous election, Alia sought to win a few votes by sabre-rattling on behalf of the Kosovars. In terms which became familiar throughout Eastern Europe after 1992, the Socialists promised to ease the pains of the transition back to capitalism by giving decent welfare benefits to those out of work, and by maintaining the value of pensions. The 60 per cent of normal wages paid to those unable to work through no fault of their own would also continue, an element of the Socialists' programme that was particularly objectionable to the international financial community. The Albanian Communist Party, formed in September 1991 under the leadership of Rosi Brahimi and Hysni Milloshi, warned of 'danger on the doorstep' as a result of the 'counter-revolution taking place in the country'. It appealed to the electorate to follow the 'teachings and instructions of the genius, Enver Hoxha, who contributed to the freedom, independence and sovereignty of the homeland as nobody before in the history of this nation'.[2]

Of the eleven parties which competed in the election, the most significant new one, the Social Democratic Party, was founded

---

[1] *East European Reporter,* March/April 1992, pp. 54-5.

[2] B. Szajkowski, 'The Albanian Elections,' *Journal of Communist Studies,* vol. 8, no. 3, (September 1992), p. 122.

in April 1991 and led by a former Minister of Education, Skender Gjinushi. Although the party was seen as genuinely reformist, it was somewhat discredited by Gjinushi having stood as a PLA candidate in the 1991 elections. The Communist Party drew most of its support again from its traditional power base in the south but also now from some northern regions, especially around Kukes, where living conditions were difficult and the huge Drin hydroelectric schemes in the 1970s and 1980s had provided a real increase in living standards under the old system. The electoral law prevented a party such as Omonia, which campaigned on 'ethnic principles', from participating in the elections. Consequently it and a smaller party, Prespa, that represented the tiny 'Macedonian' population, both fielded candidates in the list of the Human Rights Union Party. The decision by parliament on 2 February to ban Omonia from the elections was preceded by a wave of anti-Greek sentiment in parliament led by the DP member and Albanian nationalist, Abdi Balletta. Article 13 of the draft electoral law, providing for ethnic Greek candidates in areas where that population is concentrated, was duly scrapped. Relations with Greece were tense, and on 15 March there were some killings on the border. In many ways the electoral law favoured large parties; a provision was that each candidate be supported by 400 signatures from a particular constituency. This provision naturally proved difficult to meet for minor parties with small and fragmented memberships. In addition, the state's financial support for the electoral campaign was conditional, and depended on the number of candidates put forward by each party. Again smaller parties found difficulty in launching their electoral campaigns and attracting suitable candidates in view of their extremely limited, and in most cases all but non-existent, financial resources.[3]

On 22 March, with a 90.35 per cent turnout of eligible voters, the DP swept to victory with 62 per cent of the votes compared to just 25 per cent for the Socialist Party. The re-activated Communist Party polled only 2 per cent of the total votes. In the second round of voting on 29 March the DP consolidated its landslide victory by scooping up all the eleven seats at stake. The Socialists won only six seats, all in the south, their traditional power-base. Perhaps the most unexpected result was the decline

[3] Szajkowski, op. cit., p. 120.

in popular support for the Human Rights Union Party, which expected to attract the ethnic Greek and 'Macedonian' vote. It succeeded in winning only two constituencies, Saranda and Gjirokaster, out of the twenty-nine in which it presented candidates.[4] Part of the reason for this may have been the beginnings of a private enterprise culture in the Greek minority communities which led some voters to opt for the DP in the hope of benefiting from privatisation. The SP and DP both said publicly that they regretted parliament's decision to ban Omonia, and that the new parliament would amend the electoral law again in its favour. In private, however, parliamentarians agreed that there was wide public support for banning Omonia, and that to be seen supporting the ethnic Greek cause would be electorally damaging. The attacks on Greeks in Saranda on 8 and 9 February seemed to be a direct result of the ban. Anti-Greek sentiment took off after the Greek Interior Ministry's 'Operation Broom' the previous December which forcibly repatriated many of the 100,000-odd Albanians living illegally in Greece. Scenes of dishevelled Albanians (mostly ethnic Greeks) spilling out of police vans on the border crossing at Kakavia aroused indignation.[5]

The conduct of the campaign was marked by an overwhelming war-weariness and lethargy on the part of the Socialist candidates, compared to the vigorous confidence and much improved organisation of the DP machine. The DP had substantial foreign assistance for their logistical needs, whereas the Socialists had none and held few large rallies, unlike the DP which made them a centre-piece of its campaign. The DP rallies had a presidential character, and were focused on the personality of Berisha. The influence of media advisers brought in from Britain and the United States was obvious. Berisha had become an effective performer at these large-scale events, and with his superficially attractive personality, good looks and media schooling he made a much more favourable impression than the old-style ex-communist speakers. He was less effective at 'meet the people' events, where these same virtues would make him seem vain and overbearing to Albanians of modest social status.

The American connection was made tangible for the people

[4] Ibid., p. 125.
[5] *East European Newsletter*, vol. 6, no. 4, 17 February 1992.

with the presence on certain occasions of the US ambassador, William Ryerson, on the platform as a well-wisher – but one who appeared to be overstepping considerably the limits of a normal diplomatic role. At one of the largest rallies, held in the football stadium at Korça, Berisha spent much of his speech explaining to the people how, a week later, 'the doors of Europe' would be 'thrown open to Albanians'. It was a seductive prospect, however far removed it might be from reality. Ryerson spoke after him, promising US support for the new Albania. Symbolically, this event set the pattern of Albanian politics for the next three years: of a well-intentioned and charismatic President courting the United States in the face of relative indifference from the European Community. After the announcement of victory, wild celebrations swept the country. Even in tiny villages, like Dragobi, under the lee of the mighty snow-covered Dinaric Alps, there were parties – of a distinctively Albanian kind. First the statue of Enver Hoxha, which had disfigured the beautiful Valbona gorge was dynamited, and then the raki bottles were opened, and stayed open for a long time.

The first Democratic Party government

The DP now had ninety-two seats in the new 140-seat parliament – just one short of a two-thirds majority. The Socialists gained thirty-eight, the Social Democrats seven and the Human Rights Union Party two. A somewhat relieved Socialist Party accepted the election results and attributed its defeat to the current European trend towards the political right. The Party Chairman, Fatos Nano, claimed that there were some irregularities during the electoral campaign and on the election day, but that they did not alter the final results. The roll was also validated by all the international observers present. Fatos Nano wished the DP luck in solving the problems in store for it.[6] Thus ended the political framework of almost five decades of communist rule. It was difficult to avoid the impression that the Socialists did not really want to win the election: there was a strong sense in Tirana of a party wishing to relinquish power with a modicum of dignity and to allow the new political forces their chance to run the country. However

[6] Szajkowski, 'The Albanian Elections', p. 127.

great its disadvantages had been at other times, the shared political culture of the Tirana élite stood the country in good stead in this period, in helping to provide the basis for an orderly transfer of power to the DP.

The foremost task now was to make the country at least relatively governable, even though harder times were almost certainly in store. On 4 April Ramiz Alia announced his decision to resign as President. Dr Sali Berisha became Albania's first non-communist President since King Zog, elected as the only candidate by a large majority in Parliament. Berisha responded to questions about his communist past by saying that he had done for 'his people' what any true socialist would do:

> 'It is true that I have been a Communist Party member, but what I have done is in line with authentic socialist ideals. Little by little I came to believe in their failure, I understood that Albanian socialism had been transformed into a prison, into a terrible tragedy. In 1990 I demanded from Alia to eliminate the unique party, to open up the road to pluralism ideas. It was me who defined Stalin as the most hated figure of this century. Alia concealed these statements of mine, then ordered the security officers to persecute me. I am here thanks to my people. Now I must help them revive and prosper.[7]

Berisha then appointed the new government, headed rather surprisingly by a fifty-three-year-old structural engineer and expert on Byzantine buildings, Alexander Meksi. He had no previous political experience, but had won considerable respect for his even-handedness while deputy chairman of parliament from April 1991 to March 1992. Quiet and unassuming, Meksi was to prove not quite the yes-man to Berisha that many people expected him to be. The DP held the premiership and fourteen ministries, and the Social Democrats and Republicans had one portfolio each. DP politicians held the key Finance, Interior, Foreign Affairs and Defence Ministries, while independent technocrats were appointed to run the Ministries of Industry and Justice. Gramoz Pashko was conspicuously absent from any of these posts. The Socialists, whose representation in the 140-member Parliament had fallen in the elections to thirty-eight, had no post in the new government.

[7] Albanian Telegraphic Agency, 17 April 1992, p. 5.

The new Cabinet was youthful and inexperienced and the daunting array of ills that it faced without extensive foreign investment and unconditional loans could only raise doubts about the government's long-term future.

Berisha, born in 1944 in the northern town of Tropoja, had been assistant chief surgeon and teacher at Tirana's cardiology clinic. As President he has refused to alter the life-style he was forced to adopt under the old regime, and has continued to live in a small tenement apartment with his wife Liri, a paediatrician, their twenty-two-year-old daughter Argita, a law student, and their fifteen-year-old son Shkelzen. After graduating in medicine, he was one of the privileged élite allowed to travel outside the country to study. Time in Paris and Copenhagen followed, and he became internationally recognised. In his general character and outlook, Berisha was one of the new generation of post-communist Balkan politicians, with his flamboyant speeches delivered in a deep booming voice, media awareness, rugged good looks and meticulous attention to his appearance. In public meetings he has a very similar *persona* and technique to those of the Bosnian Serb leader Radovan Karadzić. He is shrewd, with an impulsive streak, a workaholic reluctant to delegate, and has an unfaltering faith in the capacity of the DP under his leadership to solve all of Albania's problems. He has claimed, inaccurately, that he only met Hoxha twice and denies that he was ever the dictator's personal doctor.

Berisha had now to satisfy the high expectations he had raised in the election campaign by claiming that foreign investment would increase dramatically if the remaining Socialists were ejected from government. He had also openly promised that immigration quotas to EC countries would be available to Albanian workers if his party won. However, there was virtually no change in the attitude of any foreign power towards Albania as the result of the election. An exception was Italy: the close links that had been built up were broken, and the Italian Ambassador did not even attend the presidential inauguration ceremony. The DP had come to hate the close relationship between the Craxi government in Rome and the Socialists in Tirana. It later proved a poisoned chalice for the Albanian politicians involved, such as Fatos Nano, as the Italian government leaders were convicted in 1993-4 of major corruption. This breach with Italy was largely irrelevant to the main issues facing the country, and here the pattern of indifference towards Albania remained. Even the warmest of political relationships with the United States resulted in little or no increase in the aid budget, or any rush of foreign companies to invest in Albania. Ironically, it was Greece and Italy, traditionally hostile neighbours, which continued to invest on a small scale. The internationally known Benetton company announced the opening of a manufacturing facility for shoes and woollen goods in Shkoder.

In terms of population movement rights, the neighbouring Former Yugoslav Republic of Macedonia (FYROM) was the only country, albeit not a recognised one, to invite Albanians – on visits only. Even this invitation was limited to just thirty-two hours, and to residents of Pogradec, a centre of Orthodoxy 80 miles south-east of Tirana. Muslims were also allowed to cross provided they could prove that they lived in Pogradec. And so on 26 April thousands of Albanians flooded into FYROM after the border was temporarily opened for the first time since 1948, in a goodwill gesture for the Orthodox Easter. A few days later the DP began its systematic campaign to eradicate all vestiges of communism. The body of Enver Hoxha was quietly exhumed from his hero's tomb and re-buried in a public grave plot in a suburban cemetery. The bodies of twelve other former senior communist officials, including the father of Gramoz Pashko, were also removed from the imposing Martyrs' Cemetery on a hill overlooking Tirana. The exhumation was carried out in secrecy in the early morning and under heavy guard. Workers removed Hoxha's lead coffin from his concrete and marble mausoleum, and only close relatives took part in the reburial. The red marble slab, imported especially from Italy at great expense in 1985 to cover the tomb, was recycled as part of the monument in Tirana to the British soldiers who died in the Second World War in Albania. At the end of May the government confiscated the hard currency account of the PLA – the predecessor of the SP – worth $1,565,000, and transferred the sum to the state budget. Another decree froze the accounts of the former communist-controlled trade unions and women's and youth organisations. More bad news for the SPA followed when the government expropriated the Party's main building in Tirana for its own purposes.

It is hardly surprising that a general air of unrest soon prevailed throughout the country: despite the political changes, living stand-ards had remained at subsistence levels for the majority of Albanians, foreign doors remained closed, and most people saw no obvious change in their lives as a result of the election of a DP government. In view of the exaggerated promises made in the campaign, this soon brought political problems for Dr Berisha. Agricultural production was still in a state of complete paralysis due to the uncontrolled seizure of state-owned co-operative land and proper-ty. Moves to secure the return of land to the peasants became so fraught with disagreements that in many cases they were aban-doned. The peasants, realising that state authority had broken down, demolished co-operative buildings and seized the bricks, machinery, livestock and implements for their own dwellings. Naturally, this greatly exacerbated the overall economic decline of the countryside, home to two-thirds of the population. But even with up to 70 per cent of co-operative land back in private hands, it could not be expected that agricultural production would rise above subsistence level; the necessary seeds, fertiliser and machinery were lacking. There were also vital issues of compen-sation for previously confiscated land, and the validity of old title deeds still had to be settled. These often acrimonious processes have continued. The largest companies have been affected by protracted land disputes as much as the owners of tiny strips in remote mountain fastnesses. Misery and despair now gripped Al-banian rural life, as most peasants had just a little milk or cheese to sell but were otherwise unemployed and without income. The young simply wanted to get out at any cost, no matter where. They continued to drift towards Tirana and the ports in search of the prosperity and freedom that had so recently been promised to them. One of the government's most important tasks was to seek ways to narrow the economic and cultural gap between the towns and the villages.

From 1 July the price of a standard large loaf of bread rose from 5 leks (which it had been for forty-five years) to 25 leks. The average daily wage was around 35 leks and nearly 300,000 people were then receiving no more than 80 per cent of their full wage. At the beginning of July, in yet another bid to flee the country, some 6,000 Albanians tried to commandeer ships in Durres and in Vlora, where police were reported to be dragging people from fishing boats. Government officials blamed 'communists' for inciting the would-be emigrants to move from their homes in an attempt to destabilise the country. The attempted exodus, however, was a spontaneous movement triggered off by the discontinuation of unemployment benefits for state workers, thus effectively cutting off all income to around 20 per cent of Albania's workforce. By now the desperate population was dependent almost entirely on foreign food aid, and although Operation Pelican, the Italian-organised food aid programme, had successfully prevented mass starvation, it could hardly be seen as a permanent solution to the country's food shortages. The overall public mood remained highly volatile.

Turmoil in the government party

In 5 June 1992 Azem Hajdari, deputy chairman of the DP, went to the United States on a 'training course' (to 'continue his studies'). Gramoz Pashko claimed that Hajdari had left because of differences with Berisha, which he voiced in a television interview that was never broadcast. After weeks of internal debate, Pashko and several others, including the former Defence Minister Perikli Teta and the former Minister of Culture Preç Zogaj, were expelled from the DP at a special conference in mid-August. Pashko's differences with Berisha had been clear to all since the decision to withdraw from the coalition the previous December. He had been persistently annoyed by the lack of parliamentary debate on the state of the economy, and made a public gesture by taking Hajdari to the airport himself because no official from the DP would go to see him off.

Berisha explained the expulsions in an interview: 'What happened, actually, was that a handful of gentlemen found themselves without power and were very unhappy about this. However, instead of simply declaring themselves a faction within the party based on a certain set of ideas, they tried to impose their ideas on the entire party. Had they not been so intolerant, they would not have been expelled from the party.'[8] In a display of 'tolerance' the Justice Ministry then banned the tiny and politically irrelevant Albanian Communist Party, a hardline splinter group from the SPA, after parliament voted to prohibit the activities of fascist

[8] *East European Reporter*, November/December 1992, p. 21.

and communist parties. On 16 July Parliament banned all political parties which were Stalinist or 'Hoxhaist'.

The DP government was still plagued by public order problems. On 26 August several hundred workers and local inhabitants from the Polican munitions complex south of Berat surrounded the town, captured as hostages the chairmen of the facilities departments and the Public Order Ministry, who were visiting the manufacturing complex, and destroyed and set fire to the office buildings. They were protesting against the non-fulfilment of several demands presented to the enterprise's directorate and the Defence Ministry. Six people were injured in violent street clashes, barricades were erected, and the government had to make major concessions on the economic issues involved in the dispute to calm the situation down. On the television news that evening, the Council of Ministers called these events an 'attempt to assassinate democracy and destabilise the country at the beginning of the reform process'. The dispute also had a wider significance since it demonstrated the unpredictability of outbreaks of violence in urban centres, and the fact that the trade unions were still an independent force. The dispute appears to have influenced government thinking on the labour front and may well have led to the bitter dispute in December when the workers at the important Bulquize chrome mine near the Yugoslav border, who had been engaged in a prolonged hunger-strike and mine occupation, were intimidated back to work by the use of paramilitary units centrally directed from Tirana. The forces of 'order' laid dynamite around the top of the mine shaft and threatened to detonate it if the underground hunger-strike continued. As part of a plan to establish strong central government and restore 'order', the trade unions, which had played such a vital and honourable role in the final demise of communism in May 1991, had to be virtually crushed as a serious bargaining force only a few months later. Similar tactics were used the next year when striking workers at Kukes, in the north-east, protested at the government's failure to honour land compensation promises made during the election. Paramilitary units were sent into the town and it was made all but impossible for either Albanian or foreign news reporters to discover what was happening and report on it.

The Split in the Democratic Party

By the summer of 1992, support for the ruling Democrats was already waning in parallel to the growing centralisation of all real power around Berisha. In local elections held on 27 August, the DP saw its share of the vote plummet approximately from two-thirds to half. The turnout of 70 per cent reflected, the third time round, the lack of enthusiasm for a process which seemed to bring no positive results. The Socialist Party was the surprise beneficiary, capturing several key DP strongholds. A prime reason for this dramatic turnabout was the social hardship caused by the government's tough economic reforms. Voting for the Socialists, who promised to slow the reform process down, was seen by many as their only defence against the huge job losses and social deprivation they were experiencing. In a public statement the DP leader Eduard Selami blamed 'people who have misunderstood the meaning of democracy' for the revival of the Socialists' fortunes. He argued that 'voters have not allowed us enough time' to reverse decades of communist mismanagement and improve the living standards of Albanians. Nevertheless, the DP saw the results as only a minor setback as they actually won more votes than the Socialists. However, as with the 1991 elections, their support declined mainly in the countryside where small centres returned Socialist mayors again. The Berisha administration was seen to have upheld neither the principle of 'national reconciliation' nor the 'constitutionalism' it had promised to the electorate.

As the principle of reasoned debate was increasingly disregarded, a climate of intolerance developed. The progress of democracy was being hampered by an obsessive desire for power, regardless of the cost, and an absence of moderation in DP circles, often encouraged by the close relationship that had grown up between Berisha and the hardline anti-communist US Ambassador, William Ryerson. In an attempt to offer a moderate and centrist democratic alternative to the Albanian people, a group of intellectuals founded a new political party, the Democratic Alliance (DA), in September 1992, following the schism in the DP's ranks. Most of the leading figures in the new centre-right party, such as Neritan Ceka and Shahin Kadare, were among the initiators of the DP; they claimed to represent the moderate wing of the DP, upholding the ideals of social peace with social justice, national reconciliation, rapid and efficient economic reforms, and integration into the European Union. The new party was against revanchism and the fundamentalist nationalist tendencies of the trend which it considered characterised the majority of the DP membership. This leading group was and is also strongly secular, and against the increasing Islamic influence that has spread to some sections of the governing party. The Alliance Party manifesto stated:

> Considering the persistent and arbitrary attacks on democratic institutions by the leadership of the Democratic Party, and heavy violations of the Constitution by the parliamentary majority and a worsening climate of intolerance that has been awakened as a result, seeing the lack of internal democracy in the DP, and having exhausted all their efforts within that movement, a big group of the founders and ex-leaders of the DP decided to create the Albanian Democratic Alliance as a true alternative for the Albanian people.

The main aims of the DA were: to provide for all Albanians the right to find a voice in the democratic process to which they contributed; the commitment to create a political climate free of rhetoric and demagoguery in which the citizen could be protected from abuses of populist action and uncontrolled party power.

In this period there was a marked increase in the direct and indirect influence of the United States over the Albanian government and over Berisha in particular. Ambassador Ryerson – a powerful personality with a long career in difficult State Department postings, mainly in Latin America – developed a strong emotional committment to Albania and to the DP. In turn his strongly interventionist concept of US diplomacy appealed strongly to Berisha, who seems to have seen in it the potential for the Albania-superpower relationships of the past to re-emerge. It also linked easily with what Berisha and most of the Albanian political élite saw as the near-total failure of the European Union to provide emigration opportunities, investment and aid that had been promised when the communists were still in power. It is questionable how far this criticism of the EU is fair; whatever the shortcomings of its performance in Albania, it did plan and finance the vital Operation Pelican which prevented mass starvation in mainland Europe, and the sums of money it disbursed to help Albania were, and still are, always much greater than those from the

United States. But the strong relationship between Berisha and the United States defied rational discussion or analysis, as love-affairs often do, and before long Berisha was taking few decisions of any importance without consulting Ryerson. This was widely commented upon by the Tirana élite. There seems little doubt that, over the split in the DP, Ryerson strongly advised the United States to back Berisha all the way and to marginalise the more moderate leaders. Interviews with participants in the leadership confirmed this. The decision brought short-term gains, but two years later, with Berisha's referendum defeat and failure to achieve democratic legitimacy, the possibility that the influence of the United States as the one super-power in the critical Balkan region would become linked exclusively to one man clearly held long-term risks. Much remains to be discovered about the rationale for US policy in Albania; at one level it seems little more than a fascination among a few people for odd little Balkan states, but at another level it could be a serious planned attempt to counter the political influence in the region of Serbia, with its Russian links. The influence of the right-wing US émigrés was certainly important in Berisha's early days; in alliance with Ryerson they appear to have attempted to influence the land reform legislation in such a way that the old pre-war great estates would be reconstructed, but unanimous Albanian public opinion would have made this impossible. The strongest basis of the DP was with the peasantry. Under privatisation they had regained their former family land or a share of the newly available collective farm land. So, just as the Albanian political project had a very narrow base focused on Berisha himself, and the often extremist-dominated émigré lobby of Albanian-Americans on Capitol Hill, so its external backers were unlikely to re-emerge as decisive forces in economic life.

The media

Before long, authoritarian tendencies began to reappear in the media, aimed at reinforcing the exclusive power of the President. There had been no attempt to end the party-state monopoly of the media, and many Albanians felt that techniques of media reporting had change little since the days of Hoxha. While the Socialist Party newspaper *Zeri-i-Popullit* was criticised in Albania and abroad for attacking the DP in an attempt to sabotage reform, the DP's paper *Rilindja Demokratike* likewise adopted a polemical style against the Socialists, sometimes devoting as much as half its meagre few pages to bitter criticism of its main rival *Zeri-i-Popullit* and lengthy and cantankerous personal attacks on the Socialist leaders. On television most news bulletins consisted of a monotonous recital of Berisha's activities during the day. In a nation plagued with strikes the media only transmitted news of workers agreeing to go back to work. The social and economic conflicts actually occurring were seldom reported, let alone explored. The first that most people knew of a two-week strike by train workers in May was when they found their stations closed. When hundreds of rioters chanting anti-government slogans went on the rampage in central Tirana in early July, smashing and looting the few shops, television deemed it unworthy of mention. As on every other day, the lead story was the day's doings by President Berisha. Teasingly, news presenters mentioned 'problems' and 'difficulties', but these were easily accounted for by the subversion of 'communists past and communists present'. Albania's media only transmitted good news.

Questioning the government line was heresy, and anyone who criticised policy had to be a 'communist'. Such was the painful discovery made by Gramoz Pashko, who in the previous month had raised the spectre of a re-emerging authoritarian strain in political life. Needless to say, his speech in parliament was not transmitted on television, yet within forty-eight hours a statement listing his shortcomings was read out on the news. His fellow-parliamentarians 'democratically' voted to expel him from the DP parliamentary group. Albania's new leaders did not want a bad press. They had an enormous task on their hands, not only to rebuild the economy but to tackle two equally pressing problems: how to restore stability to the crime-ravaged cities and confidence to a people convinced that no one can ever succeed in transforming their poverty-stricken state into one approaching West European norms. Controlling the media by the direct appointment of directors from the President's office was one of the drastic measures the DP decided to use to shock the country out of the abyss; this left the people, in their cramped apartments, to watch Italian TV for news of the latest riots in their own country.[9] In the absence

[9] Liam McDowall, *New Statesman*, 17 July 1992. p. 16.

of any press law, civil rights legislation or a modern liberal constitution, individual journalists were vulnerable to pressure and intimidation from the government. In August 1992 seven journalists on the DP paper *Rilindja Demokratike,* many of whom had played a key part in overthrowing communism, resigned from the paper because of the heavy restrictions placed on their reporting by the obligation of always having to follow the party line, and the lack of freedom to express their opinion. The government's strongest obloquy was reserved for the nascent BBC Albanian service, many of whose staff were from old *nomenklatura* family backgrounds. It was inevitable that this would happen since access to higher education in Tirana had been closely linked to political loyalty to the PLA regime. It did not, in practice, imply any particular view on the part of the BBC recruits, but that was not how recruitment policy was seen by government circles in Tirana.

Initially Albanians had expected quick returns from their investment in democracy. However, their growing political maturity was creating a crisis of confidence and disenchantment with the democratic process, which in turn led to rising social discontent. The people's patience was turning to frustration as the promised job prospects and improvement in living standards failed even marginally to materialise. There was already nostalgia among some older people for the days of communist rule. As the country sank further into economic ruin and war clouds thickened to the north, the government turned its attention to the settling of old scores. On 12 September the former president, Ramiz Alia, was placed under house arrest, accused of corruption; he was detained in his daughter's apartment in Tirana by policemen originally stationed outside it for his personal safety. Members of the DP, in particular the Party leader Eduard Selami, had repeatedly demanded his arrest, and in an interview with Agence France Presse in June, Alia complained that since his resignation he had lived without a salary or a pension; 'I could have caused another Tiananmen in Tirana. I have never liked blood. I did my best in difficult conditions.'[10] His sudden arrest could be traced to outspoken articles he had published in the Socialist newspaper *24 Hours,* in which, sensing that his arrest was imminent, he criticised the government for lowering the standard of living since it had come

[10] BBC *Summary of World Broadcasts (SWB),* 12 September 1992.

to power. In the article entitled 'Why they want to arrest me' he wrote:

> My arrest is a political question first of all as revenge for the sons of fascist collaborators. They have the goal to judge the Partisans against the anti-fascist fighters, ex-communists and their sons. Secondly, my arrest was wanted as a result of the battle between the two clans of the Democratic Party. Thirdly, they wanted to keep me quiet in this very difficult economic situation.

Rilindja Demokratike had published several articles asking why Alia was still at liberty and not in prison along with other ex-communist leaders.

At the end of December, five former Party and police officials were jailed for up to twenty years for ordering the fatal shooting of the four demonstrators in Shkoder in 1991. By then almost the whole former Politburo was under arrest and awaiting trial charged with stealing from the state. These included Nexhmije Hoxha, who in February 1993 was sentenced to nine (later raised to eleven) years in prison for corruption. She was charged with misappropriating state funds amounting to 750,000 leks between her husband's death in 1985 and the end of the 'Stalinist' regime in 1990. In March 1992, in an interview with *Der Spiegel*, Berisha urged the newly-elected Albanian government to avoid witch-hunts of former communist leaders, saying: 'If we go down that road, our courts will be busy till the year 2010.'[11] There was, however, a noticeably subdued reaction to these events from the Albanian people. Although the horrors of the Hoxha years were still sufficiently vivid for many Albanians to feel the need to 'cleanse' the country of communists, many saw the purges of former leaders as directing attention away from the real and acute problems then facing the country. As Albanians watched the country's politics being dragged down to the level of a struggle between personalities, and quarrels over what role, if any, a person had played in the former regime, many began to argue that the DP had no monopoly on democracy, and it was clear that gagging opponents could do little to heal the country's deep psychological divisions. Contradictory orders and decrees were being issued by

[11] *Der Spiegel*, 29 March 1992.

different government departments, and public life was conducted in an atmosphere of secrecy and suspicion. Some degree of co-operation with former communists was unavoidable, especially if it is remembered that a sizeable number of today's Democrats were so recently Party members themselves, not least Berisha himself. Such is the situation in almost all the countries of Eastern Europe and the former Soviet Union.

As part of the reversion to authoritarianism, the government soon reverted to the old Hoxhaist tactic of manufacturing fake external threats and plots against Albania, or wildly exaggerating real problems. The new Albanian intelligence service SHIK played a key role in this process. SHIK had been rehabilitated after a period of reorganisation in 1992-3, and it is generally believed in Tirana that advisers from the US Central Intelligence Agency assisted in this process. For example, on 28 November 1992 the BBC correspondent Nicholas Miletich reported:

> Albania's secret service has foiled several recent attempts by Yugoslav intelligence agents to launch terrorist attacks and des-tabilize their neighbour, the head of Albania's secret service said. Bashkim Gazidede, the 40-year-old head of the service, known as SHIK, told AFP [Agence France Presse] that former Albanian Communists 'acting underground' were also implicated in this subversive activity. The destabilization attempts included trouble in July at the port of Durres where thousands of people again tried to force their way on to boats bound for Italy.[...] Rioting in August in Polican, an Albanian military industrial centre, was also orchestrated from the outside, said Gazidede, a former mathematics teacher, in his first interview since he took over four months ago as head of Albania's post-communist intelligence service. Albanian television in August had also reported a bomb attack that partly destroyed an aqueduct near Kruja, 40 kilometers north of Tirana. Kruja deputy Sabedin Balla, a member of the DP, at the time accused the *Sigurimi* of planting the explosives. Gazidede, who had no prior in-telligence experience when he came to his post, said he fired 'nearly 60 per cent' of the staff of the former secret police to weed out people 'compromised by the communist period'.[12]

12 BBC, *SWB*, 28 November 1992.

However, there was no evidence that any of these events were communist plots, in particular the large-scale population movements at Durres which by their nature would have been very difficult or impossible to organise beforehand by covert means. According to Western estimates, the *Sigurimi* had between 7,000 and 10,000 agents and thousands of informers under the old regime. 'There are still problems and the cleansing process is not yet done,' Gazidede said in an interview at SHIK headquarters, a small anonymous building on Tirana's outskirts. He was reluctant to say much about *Sigurimi* 's archives since no legal decision had yet been made on whether to open them to the public. Opening the files could have a catastrophic effect on the great number of people who worked with the secret police (it is now estimated that the number was much higher than 20 per cent of Albania's 3.2 million population). There was a hint of the tension which surrounded the issue in mid-November when the parliamentary speaker Pjeter Arbnori, a former political prisoner who spent twenty-five years in communist labour camps, was himself accused by a fellow-inmate, a Catholic priest called Simon Jubani, of collaborating with the *Sigurimi* during his detention. Gazidede himself has been accused of gathering false evidence to undermine the President's political opponents by presenting them as *Sigurimi* informers, although he dismissed this as 'pure slander'.

Although much has yet to emerge about what happened between Berisha and his previous political allies during these months, they marked a major retreat from the notion of a functioning parliamentary democracy. The concept of an opposition playing a necessary political role was definitively rejected. In a country without a tradition of party politics, the Berisha project quickly took root, and there were many functionaries from the previous regime who by background and temperament were inclined to authoritarianism and took easily to the political atmosphere Berisha created. The notion of a political party as a vehicle for democracy was equally fragile, and soon all real power began to settle in and around the presidential palace. No decision of any importance could be taken without seeking the views of Berisha. Some Albanians had privileged access; among these were northern peasants from his own Tropoja region, who could be seen hanging round the palace seeking small favours, much as suppliants would have pestered an Ottoman pasha. Others were survivors from the old *nomenklatura* who had managed to change their spots, such as Shaban Murati. In 1988 Murati, the notoriously hardline foreign editor of *Zeri-i-Popullit,* had written a comprehensive attack on *perestroika*, and yet had survived to become the spokesman of Berisha's government.

The American and EC concept of Berisha as a strong president who would enforce law and order and bring 'stability' – a way of thinking heavily dependent on relationships between the United States and client states in the 'Third World' – was fatally undermined by the lack of a healthy political culture. In turn, elements of this culture were themselves evolving during the transition in a way that would make democratic progress on conventional European lines more difficult to achieve, with the revival of religion one of the most important of these components. Just as Berisha was attempting to create a new national identity based on the market, secular economic progress and Westernisation, older ideological forces were reviving strongly to reassert traditional Albanian values. It is ironic that the United States was the first Western country to become aware of the dangers of the Berisha presidency, after it had done so much to put him in place. It was equally ironic that the EC countries did not understand that political freedom was being continuously eroded under the same regime.

6

THE REVIVAL OF RELIGION

One of the most important aspects of the transition period has been the reintroduction of religion into Albanian society with the lifting of the ban imposed in 1967 on all forms of religious worship. 'Despite popular belief that the religion of Albanians is Albanianism' (from an elegy by the nineteenth-century intellectual Pashko Vasa), a poll taken in 1945 showed that some 70 per cent of the Albanian population professed to be Muslims, 20 per cent Greek Orthodox Christians, and the remaining 10 per cent Roman Catholics. Over the border in former Yugoslavia, 90 per cent of the 3 million Albanians are Muslim, the remainder being Catholic. Throughout their turbulent history Albanians have shifted with relative ease from one religion to another – being Catholic, Orthodox or Muslim according to how this best served their interests at the time. In the late Middle Ages, their lands had become the battlefield between the Catholic West and the Orthodox East. Whenever the West was advancing, the Albanian feudal lords – often followed by their populations – espoused Catholicism; whenever Byzantium was the victor and the West retreated, they embraced Orthodoxy. A notable example was Skenderbeg's father, Gion Kastrioti, who changed religion several times. He was a Catholic as an ally of Venice and turned Orthodox as an ally of Stefan Lazarević of Serbia.[1]

Despite the generally accepted view that the Ottoman state essentially aimed at the expansion of Islam, there was little official encouragement to convert the Empire's Christian subjects who were divided into groups, or *millets*. This was basically a minority home-rule policy based on religious affiliation. Thus Ottoman subjects were divided not by ethnic origin or language but by religion. Muslims were accorded the highest status: they were

[1] S. Skendi, *Balkan Cultural Studies*, Boulder, CO., 1980, p. 208.

privileged in the law courts, paid fewer taxes and were allowed to bear arms. Although Christians were not encouraged to join the military forces, they were expected to provide the tax support for them, and were required periodically to donate one healthy male child to be converted to Islam and trained either for the Ottoman administration or the élite military corps of Janissaries. Christians were also taxed on the produce of their land and home industry and on all personal possessions; also, a special capitation tax was levied on all male Christians in place of the military service required of the Muslims.

The Russo-Ottoman wars of the eighteenth century greatly accelerated the decline of the Ottoman empire, leading towards a notable reversal of the previous Ottoman policy of religious tolerance. The threat posed by the wars with Russia encouraged the Porte to levy increased taxes on all non-Muslim subjects, while those who converted to Islam had their taxes lowered and were given grants of land. Albanians who chose to convert to Islam were also given many opportunities to serve in senior administrative positions. As Muslims, they were the allies of the Ottomans, who protected them from Slavonic and Greek encroachment, offered them employment and paid them well for their military service. Along with the Bosnians, the Albanian Muslims thus became the pampered children of the empire. However, the majority of Albanian converts were men, while women, though married to Muslims, often retained their Christian beliefs and were thus a factor in creating good feeling between the adherents of the two faiths. At various times whole villages, for political advantage, voluntarily renounced the religion of their forefathers. The majority of conversions took place in the lowlands, around the Shkumbi river, where direct Ottoman pressure could most easily be exerted. Among the Albanians of Kosova there appears to have been far greater readiness to accept Islam, perhaps because of the pressure of their close proximity to the Serbs, who by the 1830s had achieved their own autonomous state. Christian Albanians who wished to retain their faith after the Ottoman conquest often found difficulty in competing with those who had converted. To make their difficult lives easier, many Albanians therefore gradually adopted at least the outer signs of the Islamic faith, thus obtaining such privileges as the right to bear arms.

Following the Ottoman defeat and the establishment of the

independent Albanian state in 1912, the government remained secular. The experiences of the Balkan Wars and the First World War resulted in a general understanding that any religious differences had to be played down in the name of common ethnicity. Therefore, no official state religion was recognised in the inter-war period, although freedom to practise any religion was guaranteed. After the communist victory in 1945 Albanians were at first, in theory, allowed freedom of worship, although religion was given no official endorsement or encouragement and the state confiscated without compensation all land and property owned by religious institutions. Relations between all religious groups were relatively friendly and, as in the past, they interacted freely. The development in the late 1960s of Albania's ideological and cultural revolution was intended to bring about a complete transformation in the mentality, psychology and general outlook of the people. The intensive drive to educate them towards understanding and accepting the new socialist ideology was aimed at destroying the old patriarchal, conservative customs and traditions – indeed all remnants of the past. By accomplishing this, the regime believed it would 'free the people from backwardness, from the shackles of the patriarchal canons, prejudices, religious beliefs and divisions, and all the decay of the past.'[2] The regime continuously emphasised that Catholicism, Islam and Orthodoxy were alien philosophies introduced into Albania by foreign elements which essentially threatened the integrity of the nation. Priests and muftis were ridiculed as backward relics of the past, easily recruited as agents of foreign powers to undermine Albanian nationalism. Thus Hoxha hoped to appeal to the Albanian people's strong sense of national identity and their deep suspicion of the intentions of foreign powers towards their small country. The decisive blow dealt to religion in 1967 by the enforced abolition of all religious practices was intended, according to Hoxha, to give the Albanian people a 'spiritual emancipation', thereby opening up 'broad vistas to the people to master a new advanced culture embued with a scientific world outlook and to adopt a new way of life and new customs'.[3] It can be argued that Hoxha outdid even Stalin and

---

[2] E. Hoxha, *Banner of Struggle for Freedom and Socialism,* Tirana, 1985, p. 107.

[3] Ibid., pp. 107-8.

Mao by officially banning the practice of religion and the sale of religious books and icons.

Up till 1967 Albania had about 1,200 mosques and 400 Catholic and Orthodox churches, and more than 300 Bektashi religious buildings (*tekkes*). In the 1967 Cultural Revolution the majority of these buildings were either destroyed or turned into warehouses, sports halls or cinemas. In the mosques concrete was plastered over prayers written on the walls, and in the churches icons were destroyed and frescoes painted over. Although some of the smaller churches and mosques were totally demolished, those religious buildings which were of great historical or architectural interest, such as the Ethem Bey mosque with its graceful minaret in the very centre of Tirana, were preserved as part of the people's traditional heritage. Secular festivals were substituted for the traditional religious ones, and a museum of atheism was set up in Shkoder, the town Hoxha considered the most religiously conservative. Yet although Albania had proclaimed itself the world's first totally atheist state, it could not eradicate all religious beliefs and practices, but merely drove them underground: young boys were secretly circumcised, mass was celebrated clandestinely, and many continued to listen to religious programmes broadcast by radio stations in Italy and Greece.

The revival of religion

In 1991 the ban on religion was lifted, resulting in a gradual revival of religious practice, together with the restoration and re-building of churches and mosques. The re-emergence of religion in Shkoder – which, along with Durres, Elbasan and Kavaja, was the most strongly Islamic town in Albania – showed this process in high relief. Shkoder is also the spiritual home of Albania's estimated 350,000 Roman Catholics, and the two religious communities helped each other when work began on opening up the closed mosques and churches. Before the war Shkoder had thirty-five mosques, but only one, the beautiful Leaden Mosque, survived the 1967 purges intact. It was also the setting for serious violence when paramilitary police fired on worshippers inside the mosque on 2 April 1991 in disturbances associated with the victory of the communists in the election at that time. In 1992, when the city's Catholic church reopened, Muslims as well as Catholics helped to get it ready, and five days later Catholics helped to open Shkoder's second mosque. Five seminaries – four Islamic and one Jesuit – reopened in Shkoder, and by 1993 there were four imams teaching in Shkoder's Islamic school, which had 130 pupils (100 others had been granted scholarships to study in Kuwait, Saudi Arabia, Egypt, Libya and Turkey).

Throughout the country wealthy expatriates from the diaspora began to finance the building of new mosques in their native villages, and foreign governments donated money for religious building and restoration. In August 1992 President Berisha part-icipated in the inauguration of a new mosque in the village of Klopcisht near Maqellare in Diber District; this was a present from Sule Bektashi, a son of the village who had lived in the United States since the 1950s. By September 1992 around 100 mosques and thirty Catholic and Orthodox churches throughout Albania had been reopened for religious use. However, the process of reopening the religious buildings was marked by severe con-tradictions. North from Shkoder on the narrow pock-marked road to the border at Hani-i-Hoti there are a number of small villages, a mixture of Catholic and Muslim. In the Muslim village of Koplik – which is no more than a cluster of two-room cottages with small courtyards, joined by a series of dirt paths which in winter are churned into a swirling sea of mud by the hooves of cows and horses – an enormous newly-built yellow-painted mosque stands in the square, paid for by the Saudi Arabian government. Looking majestically out of place, it stands alone in an inhospitable, poor and miserable locality. The inside is richly carpeted and Korans are piled high along the walls. The opulence of Koplik's mosque is in marked contrast to the church recently opened not far away in a Catholic village, which is in a bleak former agricultural building. It had no seats and the people had collected little piles of stones on which to sit, until in 1995 an Austrian-based charity furnished the church with benches.

In addition to the three principal religious groups already men-tioned there are the Bektashi (Baktashiyya), a dervish (i.e. Sufi) and mendicant order, whose mother monastery was originally at Pir-evi in Asia Minor. The Bektashi movement took root in the Balkans at the time of the Ottoman conquest. Its preachers came in tiny groups, often of just three – a baba and two dervishes. According to H.T. Norris, the monastic order of the Bektashis was planted in Albania at the latest by the mid-sixteenth century (as indicated by the numerous Albanian Bektashi saints who can be identified with certainty as of that century).[4] The Bektashis, who very loosely observed traditional Muslim practices, called for Shi'ite retaliation against the (Sunni) Ottoman power, and preached tolerance of all non-Islamic creeds. This partly explains the sect's steady growth in Albania, which enabled Bektashis to co-operate with the northern Catholics and southern Orthodox alike. Bektashism in Albania expanded greatly at the beginning of the nineteenth century, when *tekkes* were established at Gjirokaster, Tepelena and Janina. In the struggle for the Albanian national awakening and subsequent independence from Ottoman rule, the three most prominent Albanian leaders followed the Bektashi faith. Their *tekkes* became centres of cultural awakening, and bridges between Christian and Islamic communities.

The world centre of Bektashism is today in Tirana and in associated institutions in the United States, all with strong Albanian links (Detroit has a strong Bektashi presence). Since 1991 the central *tekke* in Tirana, in a poor area to the north-east of the centre, has been extensively restored, as have the nearby graves of two of its founding fathers. Under communism the sect was tolerated till the early 1960s when persecution appears to have begun sometime before the major anti-religious campaign. The current head of the Tirana *tekke*, Baba Reshat Bardhi, was sentenced under Hoxha to a long term of forced labour on a prison farm in southern Albania. The *tekke* was closed and its library burnt, the building was then used as an old people's home. Along with other religions, Bektashism revived somewhat in mid-1990, and the first formal assembly of Albanian Bektashis was held in June of that year. The renovation of the *tekke* began shortly afterwards with major financial and logistical help from Albanian Bektashis in the United States. To date it does not appear that the Bektashis have much hold over the young in Albania. Although other important *tekkes* have reopened, such as the exceptionally beautiful building in the citadel at Kruja, and a new one has been established in the eastern highlands at Fushe Bulquiza, a long struggle will be necessary before the sect can regain its previous general cultural influence, which grew in Albania as a result of particular historical

[4] H.T. Norris, *Islam in the Balkans*, London: Hurst, 1994, p. 132.

circumstances in the nineteenth century. No doubt Bektashism will survive as a minority religion, but although the *tekkes* may establish themselves as centres of local popular identity, it is doubtful on present evidence if they will ever become any more than that.

Sunni Muslims

Long before the collapse of communism, various Islamic organisations had established contacts with existing Islamic communities in Eastern Europe. This had not, however, been possible in Albania until it became obvious that communism there was finally doomed, although in diplomatic terms Ramiz Alia had moved closer to some secular left-wing Arab countries since the death of Hoxha, with the opening of a Libyan embassy and an expansion of the existing Egyptian presence. In 1990 representatives of a number of Islamic groups began visiting the country, and an aid scheme was agreed with the Turkish government for the restoration of a number of historic mosques dating from Ottoman times. This produced a rapid improvement in the physical condition of important buildings such as the central Korça mosque, the oldest in Albania, and enabled restoration of the notable Gjirokaster building to begin. Old links with the strong Islamic communities in former Yugoslav Macedonia were restored, in towns such as Tetovo and Gostivar. In Tetovo, Saudi Arabia had paid for a large new *madrasah*, which was opened in 1992. In Albania itself the Saudis paid for more than half a million copies of the Koran to be imported, which so exceeded local demand that a familiar sight in mosques in 1991 and 1992 was numerous unopened boxes of these volumes.

In February 1992 Ramiz Alia greeted a delegation from the Turkish Islamic community based in Istanbul. The discussions centred around the role of religion in Albania and the strengthening of co-operation between the religious communities of both countries. Just before the March elections of 1992, a Kuwaiti delegation presented the beleaguered Alia administration with an ambitious investment plan and, in return for promises of economic aid, asked for permission to build several mosques. It was then that major new constructions of mosques began in earnest throughout Albania. On 31 March 1992, thousands of Muslims gathered at the Leaden Mosque in Shkoder to attend the ceremony of Kadir. The Islamic leader of Shkoder, Haxhi Faik Hoxha, spoke to a curious congregation on the religious significance of the occasion, and parts from the Koran were then sung. A visitor from Egypt, Hafiz Feti Muhamet El Atari, read extracts from the Koran.

As soon as the Democratic Party's victory was confirmed in March 1992, an increasing number of delegations from around the Muslim world began visiting Albania. Among the first was one from Saudi Arabia which attended a ceremony in the mosque in the Kiras quarter of Shkoder on 17 April. The Saudi guests read from the Koran, and after the ceremony a contest was organised for the children present to test their Islamic knowledge. Already small classes had been set up in the mosques to teach children to read basic Arabic script. The chairman of the Albanian Islamic Community, which had been formed in February 1991, Hafiz Sabri Koci, spoke about religious morale and the revived spiritual formation of the people. In the chaotic and crime-ridden conditions of this immediate transition period, Muslim leaders capitalised on popular anxieties by arguing that the state should consider introducing Islamic laws if the police could not restore order. Hafiz Sabri Koci, born in 1921, was one of Albania's few surviving imams, having become one in Shkoder, where he grew up, in 1941, and mufti of Kruja and Kavaja in the 1950s. He was arrested in April 1967 for refusing to support the new drive towards complete atheism, and spent the next twenty years in prison. He has a charismatic personality and is committed to ensuring the restoration of Islam in Albania to its pre-war status.

By now international aid was arriving in Albania from several sources. On 23 April a delegation from the Alislamic Aluok Foundation, based in the Netherlands, arrived in Tirana. Four sheiks, led by the Foundation's director Imaledin Bakri Ismail, offered to help Albania through the difficult period of transition by building four complexes comprising medical clinics, schools, sports clubs and mosques for the Muslims of Tirana, Shkoder, Durres and Kavaja. They also promised investment in all kinds of industry, trade, schooling and medicine. A spokesperson for the Islamic Relief Agency (IR), said that without the help of the Democratic Party, which provided a lorry, it would have been difficult to distribute aid. Not surprisingly he found Muslims ignorant of their faith, aware that they were Muslims but not knowing what it actually meant. Islamic Relief reported that Albanian Muslims were like a dry sponge, ready to soak up anything given to them. The need for Islamic literature has continued, and the IR and Muslim Aid have sought to remedy it with their own productions.[5]

By the summer of 1992 the issue of the revival of religion had become a sensitive debating point. In June of that year Albania's most prominent intellectual and writer, Ismail Kadare, angered Albanian Muslims by his media discussions of Islamic influence among Albanians. From his base in Paris he argued in interviews that Albania was increasingly identified as an Islamic country and that Christian Europe would therefore be less inclined to help it. During the Gulf War several Albanians had been shown on European and American television declaring their support for Iraq. Kadare believed that such images damaged the Albanian cause at a time when Western assistance was urgently needed to rebuild the economy and to help the cause of Albanians in the former Yugoslavia. Kadare claimed that 'Albanians are among those people who have suffered equally from Communism and from Islam.'[6] This remark caused a storm of protest from the influential Albanian-American community. A large proportion of them are Muslims, and they gathered in Albanian Islamic centres around New York to criticise Kadare. They wanted to know why he had not been more outspoken against the former Albanian communist regime and distanced himself from the ideology it represented long before. Kadare was accused of knowing little about religion, having been born and brought up under communism, and of irresponsibility in creating divisions among Albanians by bringing the religious issue to the fore.

Unlike the other religious groups which flocked to Albania during this period, the Islamic representatives were intent on fostering an economic as well as a spiritual and cultural base in the country. In October 1992 a delegation from the Islamic Development Bank (IDB), headed by its chairman Ahmed Mohammed Ali, visited Tirana to lay the groundwork for Albania to join the bank. Ali told President Berisha that it was willing to invest in Albania and develop co-operation in all areas of the economy,

[5] *Impact International*, vol. 22, nos 7 and 8, London, 10 April-7 May 1992, p. 9.
[6] *Le Figaro*, 3 March 1992.

including agriculture, education and transport. The IDB delegation told ministers in Tirana that the bank would promote Albania's exports and imports and grant it credits as soon as it became a member of the bank. This was just the sort of talk the new DP government wanted to hear. Interviewed in Tirana, the chairman of the bank said that Albania would benefit greatly from membership, since credits would be granted at low interest rates and would be repayable over a period of twenty years. The delegation also discussed plans to build an institute to train teachers in Arabic and five schools; to dispatch a first contingent of Albanian students to undergo higher education in IDB member countries; and to promote book publishing.[7]

After the failure of American and European capital investment in Albania, the slogan 'Towards Europe or Islam' began to appear in several media discussions. However, even though many Albanians now believed that Europe had turned its back on Albania, they were alarmed by the decision of Berisha that the country should become a full member of the Organisation of the Islamic Conference (OIC). It had been made hurriedly and without consulting parliament in December 1992, and many Albanians were worried that the move would align Albania closer to the Islamic world. Alarm bells immediately rang in many quarters. The Foreign Minister, Alfred Serreqi, a Catholic from Shkoder, was staunchly opposed to Berisha's decision to join the OIC, and a sharp political debate followed, led especially by the Socialist Party which sought public support by voicing the population's general unease at what was widely interpreted as a backward step. It was also known that West European countries were deeply suspicious of Berisha's motives, fearing that Albania could become Islam's advance-post in Europe. This was perhaps somewhat alarmist, given that numerous countries have relations with Islamic countries without being turned into protégés of Iran. For a country in such desperate economic straits it was a logical move in order to provide an alternative source of potential aid and investment; it was also realistic given the country's geopolitical context, and Albanian impatience with what was seen in Tirana as a general failure of big European companies to invest in the country. Witnessing the abysmal failure of European diplomacy to stop the Serb-Croat

---

[7] *Radio Free Europe*, vol. 2, no. 7, 12 February 1993, p. 29.

conflict spreading to Bosnia, and fearing a sudden Serbian military offensive in Kosova, Albania may also possibly have joined the OIC with Islamic military support in mind. However, it can generally be assumed that the decision to join the Islamic Conference was mainly in response to Western Europe's failure to invest in Albania, to provide jobs for its people and to convince Berisha's administration that, if the conflict in Bosnia were to spread to Kosova, it could expect adequate protection.

By the spring of 1993 the biggest Muslim mission in Albania, the Islamic Charity Project International (ICPI), was funding a variety of schemes throughout the country, including an enormous battery poultry farm in Fier and the refurbishment of the Arberia Hotel in Tirana. The number of foreign Muslims living in Tirana also increased, and a few young girls could now be seen making their way to the mosques covered from head to toe in religious veils. Islamic schools were being set up following the opening of a popular Islamic educational centre in Kavaja in 1992. The Kuwait-based MAK group began an ambitious hotel building scheme in Tirana. As Albanian schools remained secular, children and young men were being sent to Turkey, Syria, Jordan, Malaysia, Libya, Saudi Arabia and Egypt to study Islamic theology. Islamic organisations helped to fund the expenses of those Albanians wishing to make the trip to Mecca; in 1991 around 170 Muslims from Albania went on the *hajj*; in 1992 the figure was 300 and in 1993 over 400. In September 1993 Egyptian craftsmen put the finishing touches to the restoration of one of Tirana's most prominent and graceful mosques, in Kavaja Street. On the external walls were instructions for children in Arabic on the correct attentions to make before going to pray. Loitering outside the building were some Egyptian men who looked at visitors furtively and suspiciously and were reluctant to talk. Some crumpled clothing was found in the women's gallery, and when asked to whom it belonged the children said that some Egyptian men were sleeping there. Although Egyptian artisans were undoubtably restoring the mosque, it was also well known that there were several fundamentalists on the run from the Egyptian authorities who were living in Tirana. Similar refugees were discovered by the authors in the Old Market mosque.

By the end of 1993 the government was becoming increasingly sensitive over the religious issue. In an interview in December

1993, Sali Berisha, who is himself of strong Muslim background, stressed impatiently that his country 'would always remain a secular state', despite the growing influence of Islam. 'There is no tendency to see religion play a political role in Albania,' he said, dismissing as 'totally unfounded' suggestions that the country could turn into an Islamic republic. He said he would like to see Albania eventually act as bridge-builder between Europe and the Islamic world.[8] Throughout 1994, however, both Christian and Muslim organisations continued their ardent missionary work. The Committee of Eastern Europe Muslim Youth, in co-ordination with the World Assembly of Muslim Youth, was working in the Albanian countryside, and groups of Saudi-trained Kosovar activists, fluent in Arabic and well-versed in the Koran, were to be found in some of the remotest towns. The campaign was intended to re-establish Islam among Albania's Muslims by touring the country to explain its basic concepts and distribute literature about it. Elderly men came with their sons and nephews, for they too needed their knowledge of Islam refreshed. For the young with little hope of finding employment, any distraction from their hopeless situation was welcome. The same vulnerability was exploited by the numerous 'New Age' sects active in the country, such as the Scientologists encamped on Mount Dajti.

The most important Islamic initiatives continued to be in education. A large secondary school established with Turkish government backing in southern Tirana had, by 1994, about 400 pupils and offered a predominantly secular curriculum with emphasis on science and vocational teaching, and joint language instruction in Turkish and English. Egyptian radicals had also set up a small computer-training facility in part of the former Palace of Culture, with lines of intense young Albanians learning computer basics under pictures of famous radical mullahs, but to date there seems to be little direct religious propaganda.

It remains to be seen if Albania's separation of state and religion can be maintained. The only tangible evidence of activity that could affect it has been a steadily increasing number of newly-built or refurbished mosques and some relatively small-scale educational and economic projects, some initiated by committed individuals rather than organisations or governments. But even where govern-

---

[8] Interview with Sali Berisha by Miranda Vickers, 7 December 1993.

ments have been involved, as in the economic development programme funded by Iran, what has been undertaken has been small-scale and largely uncontroversial. It may be however that this will change as the IDB establishes itself as a feature of the Tirana economic scene. In general, Albanians of Muslim heritage have shown little sign of mass revival, but since committed individuals have begun Islamic studies abroad the situation may change when they return. There is likely to be a large influx of young and probably relatively radical *imams* returning to Albania in the late 1990s from their training abroad. The growth of the Refah (Welfare) Party as a major political force in Turkey may also become an important factor. Although Turkey has not influenced Albania politically as much as its detractors have claimed, at a cultural level links are still close for many Albanians, and a major growth of Islamic influence in Turkey would certainly have effects in Albania.

Roman Catholics

During the period of religious persecution, it is generally accepted that more severe pressure was placed on the Catholic population than on other religious groups. The Catholic Church was seen as an instrument of the Vatican, and some Catholics, most notably in Mirditë, had undoubtedly collaborated during the war with the Axis invaders, particularly the Italians, and supported anti-Hoxhaist forces in the resistance movement. Because of this, Catholics often found themselves the victims of discrimination; Muslims tended to be favoured in the allocation of jobs and housing. In communist eyes the Church could never shake off the wartime heritage. As Hoxha came from a Muslim background and from southern Albania where he had frequent contact with Orthodox Albanians, his knowledge of the northern Catholics was limited. He consequently mistrusted them and by banning religion hoped to eliminate the bond of Catholicism linking many of the northern clans.

During the Hoxha years, Catholic priests held secret masses in people's homes whenever possible, and the last rites for the dying were secretly administered in hospitals. Only thirty-one out of 200 Catholic priests survived the ban on religion in 1967; around 140 were either executed or died in prison and others died of natural causes. Hundreds of tons of reinforced concrete were used to transform the interior of Shkoder's impressive cathedral, the largest Catholic church in the Balkans, into a volleyball court, with only its ceiling revealing its original use.

When the religious ban was lifted it was the Catholic communities that were first galvanised into religious activity. However, Christmas celebrations in 1991 in Shkoder were rather bleak. Rescued from the National Museum of Atheism, a motley collection of chipped and cracked lifesize plaster figures of Jesus and the saints stood behind a makeshift altar as mass was said in a crumbling cinema auditorium. This cinema had been a Franciscan church before the interior was ripped out and concrete cladding added to conceal the façade. While slowly being transformed back into a church, the building was the focus of Christmas worship in 1991 for all Albania's Catholics. At that time, however, most Albanians were preoccupied with the search for food, and few felt in a festive mood. The lifting of the ban on religion, could not remove another equally oppressive clamp on their ability to celebrate: poverty. Under the communists eggs, which were available throughout the year, would disappear from shops two weeks before Christmas to stop people making special Christmas sweets; they would then reappear in time for the new year.[9]

During the 1990s the Catholic Church in Western countries was experiencing an acute shortage of priests, and so with Catholicsm undergoing a revival throughout the former communist world, there were few priests available to be sent to Albania, where the youngest surviving Albanian priest was seventy-five years old. Priests were being trained in Italy and Austria, and about fifty Albanian boys entered the seminary in Shkoder in 1991, but it will take several years to train them to become priests. Throughout 1991 and 1992 financial assistance came from Catholic Albanian-Americans and from Italy, with the Vatican funding much of the restoration of the cathedral and seminary in Shkoder. In the spring of 1993, in what was seen as a bid to counter Islamic influence, Pope John Paul II was invited to Albania, on the first-ever visit by a Pope to the country. He addressed tens of thousands of people of all faiths in Tirana's main square before moving off in a motorcade to Shkoder where he conducted

[9] *The Guardian*, 24 December 1991.

a mass in the newly-restored cathedral and ordained four new Albanian bishops. Archbishop Rrok Mirdita, formerly pastor of Our Lady of Shkoder Catholic Church in the Bronx, New York, was appointed as the new archbishop of Tirana and Durres. Mirdita had a formidable task ahead of him, having to build up most parishes and church buildings again virtually from scratch.

President Berisha's official greeting to the Pope reaffirmed Albania's willingness to integrate into Europe: 'Your visit, holy father, represents great moral and political support for Albania in its efforts to be integrated into Europe and to endure the sacrifices necessary for the building of a different future. Your Holiness, you have come to a friendly country and your visit is a great contribution to the revival of religion in Albania.' Aware of the escalation of the war in Bosnia, Berisha continued to stress the traditional tolerance of Albanians towards each other's religion:

'Holy Father, Albanians welcome you today with their hearts open because Albania is a country of great religious tolerance. Our three religious communities have for centuries lived in peace and harmony. Here three different religions, like three spiritual roots, feed and enrich the great soul of our nation. Today in this square you are greeted with great love by Albanian Catholics, Muslims and Orthodox. Your visit brings them closer together because they are brothers, they have the same God, land, mother, blood, culture and language.'

To reinforce still further a commitment to assist in the reinstatement of the country's main religions, Albania's second Roman Catholic cathedral is being built behind the Dajti Hotel in Tirana on land donated by the government. President Berisha laid the cornerstone its in November 1994. He said later: 'The religious infrastructure is very important for our country. May this become a temple for the martyrs of religion.'[10] In November 1994 the Pope named Mikel Koliqi, a native of Shkoder respected by both Catholics and Muslims, as the first-ever Albanian cardinal. However, it is noteworthy that the Catholic Church seems to find difficulty in linking its building programme to the needs of believers. Very little activity and few priests are to be found in traditional Catholic areas such as Mirditë, but grandiose new

[10] *Illyria*, 10-12 November 1994.

churches are appearing in towns such as Fier, with tiny Catholic populations. Before long Tirana will have two cathedrals.

Orthodox

There are estimated to be 750,000 Orthodox Christians in Albania, and alone of Albania's four main religions the Orthodox Church is closely linked with the Greek minority in the south of the country. The Albanian Orthodox Church was founded in 1908 in Boston, Massachusetts, by Bishop Fan Noli, and was recognised as autocephalous by the Ecumenical Patriarch in 1937. During the spring and summer of 1991, when the world's churches were launching their missionary crusades into Eastern Europe, the campaign led by the Greek Orthodox Archbishop Sevastianos was among the most vigorous. The archbishop was in charge of a sprawling diocese centred on Konitsa in Epirus in northern Greece. This diocese also includes a substantial part of southern Albania (known to the Greeks as Vorio Epirus) which is home to 35,000 ethnic Greeks.[11] Sevastianos had long been the scourge of the Albanian communist regime, regarding the 'Socialist Paradise' as a contemporary hell, and the Greek Christians struggling under its rule as contemporary martyrs. His death in 1994 was almost openly celebrated in Tirana.

However, the complexity of the Greek community's position was ignored by Sevastianos: many ethnic Greeks and people with some Greek blood held leading positions under the communist regime, e.g. the former Minister of the Interior, Simon Stefani. Greeks were also prominent in Tirana in all professions: medicine, law, academic life and so on. Indeed some ethnic Greeks remained communists after 1992, especially those from hardline families who fled to Albania after ending up on the losing side in the Greek Civil War. Determined that his spiritual message would be heard by his Albanian flock, Sevastianos would conduct services in the border village of Mavropoulo using some of the most powerful loudspeakers in Greece, which blasted the Christian message over the electric fence to any Albanians who happened

---

[11] The Albanian government has always claimed a Greek minority population of about 35,000, while the Greek government usually claims around 100,000. The Vorio Epirus Organization in Greece has claimed up to 250,000. See James Pettifer's article in the Minority Rights Group publication 'The Southern Balkans', London: MRG, 1994.

to live nearby. The archbishop wrote many books on the enslavement and oppression of Albania's Greek minority, which were published by his Panhellenic Association of Northern Epirus. The Association produces maps of what it considers is the rightful border with Albania, extending as far north as Elbasan, which would deprive Albania of half its territory. Although the Panhellenic Association of Northern Epirus is very much on the fringe of contemporary Greek politics, its supporters were the first Orthodox personnel to initiate aid distribution to southern Albania in 1991. But when distributing the aid, they were careful to distinguish between Albanians and ethnic Greeks. During this time hundreds of Albanians changed their names to Greek ones and agreed to be baptised into the Orthodox faith in order not only to receive the precious aid parcels, but also to become eligible for a visa to work in Greece. In one celebrated case in February 1991, the bishop of the northern Greek town of Florina baptised fourteen Albanians in an ice-cold river. This process of 'Hellenisation' caused by immigration pressures has continued, and may have substantial long-term effects on the culture of many parts of Albania.

In 1993 an ethnic Greek, Anastasios Yannulatos, was appointed by the Patriarchate in Istanbul as Albania's archbishop, along with three archimandrites to serve under him. Yannulatos had been temporarily appointed to the post in 1991 in order to help in the initial stages of re-establishing the Albanian Church. Yannulatos is a man of much more conciliatory views than Sevastianos, and his appointment was seen in both Athens and Tirana as a sign of the Ecumenical Patriarch's wish to see church-state harmony in Albania. But while the appointment may have pleased the ethnic Greek minority in southern Albania, it inspired revulsion among many Albanians, who saw the move as a threat to the independence of the Albanian Church and, more important, as a plot by Greece to Hellenise and later annex southern Albania. They began to call for legislation which would require the chief prelate of the Albanian Orthodox Church to be of Albanian birth or heritage; in this they sought a parallel to the Turkish legislation governing the nationality of the patriarch in Istanbul. The controversy occurred when Yannulatos' appointment was made permanent, a move over which Albanians were apparently not consulted. The Albanian Church constitution of 1929 says specifically that only Albanian citizens or people of Albanian descent may be nominated for the post. President Berisha was bombarded with petitions from intellectuals, the Albanian community in the United States and the Albanian parliament, all suspicious of Greek attempts to gain influence and power in southern Albania. Roman Catholic and Muslim Albanians in the United States were also angered. This was seen as the first religious issue to divide Albanians on a serious and national level.

The controversy over the nomination of a Greek archbishop as head of the Albanian Orthodox Church grew as a delegation from the Albanian Orthodox Church in Boston, headed by Archbishop Arthur Liolin, arrived in Albania in August 1993 to find out how Yannulatos had come to be nominated. Albanian Orthodox authorities in Tirana eventually annulled his appointment, relying on an article in the Church's statute requiring its primate to be of 'Albanian nationality and citizenship'. Since 1991 little Orthodox churches have been painstakingly restored throughout the Greek minority villages in the south by artisans who are meticulously repainting the faded icons and wall-paintings. The work is largely funded from Greece and the Greek-American community. In Saranda the Greek Church is financing and building an enormous Orthodox church that dwarfs nearby shops in the centre of the town, overlooking the beach. The dispute between the Albanian and Greek governments over the number, status and rights of the ethnic Greek minority in southern Albania has inevitably made the resurrection of the Orthodox faith in Albania more controversial than that of the other principal religions. A central issue for the foreseeable future will be the high rate of 'conversions' to Orthodoxy as a result of economic pressures.

Evangelical Christian groups

Since 1991 missionaries and clerics from a variety of European and American Christian Churches have flooded into Albania. Because Albania had been officially proclaimed the world's first and only atheist country, the need for Christian teaching was deemed by these highly-motivated zealots to be more necessary there than in any of the other former communist countries. The majority of Albanians have found the arrival of many of these groups a bewildering experience, especially as many of these visitors come from the wilder fringes of cultist movements. Albanians were ignorant of the existence of so many different Christian religions, and as a result some members of Parliament proposed a law that would forbid any missionary activity unconnected with one of Albania's established religions – Islam, Bektashism, Eastern Orthodox and Roman Catholicism. This, however, was such a sensitive issue, dealing as it did with the fundamental freedom to practise one's religion, that the matter remained unsettled. In the summer of 1991 the Dutch Evangelical organisation 'God Loves Albania' was very active. Its vans, emblazoned with the words 'God Loves Albania', could be seen in several towns, where its youthful and enthusiastic members would hand out translated Bibles to incredulous groups of Albanians who gathered around them in awestruck silence. During the last years of Ramiz Alia's government, several Albanians had been encouraged to escape to the Netherlands where they were employed to translate children's Bibles into Albanian. They were quickly baptised and given meagre accommodation in return. In 1991 Mormons, Jehovah's Witnesses, a number of other Christian groups and Baha'is gathered under government recognition as the Evangelical Brotherhood. A year later these Protestants had legal recognition.

A highly controversial aspect of Christian activity in Albania is the running of orphanages for the state. The Shtepia Shpreses 'Home of Hope' in Elbasan, founded in the summer of 1992 by the American Apostolic Team Ministries, was the first privately run orphanage in the country. Another in Tirana, with 113 children aged between six and sixteen, is run by the American-based charity Hope for the World, which was given a ten-year contract to run the orphanage by the Albanian government, which was desperately short of the financial means to ensure proper provision for the children. Most of the funding for the Home of Hope orphanage came from the Austrian-based missionary group, Evangelism in Action. Other donations arrived from Evangelical groups in Europe and America. Any foreign assistance was gratefully accepted at this time.

Baptist groups have been particularly active in Albania ever since the first Baptist delegation arrived on 16 July 1992; along with other Christian groups, they offered material incentives, such as food, clothing, medicines and Coca-Cola to lure potential converts. The Seventh Day Adventists are active in Korça and the surrounding region, and in charity and aid work in Tirana. Evangelical missionaries were soon to be found in almost every remote town in Albania, and advertisements for prayer meetings appear in the press and in public places. Their dedication in preparation for their task is phenomenal. For example, most Mormon missionaries, before coming to work in Albania, studied Albanian for six hours a day five days a week for three months. They also frequently live with their Albanian neighbours in extremely primitive conditions without hot water, electricity or regular food supplies. The Christian missionaries see themselves as part of a religious war for the minds and souls of Albanians and as the vanguard of a new crusade for Christendom. Hundreds of thousands of Bibles in Albanian were feverishly printed to match a similar number of Korans being sent from the Islamic world. Some of the more extreme Christian groups would tell anyone who would listen that they were in Albania to counter not only the encroachment of Islam, but also communism and atheism, which they claimed were still active elements in Albanian society.

In July 1992 eighty members of the American Christian youth group 'Teen Mania' travelled through Albania giving performances in various towns. In the northern town of Burrel they performed concerts, of which the overall message was 'friendship with God', in the streets and parks and, according to ATA, 'were followed with interest by the artlovers of Burrel'.[12] That these concerts were called 'art' says much about the way Albanians generally interpreted the action of foreign Christian groups during the early transition period. 'Culture' was deemed to be a product of the West, especially America, and in a society where almost everything Western had been condemned the authorities were at a loss to give an appropriate name to what was now suddenly appearing from the West. This attitude was to last for about two years; by 1994 many Albanians had become irritated by these insistent, humourless and dogmatic missionaries, whether Christian or Muslim. Gjerj Mala, a factory worker, called them 'soul-buyers'. He told a journalist angrily: 'These missionaries say they have come to help Albania. If they consider building churches and mosques a help, that's fine, but that's not going to put food on my family's table. If you want to help me, how about building me a factory where I can work and make a living? The missionaries are doing

---

[12] Albanian Telegraphic Agency, 12 July 1992.

what Enver Hoxha did; brainwashing young people, but to the other extreme.'[13]

Since the average age of the Albanian population is twenty-eight and the atheist state was declared in 1967, the majority of Albanians have no inherited culture of religious practice, only an inherited identity. It is those aged between twenty and forty – the parents of the next generation of Albanians – who have been most affected by the years of atheism, a fact which has not been lost on the Christian and Muslim missions working in Albania. They have therefore to some extent given up on older people and are concentrating their efforts on the very young, but few young people in the major towns were prepared to listen to what were now termed 'crackpot' missionaries. In the summer of 1995 the crowded tables at one prominent central Tirana café quickly emptied as soon as three check-shirted, wholesome-looking American evangelists arrived. They had paid the café-owner well for the privilege of setting up their microphone and stereo equipment right in the midst of the tables and began, in a deep southern drawl, to croon a song entitled 'Jesus has come to Albania'. The young clientele evaporated into the nearby streets leaving a deflated trio of Americans and a smiling café-owner. In the more remote and impoverished rural districts, however, people were still receptive to religious workers of extremist persuasions.

In general the religious atmosphere of Albania has had a febrile, effervescent quality during the first half of the 1990s with hundreds of organisations competing against a mainstream culture which, for the moment at least, seems likely to be dominated by pro-American Western secularism, leaving the missionaries with their extreme and divergent views competing for the same somewhat bewildered potential converts. By the summer of 1995 attendance at Protestant churches throughout the country was estimated to be no more than 3,500. But as loudspeakers in the beautiful Ethem Bey mosque in central Tirana blare out the call to prayer at dawn and mid-day, smart businessmen, bearded imams, café workers and veiled women crowd into the newly-decorated mosque. No one stares any more, not even at the old men who have resumed wearing the traditional white Albanian fez, a glimpse back to the Ottoman world in the centre of a small European

[13] *Illyria*, 406, October 1993.

city. Nevertheless, despite this revival of Islamic religious practice, the population as a whole, has remained largely secular. There is no sign yet in Albania of widespread observance of Ramadan, or of the anti-alcohol campaigns that are now so pronounced among the Albanian communities of western Macedonia (FYROM). After so many decades under a rigid, stifling dictatorship which enforced intolerable rules upon the Albanian people, the last thing most Albanians want is to be told what they are allowed and not allowed to do, let alone see Sharia law or repressive Evangelical Christian codes concerning drinking and relaxion introduced. But the intellectual disorientation being caused by the religious struggle in terms of the traditional national identity is considerable, and has been an important factor in the difficulties the government has faced. Religion, culture and politics are always close companions in Balkan countries.[14]

[14] For example, Greek clergy are attempting to recover and re-consecrate abandoned churches in southern Albania. Many of these are sited on land subject to restitution claims, and ownership of the land is strongly contested.

7

SOCIAL AND CULTURAL CHANGES

As well as religion, an important element in the Albanian identity was formed under a fifty-year-long communist regime by the notion of culture. In the pre-communist period Albania's folk and oral culture was rich and distinctive, even by Balkan standards, but there were few traditional 'European' institutions such as theatres, orchestras, publishing houses and other formal and collective bodies. Enver Hoxha was a man of very conservative cultural tastes, largely formed in his days as a student in the provincial France of the 1930s. He admired the forms if not the content of this traditional European bourgeois culture, and sought to bring them to socialist Albania. It was a lofty and not unattractive ideal but, given the nature of the regime, the reality proved to be very different.

Throughout the post-war years Albanians endured a monotonous cultural scene, which was considered exceptionally dull even by the standards of other communist countries. The few dingy, shabby, ill-lit and, in winter, freezingly cold restaurants and bars did little to encourage people to linger. The acute shortage of entertainment meant that, apart from a number of new sports centres, there was little to occupy Albanians other than watching Italian, Yugoslav or Greek television programmes. These ran throughout the day whereas Albanian television transmitted only a short evening programme. For the few Western business visitors staying in Tirana's two tourist hotels, where entertainment was particularly bleak, 'early to bed' was the rule. In the evenings foreigners could be seen gloomily thumbing though the latest copy of the selected volumes of Hoxha's works which lay strewn around the hotel lobbies with their dismal 1950s decor and predominantly empty bars. Socialist realism was the only artistic form allowed. For Hoxha everything pertaining to the life of the

Albanian people had to be 'home-grown'; it could not be imported from abroad. 'Genuine culture', he maintained, 'cannot be truly so if it is not part of the blood and flesh of the people who create it and use it, if it is not conceived in their history, life, struggle and interests.'[1]

Hoxha's pride in Albania's national culture resulted in tight restrictions on the number of foreign visitors to the country. He was repelled by images of the West's 1960s youth culture, which led him to exclaim: 'Why should we turn our country into an inn with doors flung open to pigs and sows, to people with pants on or no pants at all, to the hirsute, long-haired hippies to supplant with their wild orgies the graceful dances of our people?'[2] The communist regime consequently placed great emphasis on the study and performance of Albanian folk art, songs, dance and music. The National Theatre put on revolutionary ballet, opera and folklore ensembles, which were by far the most entertaining cultural events in communist Albania. For foreign visitors these performances were often a delight; the colour and variety of the costumes and the different vocal pitches of the songs and instruments used reflected the many distinct regions of Albania, Kosova and Western Macedonia. Almost every Albturist itinerary included an evening attending a folklore concert. Under the communist regime cultural institutions had an extremely limited sphere of activity: designed for the services of propaganda, they stopped new cultural orientations while producing little of value themselves. At the expense of other sectors of the economy, Hoxha's regime put vast funds at the disposal of the film industry, which it used entirely for ideological and propaganda purposes. Around fifteen films were produced annually, mostly of mediocre quality and all propagandistic in content.

In the years after Hoxha's death some art forms were declassified as non-decadent and in 1988 two national art exhibitions were put on in Tirana, one of which was the first Albanian exhibition to show a painting of a nude woman. In terms of a foreign audience, cultural progress was exemplified by the output of the novelist and poet Ismail Kadaıe. This writer had attained an international reputation in the 1970s and '80s through work such

---

[1] E. Hoxha, *Banner of Struggle for Freedom and Socialism*, Tirana, 1985, p. 104.

[2] L. Gardiner, *Curtain Calls*, Newton Abbot: Readers Union, 1977, p. 15.

as *Chronicle in Stone,* which reflects his native Gjirokaster in wartime; *Broken April,* an analysis of the operation of the blood feud in northern Albania; and *Doruntine,* which many consider his greatest achievement. Kadare was, and is, a highly political man. Though never a member of the Party, he played an active part in the Democratic Front and for a time in the late 1970s was a favoured Party writer, producing Stalinist-style verse on approved themes. Nevertheless, he found it difficult to publish many of his most important works, which tended to criticise the communist system though allusion and metaphor and in the guise of folklore. He played an active role in the opposition immediately before the fall of communism, and at one point, early in 1990, it seemed as though he might become the Albanian Havel and stand for the presidency in a newly democratised Albania. However, he resisted this temptation and retired to France to continue his writing once it was clear to him that the dictatorship had ended.

By the late 1980s the forces of conservatism in all fields of cultural life were coming increasingly under pressure to relax their attitude towards young people. The character and direction of Albania's younger generation was of particular importance, given that the country had such a youthful population. In 1988 Professor Hamit Beqeja, Albania's leading psychologist dealing with youth affairs, continually criticised those conservatives who were against the liberal treatment of young people and of active discussion and open debate of issues involving them. The crux of the conflict between 'liberal' and 'conservative' forces in Albania during the late 1980s was the question of how to deal with increasingly apathetic, unruly and undisciplined young people who, it was claimed, were being increasingly exposed to strong foreign influences. Beqeja admitted in a newspaper article that the threat of such 'harmful' influences was great. However, he insisted that the conservatives' way of dealing with them was wrong:

> We are talking here in particular about the information provided by foreign radio and television. This information includes weeds, and poison, coarse soap operas and mind-blowing ideas, and the cult of sex and violence, and it promotes a 'rosy' life and false and unreal 'drama'. Should we not help young people to distinguish for themselves between the wheat and the chaff, to create gradually the necessary immunity from it, and to be able to judge maturely and develop a healthy taste? But

the partisans of taboos are incapable of providing such help. They may try to prevent the inflow of this information, but they are not succeeding.[3]

In August 1989 the Party-run Union of Albanian Youth held a plenum to discuss some of the issues preoccupying young Albanians. Young people were expected to spend all day at school hearing incessantly about the greatness of the PLA after which they went home and watched the opposite to everything they had been taught being broadcast on Italian television. The first secretary of the youth union, Mehmet Elezi, criticised the narrow-mindedness of the authorities attitude towards 'alien and liberal' trends among the young.[4] He then spoke of a survey of musical taste that had been carried out among young Albanians. What made the survey a novelty in the Albanian context was that the respondents were allowed to remain anonymous. Elezi described the reaction of the researchers when they found out that a number of young people had expressed a liking for rock music: 'Their anger turned quickly into rage as they demanded "Who are these people who like rock? Who could have been the persons claiming to like rock? Everything must be done to find out who they are." '[5] Once cracks had begun to appear in the Party's control of culture, it was not long in this general climate before the old system collapsed. Whereas in the 1970s Beatles songs could only be heard in clandestine conditions, by the summer of 1991 the authorities were playing such songs through loudspeakers in Skenderbeg Square to placate the young.

During the period of transition to democracy, the dizzying pace of change and the near-total reversal of state-prescribed values and loyalties left the Albanian people profoundly disoriented. The new democratic system swept aside almost every law and social code attributed to the communist regime without offering any positive alternatives. A void was thus created, allowing writers, artists, actors and film makers the chance to develop new ideas and forms. They were hampered at first by two negative factors: a severe shortage of finance and a desire to imitate mechanically

[3] Radio Free Europe, Background Report 122, 1 July 1988.

[4] Mehmet Elezi subsequently became a leader of official Tirana intellectual life under the Berisha government. He is currently head of the foreign and defence policy institute.

[5] Radio Free Europe, Background Report 177, 20 September 1989.

the culture of the West, in particular the United States. Albanian artists faced the difficult challenge of retaining the nation's, and especially young people's, interest in the national folk culture, while evolving new cultural themes that could relate to the country's belated arrival on the modern European scene. Young artists found themselves hampered by the absence of any teachers who had been trained to understand abstract art.

After 1992 the new Ministry of Culture began gearing itself up to avoid a return to the old ways by encouraging the creation of new independent companies throughout the country; administrative decentralisation, with local control over budgets, is being promoted. The Ministry of Culture now sees itself as merely a donor foundation, hoping to found specialist support organisations for different genres of art and culture. It will also continue to support national institutions such as the Prose Theatre. Nevertheless many cultural bodies which existed under communism, such as amateur symphony orchestras, disappeared during the transition period and are unlikely to revive in the foreseeable future. As part of the process of reconstruction and renewal, the government has seen it as fundamental that cultural institutions maintain independence in their activity and are subject to market disciplines, thus ensuring practical efficiency. The old institutions were full of people who obtained their posts on the basis of political rather than professional criteria. In the publishing field, because salary payments so dominated resources, the Ministry of Culture was unable to finance publications connected with the country's cultural heritage, such as poetry, ballads, legends, fables and a wealth of other material. In some fields hundreds of volumes await publication. The Academy of Sciences does not have the funds to receive guest lecturers and if academics are invited to participate in academic or cultural events, they have to come at their own expense. It has been equally difficult for young foreign scholars to travel to Albania to pursue research projects.

From the end of 1990 until the summer of 1992 the political uncertainty, social chaos and absence of funding meant there was no official cultural activity at all. Important and internationally respected academic journals such as *Illyria* (devoted to archaeology) failed to appear at all. However, at the other end of the cultural spectrum one of the easiest ways for Albania to appear on the international stage was through the Miss World contest. Because this was a Western phenomenon it was deemed untainted by communism and a symbol of Albania's new liberalism. Thus in February 1992 twenty-five young women competed in the first 'Miss Albania' contest, but in order to obtain make-up they had to scour the squalid 'émigrés' market' in central Tirana for cosmetics. Nevertheless many Albanians, especially older ones, saw the contest as an instrument designed to corrupt their daughters. The winner, eighteen-year-old Valbona Selimillari, was ignored by her father for bringing shame to the family by parading in front of television cameras in a swimsuit. However, her prize money of 30,000 leks (over £400) and a trip to Italy brought her more than her father could have hoped to earn in two years.

In general, however, Albanians set great store by the term 'intellectual', and in April 1992 the first private cultural café was inaugurated in Durres fortress tower. Its owner, the dramatist Minush Jero, wished to commemorate the life and works of renowned artists and intellectuals from the Durres region, and hoped that the new café would offer a cultural environment in which citizens of Durres could gather to discuss problems and ideas. About the same time a similar 'intellectuals' café' opened in the old town of Gjirokaster, only a short distance from where a monumental statue of Enver Hoxha had stood till August 1991. Here, having climbed up steep steps, the visitor could sit and look out over the city below while listening to Wagner or Bach and drinking local wine or *raki*. Inside the little café was an old bookcase crammed with selected works of once banned foreign literary and philosophical writers which had been hidden, under Hoxha's very nose, in the cellars of Gjirokaster. This was a far cry from the brash new cafés springing up in central Tirana, with their gaudy Coca-Cola umbrellas and raucous Western music, which sold only Western drinks; one of the authors, asking for a *raki* in one of them, was told that such old stuff was not sold as 'this is Tirana, not some village.' Those who could not afford the high prices charged in the cafés would buy a can of Coke on a Saturday night and spend the rest of the week posing with the empty can on the low walls around Skenderbeg Square. Throughout 1992 several discos began to open in Tirana, together with some private restaurants, which at first were only frequented by Kosovars and foreigners. One such establishment was named 'Tasho' after its owner, Romeo Tasho, who claimed to 'have created another image for the values of civilization'. He financed the enterprise with money earned working in Greece. said a young dancer who regularly attended discos said: 'We need human warmth – we feel ourselves equal under the influence of music at this time of transformation'.[6]

Under the old regime there was just one state-controlled general publishing house, called '8 Nentori', (8th November) along with specialist publication units for certain scientific disciplines and the armed forces. By mid-1993 over seventy companies had been given licences to publish. A much wider range of subjects was now being offered, including biography and sociology. Wartime memoirs proved popular, as did books by opponents of the dictatorship. There was a plethora of material published by former dissidents, often those severely persecuted under the communist regime. The Catholic Church in Shkoder initiated a number of publications dealing with persecution of Catholics under communism, including an important record of the fate of the clergy during that period. For the first time since the war, detailed maps of Albania became available; under communism all cartography was monopolised by the armed forces, for security reasons, and considered a military secret. However, by 1994 all publishing activity had declined considerably as the market for new books appeared to have become saturated, and the economics of publication became unfavourable. As one prominent Tirana resident observed, 'Those who want to buy books have no money, and those who have the money have no desire to read.'[7]

In the new atmosphere of freedom, modest productions in different media appeared without the influence of political dogma. After a long interval the periodicals *Nentori*, *State and Screen* and *Arber* re-appeared in the autumn of 1992. In November that year the feature film *The Death of the Horse* was shown in Tirana, the first film to be shot by Albfilm after the overthrow of communism. Its main theme was the machinations and violence visited by the dictatorship on individuals to deprive them of their personality, and indeed it was an outburst of things that had been forbidden for so long. The film showed explicit sexual scenes for the first time in Albanian cinematography since the war. The public's thirst for new cultural stimulation was dramatically expressed in the spring of 1993, when the first independent theatre production since 1990, a drama redolent of William Golding's *Lord of the Flies,* took Tirana by storm. *Crazy Island* was consistently sold out although the tickets, at 50 leks, were twice the normal price. In an expansion of the cultural horizon the play discussed topics, and contained language and behaviour, which had been strictly taboo under communist rule. The producer Edmond Tare said that the central theme was how dictatorships develop, a theme all too familiar to the audience.[8] The writings of the intellectual Faik Konitza, ignored by the communists, were revived, and others were rehabilitated in objective evaluations of their work. The trading of Hoxha memorabilia began in earnest, a process encouraged by the destruction, in 1993, of most copies of his works which had been held by the old state publishing wholesale agency.

The collapse of communism meant a lifting of the measures in force to restrict the movement of people from one place to another. The shift of rural inhabitants to urban areas led to a considerable growth of population in the cities. In 1991 alone the population of Tirana increased by at least 30,000 as people exercised their new right to live where they chose, and the newcomers virtually encircled the city with their hastily built houses. The influx was encouraged by political, economic and social instability. The absence of appropriate legislation caused many peasants, especially those in mountainous areas with little or no land, to move to the towns in the hope of somehow improving their living standards. Most were 'newcomers' who had been moved to villages under agricultural collectivisation programmes under communism, but had never really been accepted in their new communities. When the privatisation of land began after the DP victory in March 1992, they were quickly evicted. Those who settled in the Tirana environs occupied agricultural land that mainly belonged to the state farms and had formerly been used to grow food for the city.

Another visible sign of change was the sudden appearance of cars. Up till March 1992 it was illegal to own a car, and people ambled along peacefully in ox-drawn carts or on bicycles. The only private individuals allowed cars were public service workers

[8] *Illyria,* 31 March-3 April 1993.

such as doctors, and the vehicles they used remained state property. With democratisation, people rushed to acquire the premier symbol of capitalism. Within weeks of the DP victory the first private cars appeared on the streets of Tirana. However, the quality of the cars arriving in Albania was poor, reflecting the financial limits of the drivers. Many had no windscreens or lights, and some had doors held on with rope. There was no way to replace anything that was smashed. Smouldering wrecks were left to litter the roadsides. Cars belching smoke, with horns blaring and packed with young men who had been drinking, screeched through the narrow streets at breakneck speed. Terrified cyclists and pedestrians were literally forced off the streets as cars hurtled towards them on the wrong side of the road. By the summer of 1992 there were over 20,000 cars on the country's narrow, pot-holed roads, which were almost wholly without road signs or signposts or traffic-lights. By the end of 1993, 185,000 vehicles had been imported and registered. Less than one-third of Albanian roads are asphalt-surfaced and many stretches had simply disintegrated. In relation to the number of cars in the country, Albania jumped to the top of Europe's *per capita* road-death chart by the end of 1993 with 210 fatalities. By then it was fast becoming Europe's car cemetery with scrap-dealers springing up throughout Tirana and Durres, their yards full of wrecks being cannibalised for spare parts. To add to the thrills of driving at this time, stones were thrown at cars from hillsides, and bandits set up roadblocks in isolated areas to rob lone motorists.

By 1993 Albania had tentatively re-emerged on to the world's cultural circuit. In June its folk artists participated in a concert at Bursa in Turkey and won first prize. Albania also took part in the International Poetry Festival held at Struga, Macedonia, and other international festivals. In June there was an exhibition of paintings entitled 'Forbidden Art in Albania' by painters who had been imprisoned for their political beliefs under the communist regime. It was sponsored by the Helsinki Human Rights Federation in co-operation with the Catholic charity Caritas and the Austrian Ministry of Arts. Collaboration programmes were established with the Council of Europe and UNESCO.

Albanians began watching more television, but they were becoming more selective as video recordings of films became popular, and the sudden widespread use of satellite dishes gave a wide choice of programmes, ending the almost total dependence on Albanian state or Italian television, particularly in the lowland cities. In this environment pornographic material was widely circulated; all five of Tirana's cinemas showed hard-core pornographic films which were watched even by very young boys as there was no age restriction. Girls were not allowed into these films. In 1993 there was a noticeable and welcome reappearance of traditional Albanian craft artifacts in local markets, after a period when the closing of the state craft factory had caused most of them to become unobtainable. Local pottery and woven rugs suddenly appeared at roadside stalls.

On 28 February 1993 the BBC World Service re-launched its broadcasting to Albania, which had been axed in 1967 due to Foreign Office spending cuts. Using one of Radio Tirana's transmitters, the service broadcast short items of news, education and sport for thirty minutes nightly. It was revived partly because of the tense situation in Kosova, which also receives the BBC World Service. The first transmission included an interview with the then British Foreign Secretary, Douglas Hurd, a message from President Berisha and a presentation by Dervish Duma, who had opened the BBC's original Albanian service back in 1940. During the summer of 1993, the BBC sent a World Service publicity bus to Albania, which travelled around the country promoting the newly-restored service. The inhabitants of Kukes appeared bemused by the BBC bus which was besieged by children and adults alike, desperate to grab publicity pens and other material and appearing to mis-identify the bus as an aid truck. Staff were obliged to lock the doors and make a hasty retreat.[9] Initial reaction to the service in Albania was mixed, as might have been expected, but after a few years of operation it has established a solid reputation, and records much higher listening figures than its competitors, foreign or domestic. Initially the main criticism was that listeners could not take the young Albanians in London seriously when they commented on such items as Russian foreign policy. Everyone knew the political and educational background of those who had won the much sought-after jobs with the BBC; they wanted to know what criteria had been adopted in choosing them and why they were all the sons and daughters of communists. The Berisha

[9] *The Guardian*, 2 September 1993.

government indeed withdrew some transmission facilities for the BBC in 1993, and has also sought to encourage listeners to tune in to the Voice of America.

The crime wave

During 1991 and 1992 Albania witnessed the almost total break-down of state authority, resulting not only in the collapse of the economy but also in an escalation of serious crime, especially in Vlora, Durres and Tirana. Robbery and rape became daily oc-currences, and foreigners were advised only to travel about the country with an armed guard. Albania had no laws controlling the ownership of weapons, and the firing of pistols, rifles and occasionally machine-guns often disturbed the still Tirana nights. Guns were cheap and plentiful. A handgun could be bought for about $20, and a rifle often cost less because Albanian conscripts would sell their weapons to the black market before fleeing the country. Although the government attempted to clamp down on illegal weapons in 1992, the black market in small arms has flourished in Tirana ever since. The Albanian tradition of taking an evening stroll came to an end during the winter of anarchy; public order had decayed to the point where people were afraid to venture out after dusk. In desperation the new DP government turned to the United Nations for help in restoring law and order, and the UN agreed to set up 'laboratories' in Tirana to assist in reorganising the police force, and so help to restore its morale and curb the increased drug dealing.

As the unemployed young saw no chance of emigrating, their frustration and anger exploded on the streets. The slackening of border controls enabled easier trafficking in drugs and other illegal goods. In July 1991 a group of youths entered a children's hospital in Tirana and threatened staff before stealing a large supply of amphetamines. The following month another group of drunken youths demanded medicinal drugs from frightened staff at Tirana's central hospital. With the collapse of the communist system, drugs had suddenly become an issue, albeit on a small scale compared to other countries. The knowledge that Albania lacked the capacity to cope with the escalating crime wave prompted the Italian Minister of the Interior, Vincenzo Scotti, to come on a visit in August 1991. He was accompanied by the commissioner responsible for fighting the Mafia, reflecting the concern of the Italian government over the possibility of Albanian criminals operating in Italy. The delegation promised to assist Ramiz Alia's beleaguered administration with technical equipment, training and specialised instruction, and joint naval patrols in the straits of Otranto. Scotti also advised the Albanians to apply to join Interpol, promising his government's resolute support for their application.

In February 1992 teachers and pupils in the Shkoder district boycotted lessons in protest against crime, violence and terror in all schools. They took part in a rally organised by the independent educational union in the city, whose secretary Robert Jaubelli spoke of the schools being a prey to destabilising acts of theft and vandalism. An appeal was made for order and tranquility as youths even walked into the University of Tirana and accosted female students in their classrooms. In the north brigands freely blocked the roads with logs and held up cars at gunpoint. On a visit to Albania in 1992, the leader of the Social Democratic Party for Kosova, Shkelzen Maliqi, was attacked by a gang of youths, robbed of his personal possessions, stripped of his clothing, and forced to wait in a car until someone brought him a pair of trousers. A German journalist had his throat cut behind the Hotel Tirana by two youths who stole his watch. These and similar crimes, in a society that had hitherto been notably crime-free, only enhanced the already bewildered population's sense of insecurity, as well as deterring foreign investment.

The new Minister for Public Order, Bajram Yzeiri, said in an interview that the steep rise in crime had 'shattered' the confidence of the people, who had begun to question the 'existence and the power of the state'. Reasons given by Yzeiri for the deterioration in public order included the terrible economic situation; the prolonged high unemployment; the early release from prison of criminals (the prisons, to all intents and purposes, opened their doors with the fall of the communist system); the inability of the state and bodies responsible for public order to function; and a police force ill-equipped to function in the new democratic environment. Because of legal and organisational deficiencies, the police suffered from lack of confidence, indifference and even fear.[10] Albania was not alone in experiencing a crime wave: all

---

[10] Radio Free Europe, 27 September 1991, p. 2.

the former communist states faced a similar situation. In Albania, however, the situation appeared worse because there were so many other social problems. The police and the legal system barely functioned throughout 1991-2 and the media fed people a daily diet of often horrific stories of violent crime.

Foreigners, as already noted, were especially easy targets. In 1992 the Associated Press correspondent Liam McDowell was driving near Fier, and in very poor road conditions had to make a choice between driving into the ditch and hitting a lorry. He chose the ditch, crashed the car and hit his head in the process. A crowd then assembled and started to strip him of his clothing and the car of all its equipment. In trying to resist he gained more cuts and bruises before being picked up by a passing motorist and taken to the outskirts of Tirana, at which point the driver stopped the car by a wood and demanded $600 at knifepoint. Having managed to convince the man that he had nothing left, the correspondent got away and had to walk into town. Similar occurrences were frequent during this period.

Many of Albania's more serious crimes were blamed on Kosovars, especially since their arrival in Albania coincided with the crime wave, and the press frequently alluded to Kosovar involvement in drug-related crimes. This was probably unjustified, although some of the Kosovars had criminal connections. A common sight in Tirana during the summer and winter of 1991 was the Kosovar Hajdin Sejdija cruising around in his white Rolls-Royce. Sejdija, president of Illyria Holdings based in Switzerland, was responsible for a series of extravagant investment projects which culminated when his proposed Sheraton Hotel complex in central Tirana collapsed. The foundations were dug and then abandoned, leaving an enormous hole which has gradually filled with weeds and rubbish. It has since become known as Sejdija's hole, and by the summer of 1996 was home to a colony of rats and stray cats. Sejdija's parent company, the Swiss-Albanian Illyrian Bank, was presented to the government as a vehicle for mobilising Kosovar savings in the diaspora for the rejuvenation of the Albanian economy, but however attractive this idea seemed in theory, in practice the type of project Sejdija envisaged was highly speculative and involved the virtual surrender of control over developments to foreign interests. It was also far in advance of what the industrial infrastructure of Albania was capable of sustaining at the time. It seems that the Albanian authorities were unaware when Sejdija came to set up in business in Tirana that he had been charged in Britain with a major fraud involving equipment for the North Sea oil industry, a sign of the total lack of supervision of the emerging private banking system. Sejdija was subsequently arrested in Switzerland.

The new political situation created by the establishment of democracy and the subsequent increase in crime required a restructuring of the organs of public order. In April 1992, in an address to a UN commission, the Minister of Public Order Bashkim Kopliku stated that parliament had passed a new law on the police forces, ensuring their depoliticisation and complete detachment from the *Sigurimi*, and on the status of the armed forces and public order in general. However, it remains open to doubt how far this depoliticisation has gone. The new secret service, SHIK, is regarded by Albanians as a personal arm of the Presidency, and appointments in the senior ranks of the police and armed forces have been heavily influenced by political considerations.

Drug trafficking was of particular concern. Not only were police and customs officers inadequately trained to deal with what was already recognised as a dangerous problem, but the country lacked sufficient personnel, equipment and finance to tackle it. The very low pay of the police encouraged bribery and corruption, and the slackening of border controls greatly assisted the drug traffickers. Kopliku therefore made a plea, now that Albania was a member of Interpol, for international assistance to combat serious crime. The People's Assembly passed a gun law at the end of May 1992, limiting possession of firearms to ministers and parliamentarians, leaders of political parties, judges, local authority leaders, drivers employed by these persons, and civilian guards in government buildings, media facilities and trains. Anyone found guilty of carrying weapons without authorisation was to be liable to up to fifteen years' imprisonment. Within two weeks, more than 4,000 weapons had been surrendered to the police. In a related move President Berisha issued an order earlier the same month which curbed the use of firearms by soldiers and police on guard duty at various government installations. This was on the grounds that the frequent firing of warning shots 'creates a mood of terror and insecurity among the people'.[11]

The blood feud and the increase in organised crime

In the north, where land and food are scarce, the peasants were re-establishing the *hakmarrje* (blood feud) to end the many unsettled disputes which had either remained dormant since before the Second World War or had recently arisen over the redistribution of land in the wake of land privatisation.

The blood feud, a system of revenge killing, remained a festering wound in northern Albanian society. The communists claimed to have wiped it out, but it had only been suppressed. In Ottoman times, tribes in the more inaccessible mountain regions remained virtually free of state control, and the populations there preserved their own self-administration by paying the Albanian lords fixed tributes to live by the rules of their own common law. This was known as the *Doke* and later as the *Kanun* of Lek, and remained in widespread formal use till the 1930s; it survives in oral and popular tradition up to the present day. Although this law is said to have been laid down by the chieftain Lek Dukagjin (1410-81), most of the laws and customs ascribed to him date from long before the fifteenth century. Dukagjin was responsible for classifying the unwritten laws enshrined in the *Kanun,* the form of primitive constitution inherited from the Illyrians, which outlined the social customs and organising principles of northern Albanian society. Its decrees regulated all aspects of life, including such matters as the arrangement of marriages, the boundaries of fields and the payment of taxes. It was transmitted orally from one generation to the next and arbitrated by a council of elders. It was only written down in the nineteenth century.

The *Kanun* had a highly complex legal code, which attempted to regulate the widespread system of *hakmarrje.* The code of Lek could not prevent the endemic feuds, as families set great store by the *hakmarrje* as a means of regaining their honour if it had been slighted. However, it prescribed strict rules in an attempt to contain and discourage these feuds. Hence the *Kanun* of Lek decreed that if a man had been seriously insulted, his family had the right to assassinate the offender, but in undertaking this it

[11] Economist Intelligence Unit, Country Report no. 3, 1992, p. 37.

would then be liable to a revenge assassination by the victim's family. The original victim's nearest male relative was then obliged to assassinate his relative's murderer. And so a pattern of revenge killing was established that ran through generations of a family and resulted in the death of countless young men. Serious social and economic hardship was caused, not only by the death of these able-bodied young men, but also because so many others had to go into hiding with distant relatives, often for several years, in order to escape a revenge killing. The *besa,* or oath, could be used to cover a certain period or purpose, and during its duration the feud was temporarily halted.[12]

With the collapse of communism, years of pent-up revenge erupted. In the first half of 1992 there were nineteen blood-feud murders around the city of Shkoder. In a well-publicised instance in February 1992, a man was beheaded with an axe in the lobby of the Hotel Arberia in Tirana in revenge for a blood-feud killing his father had committed in northern Albania more than forty years before. With the discovery of the victim's whereabouts in Tirana, and movement around the country having become free with the end of the one-party state, the widow of the murdered man had sent her son to the capital city on a mission of revenge.

By mid-1993 the Albanian government had become conscious of the highly negative effect on international public opinion of such blood-feud killings, added to the riots and ship seizures of the previous two years. Considerable resources were therefore channelled into improvements in policing. Violent crime had to some extent been discouraged by the frequent application of the death penalty (in 1993 there were fifteen executions for murder in Tirana alone). As soon as prisoners were convicted, they were led to their open graves, then shot in the head, put into their coffins and quickly buried. The most notorious execution occurred in Fier in June 1992 when two brothers, Ditbardth and Joseph Cuko, aged twenty-one and twenty-four, were convicted of battering to death a family of five, including a seven-months-old baby, in a robbery which netted them only 5,000 *leks* (then equivalent to $50). They were publicly hanged from plane trees

---

[12] For a detailed description of the *Kanun* of Lek, see *The Kanun of Skendebeg*, New York: Illyria Press, 1993. There are extensive discussions of the *Kanun* and its significance in the works of Edith Durham and Margaret Hasluck, both of whom studied northern Albania. See also Ismail Kadare's novel *Broken April*, London: Saqi, 1992.

in the city centre. Although Albania was then experiencing a tidal wave of crime, this particularly brutal murder caused deep shock and anger throughout the country, and public pressure for the executions had guaranteed that there would be no last minute reprieve for the killers. The bodies were left hanging for eighteen hours from this improvised gallows in the town's main square, and crowds, including many children, gathered throughout the hot day to gaze at the corpses. There were many who journeyed to Fier especially to witness Albania's first public execution since 1986. President Berisha had his own personal video made of the event. The international community was horrified at such a 'primitive' and 'barbaric' act being permitted by a democratically elected European government.

By the winter of 1993 the atmosphere of the 'winter of anarchy' of 1991-2 had generally been dispelled, and basic law and order re-established. Nevertheless, although public order in the streets had been at least partly restored, the increasing influence of Mafia-linked groups from southern Italy was being recorded. A more sophisticated culture of organised crime was developing, integrated within the state itself despite the existence of a separate department of 'financial police' which had been set up to combat corruption. There were a number of seizures of heroin supplies, and drug-processing laboratories and proliferating extortion and protection rackets were exposed. Apart from small arms stolen from army posts and sold on the black market, others were smuggled by criminal gangs from former Yugoslavia, or stolen from the small-arms manufacturing complex near Berat. The port of Durres became an important centre in the illegal arms trade to former Yugoslavia and as a transit point for drugs from Macedonia and Turkey. In northern and north-eastern Albania a pattern of organised crime developed which was closely involved with breaking the United Nations sanctions against Serbia, with Shkoder the centre for the smuggling of petrol and diesel oil. Fuel was moved into Montenegro and Serbia by road, across the mountains by pack animals, or across Lake Shkoder by boat.

In southern Albania there was an increase in organised crime linked to former members of the *Sigurimi* who fled to Greece when communist rule collapsed. Thefts of important antiquities, attacks on police posts with the aim of stealing the small arms held in them, and a lucrative black-market trade in stolen passports and highly sought-after forged Greek entry visas were traced to these groups. Fields sown with drug-producing plants have also been discovered in southern Albania. The war in former Yugoslavia prevented heroin produced in Istanbul from being transported to Western Europe via Belgrade, but there was a more secure route through Albania and Kosova. Thus Albanians have become powerful traders in drugs to rival the Italian Mafia, and it has been alleged that by 1995 they controlled around 70 per cent of the Swiss heroin trade and a sizeable share of the wider European market. These allegations, which have been used by Serbia, and other anti-Albanian interests, against the Tirana government, have not been fully substantiated and should be treated with some caution. In mid-1994 the Swiss government increased by 20,000 the number of work-permits for ethnic Albanians, after prolonged negotiations with the leaders of the Swiss Kosovar community. It is unlikely that this decision could have been taken if many of the Albanians were thought to be involved in the hard drug trade.[13]

Food aid

The announcement in the winter of 1991 of the first alarming figures on Albania's desperate economic situation and chronic food shortages led to the establishment of a Red Cross food aid programme. The distribution began in the north-east, the region generally considered the poorest in the country. It was then that astonished Western television audiences saw ragged, malnourished and barefooted children standing in a sea of mud with their arms held aloft trying to grab at parcels being lowered to them from helicopters. Such scenes galvanised groups across Europe and America to begin appeals for aid to this miserable little country that had so suddenly reappeared on the European map and of which everyone knew so little. Throughout the spring of 1992 large groups of hungry people attacked stores containing food aid and other foreign-donated goods, and aid lorries were routinely looted by armed gangs. A year later, much of the aid intended for hospitals and orphanages in Albania was being sold by criminal

---

[13] For an account of the heroin trade in Albania and Kosova see *The Guardian*, 1 November 1994.

gangs at the port of Durres. The material stolen from the stern of ships as they were unloaded by the bows was then quickly driven to Tirana and resold on the black market. As well as food, large quantities of clothing, shoes and medical supplies were distributed by the Red Cross and Caritas, an estimated 800 tons a month. Much of this too was stolen and sold off. There were immense logistical and security problems to be overcome before the aid could be delivered, In order to run such an operation, appropriate infrastructure – suitable transport, telecommunication and administrative services – needed to be set up. Most of the transport, technology and machinery material had to be imported, and Albanian Red Cross workers trained in their use.

Domestic food production was negligible since the co- operative farms had collapsed, and in the high mountain areas, which constitute over 60 per cent of the country, fertile agricultural land was scarce. Almost the entire population was dependent on outside food aid. The Red Cross, Oxfam and Save the Children, as well as newly-formed agencies inside the country, mounted the beginning of a rescue effort. In an important report on Albania published in December 1992, OXFAM highlighted the threat to many rural dwellers in the north and north-east, where conditions were described as being no better than those found in famine emergencies in the Third World. It called for a massive internationally-funded programme of agricultural development; otherwise stability and public order in cities would again collapse.

On 12 August 1991 Italy began an airlift of emergency food supplies to Albania following the deportation of thousands of refugees who had fled to southern Italy in the previous months. The aid was announced by the then Italian Foreign Minister, Gianni de Michelis, on one of his numerous visits to Tirana that summer. The Italian offer followed a European Community aid offer of ECU 2 million. From September 1991 till December 1993 the Italian humanitarian aid mission known as 'Operation Pelican' delivered thousands of tons of basic food items throughout Albania, and the huge Pelican convoys became an everyday sight, winding their way slowly over the country's perilous road network to be used for emergency supplies of food and medicine. Rome's offer of assistance was seen as a means of stemming the flow of would-be refugees. Since the March 1991 exodus the Italian government had taken a much tougher stance towards Albanians, on the grounds that many were escaping economic misery and were not genuine political refugees. The Italian police offered $40 and new clothing to each Albanian who agreed to return home. However, several thousand refused to be deported. Meanwhile throughout 1992 between 2,000 and 2,500 tonnes of EC food aid were unloaded in the port of Durres every day. The Albanians did not know about properly defrosting the very old meat, and consequently there were many cases of food poisoning.

By the end of 1991 the health service was in almost total paralysis, with acute shortages even of basic medical supplies. In July 1992 a working group of skilled specialists and WHO representatives was established to begin its reorganisation, with privatisation the ultimate goal. Organisations working in the field included Feed the Children, the Islamic Foundation of Aid, the International Red Cross and Médecins Sans Frontières. Conditions in hospitals were very poor, and deficiencies in the care of children and the mentally handicapped were publicised in the foreign media, to the government's great chagrin. Although extensive aid was received from the European Community and other international bodies, for most Albanians the prospect of any universal system of health care had quite disappeared, with payment being required for almost all medical treatment. With the declining social infrastructure, combined with large-scale emigration of medical and ancillary staff, public health problems proliferated. These culminated in the cholera epidemic which started in August 1994 in the Berat region and continued into the winter, claiming at least thirty lives.

On 2 December 1993 Operation Pelican ended, itself something of a symbolic landmark in a period full of landmarks. When Pelican started, Albania was virtually destitute, facing widespread malnutrition and economic collapse. By the beginning of 1994 those problems had been largely overcome, foreign aid was being withdrawn, and the country was seen as relatively stable and increasingly able to feed itself.

The family, women and general social issues

Clan identity and traditional values are still fairly strong in rural Kosova, which in social terms was left very much to its own devices under Tito's rule. However, in Albania the state waged a relentless war against the customs of the past. This intensified after the country's Cultural Revolution in 1967. Clan identity was seen as a major impediment to the creation of a truly communist state. The ideological campaign against clans was seen by the public as a campaign against class, and in fear of being scorned as part of the wealthy land-owning class, families severed their ties with other segments of their clans. In Kosova extended families numbering from fifteen to thirty people are still the norm in rural districts, and constitute a profound influence on behaviour and thought. In Albania forced collectivisation led, by contrast, to a break-up of the large extended families which had been especially widespread in the northern districts. Extended families are now very rare in Albania, and there is general agreement that it would be very difficult to return to the arrangements which they entail. People have become accustomed to life in nuclear families. Because of its association with the years of repression under communism, Albanians have developed an aversion to collective life in any form, even where it would make economic sense, as it would in many of the poorer parts of the north and north-east.

Women generally had a very uncertain status once the state no longer provided a 'guaranteed job' for all. In the past they had, theoretically at least, enjoyed equality with men. With the arrival of democracy much of the job market collapsed, together with the crêches and other social benefits which the communist state had provided. The religious revival among Muslim Albanians also affected women, as conservative family values gained ground and some women were forced back into the conventional roles of homemaker and mother. From 1992 onwards young girls were lured to Athens and Italy with promises of jobs in bars and restaurants, only to find themselves compelled to become prostitutes. Once abroad, they were trapped: as illegal residents they had no legal protection, and having lost their virginity they would not generally be regarded as marriageable back in Albania. The trade in girls is tightly organised by the Mafia, and the subject is still taboo in Albania; much research remains to be done on the structure of this trade, and the identity of those responsible for it. Prostitution has now openly reappeared in Albania itself, particularly in Tirana and the coastal towns. Under communism homosexuality, deemed a 'crime against social morals', was illegal and was punishable by up to ten years in prison. Albania's Balkan, macho mentality was therefore deeply unsupportive of the country's first-ever Gay Rights Society, which was formed in Tirana in March 1994 with the slogan: 'Albania, the only country in Europe without a gay organisation. No longer.' These were brave words and, fearful that they would be the target of abuse, the society's founders gave a post-office box number as their contact address. Up to the time of writing, there has been no discussion of legalising homosexuality, a move that would be considered political suicide by all the country's political parties.

In marked contrast to Kosova, the number of marriages in Albania decreased sharply after 1992. Previously there had been an average of 2,700 marriages annually at the Matrimonial Agency in Tirana, but in 1991 only about 1,000 were recorded. The fact that thousands of young men had left the country to find work abroad also had a dramatic effect on the marriage statistics. The reduction is also due in part to the overall economic decline, unemployment, and emigration of both men and women in the marriageable age-group. A sociologist explained the reduction as due to the 'difficult economic situation, insecurity of life at home, and unemployment'. [14] Inadequate housing was another problem, leaving young couples unable to marry because they had nowhere to live; this appears also to have become a major factor in emigration pressure. In 1993 government statistics revealed that over 50,000 people were classified as completely homeless, with a further 100,000 living in defective accommodation. During the immediate transition period, in 1991-2, many Albanian girls married Kosovar men, lured by the relative wealth and sophistication of the Kosovars in contrast to the unemployed or poorly-paid Albanian youth who did not know how to drive a car and owned no flashy clothes, gold neck-chain or cassettes of Western music. By 1993, however, the glamour of the Kosovars had worn off as some Albanian women began describing them as rough, violent and uneducated, and by this time Albanian men had begun, at least in Tirana, to discard their 1970s bell-bottoms for more fashionable clothes that came via Greece or from foreign aid charities. At the end of 1992 Albania's first beauty salon opened, offering facial treatment, massage and hair dressing services – under communist

[14] Albanian Telegraphic Agency, 9 July 1992.

rule women has been discouraged from wearing make-up and jewellery. At the same time a course opened in Tirana to teach women how to drive. In general the position of women in the new society appears to contain many contradictions. However, while this became a social phenomenon in Tirana, it remained virtually unknown elsewhere in the country, such was the ever-widening gap between the capital and the rural districts where most of the population still lived.

During the 1980s Albania had persistently struggled to keep pace with steady population growth. In 1989 the population stood at 2.8 million, and was growing at annual rate of 2.1 per cent – after Kosova, by far the highest rate in Europe. By 1990 almost two-thirds of the population were under the age of twenty-six and the annual addition to the labour force was around 40,000. Hoxha's policy of encouraging population growth had been based on economic and military assumptions. Abortion and all forms of contraception were illegal, with the result that illegal abortions caused the death and sickness of thousands of women. Under the Alia administration condoms were periodically available, but they were of poor quality and unreliable. Although Italian contraceptives could be found on sale in kiosks during the 1980s, they were expensive for most young men and their sale was not encouraged. Amidst the political turmoil of the winter of anarchy, one constructive piece of legislation was enacted which had a considerable social impact. In January 1992, in an attempt to curb the many deaths resulting from unhygienic illegal home abortions, the government passed the new Abortion Law, which allows abortion for anyone over the age of sixteen, but stipulates that it must be performed before the twelfth week of pregnancy. Women who want an abortion after the twelfth week and girls under sixteen must face a special commission which decides if the abortion is necessary.

Within six months of the new law being passed, the number of reported abortions exceeded live births by a ratio of 0.8 births to one abortion. This is a consequence of the country's dire economic situation, together with the continued lack of adequate contraception and family-planning facilities. The majority of those taking advantage of the new law were married women wishing to avoid the financial burden of another child. By 1995 the average family size was down to two children in urban areas and three in the countryside. The state founded a family planning clinic but it has very few supplies. The poor economic situation causes family planning to be treated as a low priority, but three doctors from the new clinic were sent to France to learn progressive methods, and some Italian doctors were invited to Albania to provide more information on the issue and help to develop solutions. It is likely that family planning will be a priority for all future Albanian governments as the relatively high birth-rate is an important factor in the country's numerous social problems.

8

KOSOVA AND THE QUESTION OF NATIONAL UNIFICATION

'There is no Albania without Kosova and vice versa.' (Albanian Telegraphic Agency, 22 March 1992)

The Kosova problem was by far the most important element in Albanian Balkan policy in the years of transition, with its capacity to draw Albania into war with Serbia and into the heart of the wider Balkan crisis. It is also a prime element of the Albanian national identity: the Kosova crisis goes to the heart of the definition of Albania itself. Since 1992 the influence of Kosovars in Albanian politics and society has been deep and far-reaching, and it continues to grow.

On one wall of the Tirana office of the National Unity Party there hangs an enormous map of 'Greater Albania', to which the party's excitable and flamboyant leader Idajet Beqiri points proudly. As well as the territory of present-day Albania, it includes large areas of Serbia, Montenegro, Macedonia, and northern Greece as far south as the city of Ioannina. It is significant that there are few places in post-communist Albania where such a map could be found. To most Albanians the concept of a Greater Albania, including Kosova, is a myth or a dream rather than a possible geographical reality. But nations, particularly in the Balkans, are founded and strengthened on myths and dreams, and the force which this idea exercises in some Albanian minds should not be underestimated.

In general the Albanian national question and the Kosova problem are very much bound up with the belief of Kosovars that the communist Albanian government never did anything to chastise the Yugoslav government for its denial of Albanian national rights in Yugoslavia or to help the process of the unification of all

Albanians. Due to the very restricted media and propaganda turned out by the Hoxha regime, Albanians in Albania knew more about what was happening in Mozambique than in Kosova. Distance was important in this argument. Although Enver Hoxha tried to pursue the national question in the midst of the wartime resistance period, in the post-war period he consistently betrayed the national unity question in the interests of the stability of his own regime in Tirana. Albania's superpower communist backers were un-interested in its national question, and the period of isolation after 1976 deprived the country of the capacity to influence events in Yugoslavia in any meaningful way. It was also widely believed in Kosova that a democratic government in Tirana would reverse this policy, especially since the disintegration of Yugoslavia was expected to encourage the international community to redefine the 'unjust' borders to which the Albanian people had been sub-jected for more than eighty years. Albanians have never forgotten that after the First World War important parts of their country, such as the Diber region of former Yugoslav Macedonia, were given to Serbia by the victorious powers as a reward for its loyalty.

During the Hoxha years Kosova was seen as Albania's stake in Yugoslavia – a kind of buffer zone. It so happened that in 1968 the first large-scale Albanian demonstrations against Belgrade rule took place, as well as the 'Prague Spring' – followed by the invasion of Czechoslovakia by the Warsaw Pact countries. In the complex international situation that followed, the constant fear of invasion by the Soviet Union, which Belgrade shared, led Tirana more than once to go so far as to say that, if Yugoslavia were attacked, Albania would come to its aid. Consequently the Albanian govern-ment never pleaded the Kosovar cause before such international forums as the UN and the European Commission on Human Rights, or interfered directly in Kosova's internal politics. When persecuted members of illegal Kosovar groups sought shelter in Albania, they were usually handed straight back to the Yugoslav authorities in what the young Kosovar activists understandably saw as intolerable violations of basic rights of asylum. During these bitter and difficult years of communist betrayal of the national cause, the much maligned Swiss and Federal German authorities undoubtedly gave far more helpful and generous treatment to Kosovar asylum-seekers than the corrupt and complacent com-munist élite of Tirana, most of whom had never left Albania except as honoured guests of foreign partners in delegations. People were also ignorant of the severe persecution of Albanian activists in Kosova, the depredation of the natural resources of the region, and the repression of normal Albanian cultural activity. Even those who privately dissented or were critical of communism often believed that the Kosovars enjoyed a much higher standard of living and a freer political system. While this may have been true in the 1970s and early '80s, it has certainly not been so more recently, especially since the start of the Yugoslav war. This background of betrayal by the Tirana authorities has never been forgotten by many Albanians in Kosova.

Following the campaign of 'Brotherhood and Unity' launched by Tito to encourage a form of patriotic Yugoslavism, it became Yugoslav policy that the country's minorities could serve as a 'bridge' between different countries rather than as a source of conflict as in the past. It suited the Albanian regime to accept Tito's bridge-building role for Kosova. Serbs, meanwhile, were generally convinced that Tirana was constantly encouraging Kosovar dissent in preparation for moves to create a 'Greater Albania'. However, the Serbs and the majority of Kosovars were unaware of the true nature of the regime in Tirana, which was preserved as if in aspic and only able to survive in a state of total isolation. It was not in Tirana's interest to include Kosova within Albania's borders; this would have been a careless move guaranteed to destabilise Hoxhaism. Although the Albanian leadership often used the situation in Kosova as a means of deflecting domestic discontent, they realised only too well how impractical the unification of the two Albanian communities would be. Decades of separation had widened the many social and psychological differences between the internationally isolated Albanians and the relatively cosmopolitan Kosovars.

After Enver Hoxha's death in 1985, progress in Yugoslav-Albanian relations continued despite serious rioting in Kosova in 1981. In the early 1980s Yugoslavia became one of Albania's major trading partners, and ideological differences between the two countries were played down. A rail link between northern Albania and Montenegro was opened in 1986, and at the end of December 1987 it was Tirana that called for a resumption of talks on cultural co-operation. The Tirana regime had far better relations with Belgrade than the Kosovars did at a time when relations among all Yugoslavia's minorities were unpromising. During the Balkan Foreign Ministers' Conference in Belgrade in February 1988, the Yugoslav press commented that the speech of the Albanian Foreign Minister Reis Malile had been 'delicate' and 'pragmatic', and that he had avoided stirring up any controversy; for example, he had skilfully skirted the Kosovar issue by declaring that the national minorities should help build bridges between states,[1] thereby echoing Tito's earlier 'bridge-building' concept for relations between minorities. For the first time Malile granted an interview to the Kosova Albanian-language daily *Rilindja,* in which he said that Albania favoured a 'high standard of integrity' in relations with Yugoslavia. He reiterated his proposal that the minorities act as bridges linking states and, with specific reference to Kosova, added: 'We have not demanded and do not demand anything.' This was an apparent response to Yugoslav allegations that Albania had territorial claims on Yugoslavia.[2]

The only commitment demonstrated by Albania to Kosova was rhetorical. The general atmosphere among the Tirana élite who determined Albanian foreign policy was insular, uncertain and very conservative in its attitude to Kosovar aspirations. Tirana's general policy was to make a periodic announcement about the ongoing conflict, for example on the 'equality of rights' of the Kosovars, and from time to time to publish volumes of documents on the issue. During the 1980s, for economic as well as security reasons, Tirana strove to establish good relations with Belgrade rather than Priština, and although some groups ideologically related to Tirana were engaged in subversive activity in Kosova, they served only as an embarrassment to the Albanian leadership. For a long while Yugoslavia had been Albania's major trading partner, with increasing integration of the mineral and electricity industries. The smelter at Gjakova in Kosova was supplied with both hydro-electricity and chromite ore from Albania. Both countries were keen to continue strengthening the ties of Balkan co-operation established during the Foreign Ministers' Conference, but in later years this type of arrangement was increasingly seen as an example of the way that the pillage of raw materials and basic resources from Kosova by Belgrade had even begun to extend to Albania

[1] Radio Free Europe, BR/36, 4 March 1988.
[2] Ibid.

itself. With the imposition of UN economic sanctions on Serbia, these arrangements collapsed, to the serious detriment of the Albanian economy.

A mood of general apprehension prevailed throughout Kosova, and Yugoslavia, following the rise to power in Serbia of Slobodan Milosević. In November 1988 some 100,000 Albanians gathered in Priština to demand the reinstatement of two Kosovar Communist Party leaders who had been forced to resign. This was matched by half a million Serbs demonstrating in Belgrade against alleged maltreatment of Kosova's Serbs by their Albanian neighbours. The Albanian leadership showed its concern by issuing the following statement:

> The PSR of Albania has clearly expressed that it is for relations of good neighbourliness with Yugoslavia, for a stable and independent Yugoslavia, and that its people live in harmony with one another and with equal rights. Albania also expressed this desire at the meeting of Foreign Ministers in Belgrade, which marked a positive step towards understanding and confidence in our region. But it is a pity that winds are blowing precisely from the organising country where this hopeful meeting was held, which destroyed this climate.[3]

In retrospect the reaction of the Tirana leadership to the Milosević-engineered coup in the Yugoslav party seems feeble in the extreme. The serious human rights violations associated with these events, which were so seminal for the future of Yugoslavia, were played down for the sake of peaceful relations with Belgrade. The Albanian leaders were in a position of unique knowledge and opportunity to make the international community aware of the importance of what was happening, but they totally failed to do so.

In 1989, as a follow-up to the previous year's conference in Belgrade, the deputy foreign ministers of the Balkan countries met for the first international political gathering of its kind to take place in Tirana. They agreed once again not to deal with specific problems in bilateral relations, but to seek to establish a general framework for co-operation. However, this notion was immediately put to the test by yet more violent unrest in Kosova.

[3] Albanian Telegraphic Agency, 21-24 September 1988.

In February 1989 militant Albanian miners from the Trepca mine in northern Kosova went on strike and occupied the mine management offices. Trepca is one of the largest and most productive mines in Eastern Europe, a giant lead, nickel and silver complex with an associated smelter in nearby Mitrovica; it has been in production since before the Second World War, and is a cornerstone of the Kosovar economy. They demanded the resignation of three provincial officials imposed on them by the Serbian Party and considered by the Albanians to be 'Uncle Toms' because of their excessive deference to the Serbian Party leadership. The miners also asked that any constitutional limitation of Kosova's autonomy, for which Belgrade had been pressing, should be subject to democratic debate. On 23 February Serbia's National Assembly passed the controversial amendments that would, in effect, return Kosova to Serbian control. By March there was widespread rioting which left at least twenty-seven Albanians dead, shot by troops during the latest 'state of emergency' imposed on the province by Belgrade.

This crisis in Kosova severely strained the spirit of Balkan co-operation that had been painstakingly built up over the previous year. By now it was clear, even to the most anti-Kosova elements in the Albanian leadership, that they could not ignore these events, which severely damaged the most promising process of reconciliation between Albania and Yugoslavia in the post-war era. Albania's reaction was swift and unusually extensive. A statement by Foto Çami, right-hand man to Ramiz Alia, strongly criticised the 'erroneous policies' of the Yugoslav authorities towards their Albanian minority, and warned that Belgrade's policy could not fail to have a negative impact on Balkan co-operation. Çami's statement set in motion the first-ever nationwide protest campaign throughout Albania in support of the Kosovars. Belgrade's response to the demonstrations in Albania was to accuse Tirana of a 'dual track policy', of preaching good-neighbourliness while in practice conducting a hostile policy against Yugoslavia. Some of the emerging leaders of the opposition in Tirana, particularly the northerner Azem Hajdari, were quick to take up the Kosovar cause, and the PLA leadership's inertia on the issue became yet another focus for popular discontent. In July 1990s the situation quickly deteriorated as the Serbian government amended Serbia's constitution to remove the legal basis for Kosova's autonomy. Kosova's parliament was suspended and direct rule was imposed from Belgrade. In response, the Kosovars established an 'Assembly of the Republic of Kosova', initially with headquarters in Zagreb, where it was decided to organise a referendum on Kosova's sovereignty. During this period Dr Ibrahim Rugova, leader of the mass-membership Kosova Democratic League (LDK), began to emerge on to the international stage as a human rights leader.

These events caused concern in Tirana, interpreted as they were as part of the general process of self-determination being enacted throughout Eastern Europe and the Soviet Union. The Albanian government was caught in an acute dilemma. With the exception of those living in the south of the country, most Albanians could watch Yugoslav television – at this stage relatively independent of state control – and were thus aware of what was happening in Kosova. The Tirana government had, at the very least, to make some protests over the treatment of Kosovars to appease nationalist sentiment. It was around this time that Tirana began to publish a spate of English-, French- and Albanian-language books and pamphlets, such as 'What the Kosovars Say and Demand', which initiated not only the world at large but also many younger Albanians into the nature of the major issues involved in Kosova. Little had been published on Kosova by state publishers for many years, but Ramiz Alia's administration could not risk encouraging the Kosovars to push for fundamental political change since this would jeopardise the Albanian regime's stability.

Events in Eastern Europe were dictating the new tone of pan-Albanianism emanating from Tirana, which was linked to the social and political chaos in Albania itself during this critical summer for the PLA and Alia. At the 10th Party Congress of the PLA in June 1991, Xhelil Gjoni, one of three Party secretaries who led the PLA after Alia resigned as First Party Secretary the previous month, gave a lengthy address on the issue of Kosova. Having stressed that a solution to the Kosova problem had to be in line with the current political liberalisation of Europe, Gjoni went on to demand that Yugoslavia's Albanians be given the same rights as the other peoples of that country. He concluded with an important and provocative statement: 'We, the Albanians, are a nation unjustly divided. But it would be a further injustice if the wall separating Albanians on each side of the border were not torn down. We should resolutely demand ... that this wall be demolished and Albanians be able to communicate freely with one another, as do other European peoples and nations.'[4]

The collapse of the Berlin Wall emphasised the implications of Gjoni's speech, and indicated how even a hardline isolationist such as Gjoni was having to come to terms with the imminent disintegration of Yugoslavia. But it was a leap of understanding they were ill-equipped either by temperament or by ideology to make. In July Albania, with its newly-acquired status as a member of the European Security Conference, whose Helsinki Act and Paris Charter guaranteed the inviolability of European borders, was facing a fully-fledged civil war in Yugoslavia and the possibility that the fighting would spread across its own borders. Albania's relations with Belgrade, meanwhile, were becoming increasingly strained, as the systematic erosion of Albanian civil and human rights in Kosova continued apace. On 6 July the Albanian Council of Ministers held an emergency meeting on the critical situation in Yugoslavia, at which Ramiz Alia called for reinforcement of the state border. The very first official delegation from the LDK had come to Tirana on 22 February 1991, the day after the statue of Hoxha was toppled. Ali Aliu, who had been a professor at Priština University before being sacked by the Serbs, became the LDK's first representative to Albania. In an interview he stated: 'We want Tirana to treat Kosova not just as a matter of foreign policy but as a national matter. For two years Kosova hasn't had mass media, so we must exert maximum effort to ensure that the Albanian media based in Tirana concentrates on the Kosova issue so as to inform the entire nation.' Aliu expressed the wish that as well as giving assistance in medicine and education, Albania would somehow accommodate the thousands of Kosovars fleeing the JNA (Yugoslav army): 'We want the 100,000 Albanians to be offered shelter. We do not want to see our young men fleeing to Western Europe, we ask that they be given sanctuary and safety here.'[5] Aliu was asked why the Kosovars were waiting for the Albanian army to come to their rescue when in fact there was a high level of apathy – even antipathy – towards Kosovars in Albania. Aliu replied: 'The truth is that we did not fully comprehend what took place here these last fifty years. In the 1970s

---

[4] *Zeri-i-Popullit*, 11 June 1991.

[5] *East European Reporter*, March/April 1992, p. 58.

I was here as a guest of Tirana University. None of us understood the dimensions of the terror and the dictatorship here. The government blinded us from reality; we saw only the façade.'[6] Still, however poverty-stricken Albania was, most Kosovars believed this to be a temporary phenomenon that would be eradicated by massive injections of international economic assistance soon after the DP's anticipated win in the forthcoming elections.

On 24 May 1991 the Kosova Assembly in Zagreb held a presidential election. Ibrahim Rugova was duly elected President of the 'Republic of Kosova' with 99.5 per cent of the vote. On 30 September Kosovars voted in a referendum, which overwhelmingly endorsed Kosova as a 'sovereign and independent state'. The escalating conflict in Yugoslavia, with bloody fighting continuing in Croatia and threatening Bosnia-Hercegovina, meant that Albania's politicians could no longer ignore the fate of the Kosovars. Fearing a massive influx of Kosovar refugees, the Tirana government issued statements containing by far the strongest criticism to date of the policies of Kosova's Serbian leadership. Albania's armed forces were placed on alert following reported incidents between Yugoslav and Albanian border guards, and in October Albania officially recognised the 'Republic of Kosova' as a sovereign and independent state. This gesture, it was hoped, would spur the international community to recognise Kosova. By November, movements of artillery and motorised units of the Serbian army were reported in all Kosova's main towns, and Serbian reservist forces had been considerably enlarged, with many being deployed along the Albanian border. After the withdrawal of the JNA from Macedonia, the majority of the forces were redeployed in Kosova.

The situation in former Yugoslavia had deteriorated sharply following international recognition of Croatia and Slovenia in January 1992, and this led directly to the conflict escalating into Bosnia-Hercegovina. There was a corresponding tightening of Serbian control in Kosova, and at the end of January a large rally was held in Tirana in support of the Kosovars. At this stage the opposition DP associated itself firmly with the Kosovar cause, claiming that once in power it would bring down the 'Balkan Wall'. In return for such stirring statements, considerable quantities

[6] Ibid.

of material aid to the DP were made available from Kosovar diaspora groups. Campaigning equipment such as cars and fax machines was purchased in Switzerland and sent to the DP before the election in March 1992. Just as the government in Tirana watched the events in Yugoslavia unfurl, so the dramatic political changes in Albania were watched with avid attention by the Kosovars, who were mobilising their émigré communities to raise funds for the newly-formed DP. The Kosovars believed that a democratic government in Albania would use its new power and energy more responsibly for the benefit and progress of Kosova, and so repay the Kosovar blood spilt in earlier generations for Albania's independence. Throughout Kosova there was talk of how the tanks would come rolling over the mountains from Albania to defend their brothers as soon as the DP gained power.

The émigré factor is of the greatest importance in Kosovar politics. The notion of a 'Unified Albania' has much more active support in New York than it does in Albania. There are estimated to be 350,000-400,000 Albanian-Americans, and the leaders of their various communities were active in promoting the issue of Kosova. In 1986 Congressman Joseph DioGuardi founded the Albanian-American Civic League, with the purpose of bringing together the various influential groups of Albanian-Americans to campaign on behalf of Albanians in Yugoslavia, especially to cover human rights abuses in Kosova, and get the problems of Kosova publicised in the US Congress. The League has since been dogged by controversy and has not entirely fulfilled the role its founders envisaged, although on Capitol Hill it has a strong Kosovar lobby, developed under the leadership of the then Senator Robert Dole. Furthermore, it has undoubtedly contributed to anti-Serbian feeling in the United States and has played some part in the development of wider US Balkan policy in its opposition to EU policy positions.

The Albanians in the United States can be divided into two groups. The first are the descendants of earlier migrants, most of whom came at the end of the nineteenth century either from the southern Korce region or from the coastal area near Himara. They were predominantly Orthodox Christians, and were responsible for founding the Albanian Orthodox Church. The second and much larger group is made up of those who fled after the Second World War to avoid political persecution, and from repression and lack of opportunity in the former Yugoslavia. These émigrés, especially the large number from Kosova, have put pressure on the Tirana government to keep the Kosova issue alive. There are about 100,000 Kosovars in Switzerland and 120,000 in Germany, both groups well organised and financed. Those in Switzerland are especially militant; they have benefited from a good educational system which is open to *Gastarbeiters,* and from the traditional efficiency and discretion of the Swiss banks, which have been used as a channel for funds to the emergent DP in Albania. Many of the leaders of the Swiss émigrés were hardline nationalists involved in the 1989 Trepca miners' strikes, and formed a formidable organised core of opposition to Serbian ambitions. At the same time, demands were made within Albania for more forthright government action on the issue of Kosova, and Serbian warnings against any Albanian involvement in Yugoslavia consequently became more strident.

Berisha told DP supporters that one of the party's aims was to fight until the great dream of uniting the Albanian nation came true,[7] a provocative statement to make at such a sensitive time, but Berisha was in a buoyant and expectant mood. Like many European politicians, he believed that with the international recognition of three of the former Yugoslav republics, Kosova's turn would perhaps follow. The DP had also previously endorsed an eventual 'democratic' union with Kosova in its initial 1990 programme. Also Berisha felt, like most Albanians, that history was now offering his nation a chance to unite. As a Gheg with many close Kosovar family connections, he attached greater importance to unification with Kosova than did many Tosk politicians. On 9 February 1992 there was a gathering to commemorate the first anniversary of the founding of the patriotic association called 'Kosova', centred in Shkoder. This body had as its main objectives the enhancement of national consciousness and, in the words of the society's official programme, to 'make the international community finally and correctly solve the destiny of the Albanian people residing in their territories in the former Yugoslavia'. Following a stirring recital of poems from Kosova, several distinguished guests, headed by the outspoken Kosovar academic Rexhep Qosja, were invited to talk. Qosja spoke of the Albanian nation being at an historic crossroads, and of 'the great idea of uniting our

[7] BBC, *SWB*, EE/1336 B/3,23 March 1992.

nation. It is our historic duty to carry it out since a great injustice has been done against the Albanian people. The nation is divided into five parts [Albania, Kosova, Macedonia, Montenegro and Greece], but new conditions have now arisen which must be exploited to solve the great national question.'[8]

At the Academy of Sciences the following day, Professor Qosja told an assembly of academics and politicians of the symbolism attached to his visit and what he referred to as the 'sacred land'. He said:

'We [Kosovars] come to the land of our dreams and ideals, to the land of our symbols and apostles of Albania, where there is Kruja and Vlora, where there are the graves of Skenderbeg and Naim Frashëri. Albania's poverty has deep roots and is a result of historic injustice done to the Albanian people. The neighbouring countries try to make impossible the correct solution to our question; Serbia, Montenegro, Greece and now Macedonia have divided up our territories. So the same opponents we had in 1878 and in 1912-13 are against us now. But neither our international position nor theirs at present is as it was 115 years ago or eighty years ago. They are not in as favourable a political position as they were then. With the correct solution of the Albanian question, the unification of the Albanians, one of the greatest injustices in Europe will be solved.'[9]

This speech exemplified the romantic and unrealistic impression many Kosovars had of Albania and in particular the prevailing belief that they were now faced with an historic chance finally to solve the Albanian national question. It is not surprising that they thought their moment had come with the advent of the New World Order following the collapse of Communism in Eastern Europe and the Soviet Union, the swift disintegration of Yugoslavia, and the radical changes in Albania. They understandably believed that these tumultuous events had shown the Albanian national question in a new light. However, it was recognised at the same time that throughout the Albanian world there were enormous issues apart from frontiers still dividing the Albanian

[8] Albanian Telegraphic Agency, 9 February 1992, p. 3.
[9] Ibid., 11 February 1992, pp. 2-3.

nation. Further, if they were to have any chance of finally solving their 'national question', they must first meet to address the problems that caused discord among them. Thus on 12 February 1992 an Assembly for National Reconciliation and Unity was held in Tirana with the purpose defining and then implementing an all-national strategy, leading to the realisation of all Albanian national interests. Those present included leading Kosovar academics including Rexhep Qosja, representatives of the Albanian political parties, the Albanian People's League, the Islamic Community, and the organisations Chameria, Kosova, Bashkimi Kombetar, and the Association for the Martyrs of the Albanian Nation, 'Mëmedheu'. The Initiating Council of the Assembly had already convened at Thessaloniki on 13 December 1991, when representatives from Kosova and Albania set about turning what till then had been a loose gathering into an organising Council for the Assembly for National Reconciliation and Unity. Ismail Kadare was elected Chairman of the Assembly, with Rexhep Qosja as co-chairman.

Once a permanent office for the LDK was established in Tirana in October 1991, there was much coming and going by its representatives. Kosovars in general were convinced that Albania would only understand and support them in their own crisis if Sali Berisha and the DP were elected to power in Albania. When that victory occurred in March 1992 and Berisha became President it was hailed throughout the Albanian diaspora as a triumph for the whole Albanian nation – which indeed achieved, albeit briefly, a form of spiritual reunification. Both before and immediately after his victory, Berisha claimed strong support for unification. He and the Kosovars believed that the international community would see the DP's victory as so momentous that it would quickly raise Albania's status by giving massive injections of financial aid and thus making it a more important player on the international negotiating scene. The belief that a politically and economically stabilised Albania could do more for Kosova was echoed by Ibrahim Rugova, then chairman of the LDK, in an interview with 'Voice of America' immediately after the DP election victory: 'This victory', he said, 'will be significant to the Albanians in Kosova because Albania will appear with a new authority on the international scene. It will strengthen economically, and naturally will be better able to help the general Albanian issue.'[10]

However, Kosovars in general were still unaware of the full dimensions of Albania's desperate socio-economic state and how the conflict in what had been Yugoslavia would restrict international investment in the whole of the Balkans. Apart from the dire economic situation in Albania, the new democratic government faced the ever-increasing threat that the savage conflict to the north would engulf Kosova and Macedonia. Albania could not afford a war in Kosova. Albanian politicians were therefore severely limited in their options, and their only hope was to persuade the international community to intervene on their behalf. A strong sense of national pride was now being put to a severe test. For the right-wing Balli-Kombetar (BK), which was largely made up of émigrés, the abandonment of Kosova to Yugoslavia after the Second World War had been one of the greatest crimes of the communists. The Ballists tried to push the DP government to take a tougher line on the Kosova question – especially hardline nationalists like Tomor Dosti, whose father Hasan Dosti had been leader of the BK after the war and was considered by the communists to be one of Albania's greatest enemies.

In July 1992, members of the Albanian government and Kosovar leaders met to discuss socio-economic co-operation. The Albanian Prime Minister, Alexander Meksi, received Kosova's President, Ibrahim Rugova, for whom this was the first meeting with members of the new Albanian democratic government. Throughout the previous two years the Kosovar living standard had been rapidly dropping towards Albanian levels. Talks concentrated on creating opportunities for co-operation between Albania and Kosova in all fields but especially in education, where it was agreed to bring experts from Kosova to Albania. These were primarily university lecturers in philosophy, jurisprudence and sociology, subjects which had been totally distorted and politicised in Albanian institutions. Unable to assist Kosova financially, Meksi could only stress his government's unwavering support for the cause of Kosova's independence. In an interview after his appointment as the new Albanian Foreign Minister, Alfred Serçei tried to maintain the upbeat mood, and told a reporter: 'We will not hesitate to demand that all Albanians live in their own ethnic territories. It is not

[10] Albanian Telegraphic Agency, 24 March 1992, p. 6.

just to keep them apart and refuse their self-determination. Obviously our only means will be democratic.'[11] In July 1992 Ramush Tahiri, then Vice-President of the Kosova government, told the Zagreb daily *Večernji List*: '[Before Berisha] Albania did not understand the Kosova issue. But we have harmonised our opinions with the present leadership. Albania has openly declared that it would protect its brothers in the former Yugoslavia. There is no doubt, therefore, whether Albania would participate in a conflict. The Albanian army is prepared and is in a state of alert. Large forces are positioned on its border with Kosova.'[12]

This statement was simply untrue and somewhat irresponsible given the existing tensions in the region and the military realities in Albania. Far from protecting the Kosovars, the Tirana regime had hastily signed a defensive military pact with Turkey. Any involvement in a war in Kosova would have seriously damaged Albania's economic and political recovery. Despite the election of the new government, little had changed in the political mentality of the foreign and defence policy establishments in Tirana. Resembling the equally abstracted wishful thinking of Athens officialdom, the Foreign Ministry in particular, always a stronghold of conservatism and isolationism, was unwilling to encounter the untidy and often bloody realities of former Yugoslavia in any form. The DP government had to grasp the reality of how painfully slow this was going to be in the absence of any clear understanding of the Albanian national question in the international community.

In November 1992 the Albanian Defence Minister, Safet Zhulali, denied to the international press that Albania was training Kosova Albanians for guerrilla fighting in Kosova, although a training camp for this purpose actually existed in central Albania at Labinot, near Elbasan. Zhulali made this statement in response to Serbian allegations that Albania had built a system of tunnels under its mountains to smuggle armed insurgents into Kosova. Although some military movements in the north-east were taking place, and continued to do so, these deployments were strictly defensive and limited to the digging in of artillery pieces along the main roads.[13]

A realistic attitude to the situation came from the Tirana film-

[11] *Illyria*, 3 June 1992.
[12] Ibid., 11 July 1992, p. 3.
[13] See story by James Pettifer in *The Times*, 9 December 1992, which resulted in a dispute with the Albanian government.

director Kujtim Cashku, who participated in the 'Citizens and Municipalities' peace conference held in Ohrid in October 1992. He told a journalist: 'The Albanian question can only be solved if the interests of all the Balkan nations are taken into consideration. We must not think in terms of separate solutions just for Albanians. We must instead think in terms of a common process of integration.' Shkelzen Maliqi, Vice-President of the Social Democratic Party of Kosova, who was present at the discussion, said:

> 'The creation of a united Albanian state is the ideal framework for a discussion on the Albanian question, but that is not the only solution. The first goal of Albanian parties in Kosova today is independence for Kosova, not unification. Some people argue that a hasty unification now would produce more damage than good, because of the large differences in the level of economic development, as well as lifestyle, way of thinking and some basic values. The predominant view is that the least painful way to work towards the long-term goal is for both Albania and Kosova to join the EC.'[14]

Maliqi, as a Kosovar, had a much more immediate and practical response to the problem. Casku's approach, on the other hand, was more detached and philosophical, typifying the way the subject had been dealt with in educated Tirana circles if it was seriously discussed at all. At this time the thinking of all participants in the debate was conditioned by the assumption that living standards in Kosova were much higher than those in Albania, and would remain so for a long time. Although some conservatives across all parties in Tirana still make this assumption, it is increasingly unreal as a yardstick for policy-making. In fact, this had ceased to be the case in the early 1990s, and by 1994 convergence had taken place, with the destruction of the Kosovar economy as a result of the prolonged war in former Yugoslavia and some real improvement in national income in Albania after 1993. Accurate statistics are not available, but it appears that national income *per capita* in the urban centres of both countries is about US $800.

There has been considerable emigration of Kosovars to Albania, especially after the start of the conflict in former Yugoslavia. By 1993 an estimated 75,000 had arrived, most settling in Tirana.

[14] *War Report*, Nov./Dec. 1992, p. 14.

Even with the border officially closed, there was a steady flow of Albanian men crossing in both directions, despite the obvious danger on the volatile Kosova border, where tension increased dramatically throughout 1992 as nervous Serbian border guards shot at any moving object on sight. Every night small groups of young men headed for it and crossed by remote, forest-clad mountain paths. The United Nations High Commission for Refugees had contingency plans in December 1992 for an influx of Kosovar refugees. An emergency hospital was set up just inside Albania at Kruma, and hut accommodation was organised by a German charity at Kukes and Bajram Curi. Relief agencies estimated that up to 500,000 Kosovars might cross if the war eventually spread to Kosova. However, the people of nearby, poverty-stricken Kukes were resentful at the very possibility that Kosovar refugees might be given international relief assistance which they believed should rightly be granted to them. They had little in the way of medical supplies and food and were therefore reluctant to see their scanty provisions allocated to Kosovars. Another, safer exit route was for Kosovars to obtain an exit visa to the Former Yugoslav Republic of Macedonia (FYROM) and then to cross what was, at this stage, the less dangerous border from there into Albania at well-known crossing points, such as the paths through the mountainous forests near Diber. In 1993 this situation changed, largely because of deteriorating inter-ethnic relations in FYROM, and there were more than twenty killings on this border, mostly of Albanian nationals entering FYROM illegally.

In April 1993 five young men were killed by Serbian guards 300 yards inside Kosova after crossing the border illegally north of Kukes a few days after three others were shot near the border crossing of Tropoja. Despite the large number of deaths and injuries in numerous border incidents, hundreds still risked the crossing. Unlike the young men trekking south to Greece in search of work, these went in search of food. Most had relatives on the other side who hid them for a few weeks until they were ready to return. Driven by poverty and hunger stemming from unemployment and lack of land, they made repeated visits to Kosova to partake of the relative comforts denied them back in Albania. Once united with their Kosovar relatives, they were able to eat from abundant supplies of meat and fruit such as could never be found in their own villages. Many of the Kosovars who crossed in the reverse direction made their way directly to Tirana, where their arrival initially had a dramatic impact. Even with the modest amounts of hard currency they had available, they quickly began to control several areas of economic activity, notably car imports, drug-dealing and gun-running. Kosovar immigrants bore some initial responsibility for the spiralling crime rate and the growth of Mafia-type activities that became so prevalent over the transition period. Because of the difficult and unpredictable situation in Kosova, and their expulsion from countries such as Sweden, Kosovars were anxious to consolidate their economic position in Albania.

The Kosovars, together with returning Albanian-American émigrés, quickly became big fish in a little pond, and through their large extended families made use of widespread international connections to develop their economic interests. Many Albanians, especially those in Tirana from the old communist educated élite, saw the Kosovars as uncouth, ill-educated, prone to criminality, untrustworthy, aggressive, unable to speak Albanian properly and patronising in their attitude towards Albanians. For their part Kosovars tended to regard their co-nationals from Albania proper as naive, backward, primitive, élitist, too 'purely Albanian' through isolation, and incapable of operating successfully in the modern world. Some of these criticisms must be regarded as true, particularly those relating to economic competence. Kosovars were the first to exploit Albania's genuine commercial opportunities. The particularly narrow influence of high-minded 'professional' specialisation in education and culture under Hoxha left the educated Tiranan at a severe disadvantage in the new populist business culture, with its wheeler-dealers and the almost universal use of bribery and Mafia-style business methods. Communist education had left many ex-PLA Tirana intellectuals with an almost aristocratic mentality: they viewed business as a low and degrading activity, unfit for the élite, and a 'them and us' attitude began to develop. On the question of national unity, the Kosovars did not realise that at the political level the issue had to be dealt with first in Albania proper. The lack of support for the Kosovar struggle in Tirana was part of a wider crisis of national identity in Albania. Many Albanians were not prepared to heed any more demands for self-sacrifice, and were becoming generally indifferent to the plight of the Kosovars. President-Berisha, conscious that the 'blank cheque' promised by the United States would not be forthcoming, and of the anarchic and catastrophic situation his country faced, turned his energies away from Kosova and concentrated on finding foreign aid.

A first indication that Berisha was falling out of favour with some Kosovar circles came at the beginning of 1993. As an example of the widely differing views on Albanian-Kosovar dialogue, Rexhep Qosja wrote in February 1993 a rather hysterical open letter to Berisha accusing him of 'damaging our [the Kosovars'] historical image and rejecting our ideals'. This was after Berisha had said, in an interview in *Bujku*: 'The idea of a Greater Albania is not considered in serious Albanian political circles.' Qosja angrily replied:

> You are confusing the term 'Greater Albania' with 'Original Albania'. Albania and Kosova cannot be called a Greater Albania. There is, however, Mr President, an Original Albania...a natural Albania...a true Albania. You have belittled the sacrifices of all those Albanian historians, scientists and writers who have suffered in Serbian prisons for fighting for an Original Albania and a Republic of Kosova. You also said 'Albania does not want and will not ask for any changes in borders.' At first, this seems reasonable and understandable. Albania is a member of the UN and the CSCE and must comply with international rules and regulations. But, as President, you do not speak in your own name but in the name of history and the future. Albania has never accepted its existing borders and has always tried to remind international circles that these borders are unjust, dividing the Albanian land in two. They are borders that go through the heart of the Albanian people. As President, you should know the history of your own people and of the year 1912. None of us has the moral right to speak in the name of future generations.[15]

To this Berisha replied angrily in an open letter published in *Zeri-i-Popullit* and *Bujku*. Accusing Qosja of being a 'radical', he wrote: 'The Kosova issue can never be solved through terrorism. The Albanian movement in Kosova has been successful particularly because of its civilised and unterroristic methods.' He added that

[15] *Illyria*, 3 February 1993, p. 5.

Albania would not allow borders to be changed through violence, saying that 'Other ideas that promote violence would legalise violence and aggression in the Balkans and would lead to a true Balkan and Albanian tragedy.'[16]

In March the NATO Secretary-General, Manfred Wörner, urged Albania to assist in preventing the spread of war through the Balkans by continuing to show restraint over the increasing maltreatment of Albanians in Kosova. Concerning the Albanian national question, DP policy had persistently to alternate between hardline and moderate positions. Berisha was much commended by the UN and NATO for his policy of restraint. Having to swallow this bitter pill, he could only hope that the international community would act once it was fully informed of what was really happening in Kosova. Also, he had to convince the Albanian diaspora, especially in the United States where he still needed their support, that he was doing his best to alert the world to Kosova's plight. Beset by the country's increasingly serious problems with Greece, as well as domestic issues, Berisha spoke to numerous international forums of the apartheid system operating in Kosova and the military occupation of the region. In many ways the Tirana leadership was becoming the victim of its own economic achievements. While exact information is lacking, a convergence of living standards was undoubtedly taking place, as already mentioned, between Kosova and in Albania, with Kosova the poorest part of sanction-ridden Serbia and Albanian GNP improving each year. The traditional Tirana stereotype of the rich Kosovar was becoming irrelevant.

In the same context, the nightmare of life in Kosova under the Serbian martial law regime had become apparent to all Albanians, however instinctively unsympathetic they were to the Kosovar cause. The consistent violence, the denial of many basic human rights, and the effective end of all conventional education and economic life, had all produced a sense in the most patient ethnic Albanian that the status was intolerable. Shops were almost empty, exactly as they had been in Albania two or three years earlier, and the population was increasingly subject to various forms of repression. The Tirana government's policy still depended on a model of economic and social development for Kosova as

---

[16] Ibid.

an autonomous regime in a reconstructed Serbia and/or wider Yugoslavia, a model which had no basis in any likely political reality. In these circumstances pressure on the government increased during 1993 to articulate a new policy that would take account of the deteriorating situation in Kosova but still keep within the guidelines of permitted action largely laid down by the United States through its interventionist and powerful ambassador in Tirana, William Ryerson.

In June Berisha proposed a six-point plan for a 'just solution' to the Kosova issue:

(1) an objective assessment of the position of the Albanian nation and a selection of concrete means for achieving peace and stability in the Balkans;

(2) the immediate involvement of the European Community, the UN Security Council, the United States and NATO in discussion of the issue;

(3) new sanctions and other measures against Serbia, and deployment of NATO troops to Kosova;

(4) the placing of Kosova under full UN protection as a neutral zone;

(5) the lifting of the UN embargo and sanctions against Serbia after Serbia's agreement to a political solution for Kosova; and

(6) a definitive statement on Kosova's status in compliance with the Helsinki Accords and other international documents.

Towards the end of summer, as he found domestic opposition against him growing, Berisha tried to divert attention from troublesome issues at home by advocating a more radical line in Macedonia and Kosova. By playing the nationalist card, he hoped to win the allegiance of the extreme nationalists. At the end of 1993 he backed militants in Macedonia, led by Menduh Thaci, in a power struggle. That country's main Albanian political party, the Party for Democratic Prosperity (PDP), had split into moderate and militant factions, and the militants threatened armed revolt unless the Albanians were granted autonomy. This prompted fears that Berisha was plotting to annex western Macedonia.

This was very different from the DP's policy at the beginning of 1994, when it engineered the replacement in Macedonia of the moderate PDP leadership by hardliners.[17] The moderates were branded as Serbian agents, and in April Berisha refused to meet

[17] See Chapter 8, following.

the Macedonia Deputy Prime Minister, a PDP moderate, when he visited Tirana as part of an official delegation. In November 1993 several members of the Democratic Alliance (DA) had gone to Belgrade to meet both the government and opposition parties. Albanian TV accused the DA of planning to hand over Kosova in exchange for financial support. Also Gazmend Pula, President of the Kosova Helsinki Committee, and Veton Surroi, editor of the Priština weekly *Koha,* had been attacked on Albanian TV for attending meetings with Serbs, even though Rugova himself had signed a statement back in July 1992 calling for dialogue with them. It read: 'We propose that representatives of Serbia and the Republic of Kosova meet to decide on the framework for talks regarding Kosova.'[18]

As the situation in Bosnia seemed ever more intractable, Western pressure on Tirana to recognise the inviolability of Albania's frontiers with Serbia and Montenegro increased. Consequently, Berisha radically changed policy in the spring of 1994 by calling for talks between the local Kosovar leadership and Belgrade. Berisha was aware that any move towards a forcible change of borders and the creation of a unified Albania would cause a bloodbath and lose Albania its essential and desperately-needed foreign assistance. It would also lose the Kosovars the respect they had gained internationally for their years of Gandhi-like passivity in the face of Serbian aggression. Following a visit to Tirana in May 1994, 'President' Ibrahim Rugova left somewhat disillusioned after a communiqué had been issued in the joint names of himself and Berisha stating: 'Dialogue with Serbia is inevitable. Belgrade and Priština must negotiate in the presence of a third party in order to normalise the situation in Kosova.' In August Rugova proposed opening a Kosova bureau in Belgrade to facilitate communications with Serbia and talks with its officials.

In the autumn of 1994 tensions arose within the Kosovar leadership over the possibility of acceptance of autonomy over independence. The rift in the LDK (Kosova Democratic League) between hardliners pushing for total independence for Kosova and moderates advocating autonomy within a new Yugoslavia was set to widen in what was the first public conflict within the LDK since its formation in 1991. Rugova insisted that the LDK

[18] *Illyria,* 11 July 1992, p. 3.

would not split, but his efforts to keep the moderates on the main board of the LDK presidency, thus hoping to maintain a balance and ensure more tolerance within the party, could be no more than a temporary measure. The division between the moderates and the 'independentists', not only in Kosova but throughout the Kosovar diaspora, especially in the United States and Germany, was escalating. Talk about autonomy was political suicide in Kosova, but the key issue now centred around the situation in Albania itself as Sali Berisha, under US pressure, had to accept the notion of autonomy for Kosova. It remains to be seen how much longer the young activists of the LDK will accept these political positions. They depend on a view of the United States as arbiter of the New World Order, which some would argue is misconceived given the impotence in the early stages of Bosnian crisis, and on a notion of the international community as a moral body capable of producing human rights improvements in defaulting states. The rhetoric of the Rugova leadership group seemed increasingly to belong to a political world that was being superseded; it suited the Serbian authorities to pretend that it contained a threat, when it was in fact largely a feeble human rights campaign masquerading as a political struggle. Reassessment of policy was forced on the Rugova group in 1996 by the pressure of events.

For the Berisha administration the first priority had to be to prevent conflict. While international peace efforts in the Balkans were concentrated mainly on ending the war in Bosnia, the policy for Kosova was one of containment and insistence that the Kosovars settle for autonomous status within a new Yugoslav framework. However it could not be expected that radicals in Kosova would accept this arrangement as Serbian repression worsened and they saw the LDK goals rejected and their struggle abandoned once again by Albania. Both Berisha and Rugova had to beat a tactical retreat by accepting Balkan realities. By backtracking on the question of independence, Berisha was forcing Kosovars to face what he saw as reality. The 'Albanian question' and the 'Serbian question' had now emerged as the two most important factors in the future development of stability in the Balkans.[19]

The paramount concern of the average Albanian citizen is that

[19] See Kosova 'Infofax', New York, 12 September 1995.

Berisha reduces the chances of Albania's involvement in any conflict with its neighbours. For the country to be engaged in a war now would be economic and political suicide for Berisha, but he may not be able to control events. Despite the seriousness of the internal problems he faces, Berisha's outspoken support for the Kosovars has helped to keep Kosova on the international agenda. He presented the world with a united Albanian front: Albania would not be able to stand aside while other Albanians were being killed and would be compelled to intervene – however ill-equipped it might be for such a task. However, as the Serbs were well aware, Berisha had to plan to avoid this possibility at all costs. Thus a new phase of the Albanian national question is emerging in which Kosova is a critical factor but by no means the only possible *casus belli*. The Albanians living in Macedonia may prove equally important in future developments.[20]

[20] For accounts of the escalation of violence in Kosova in 1996, see articles by Miranda Vickers in *The European*, 20-26 June 1996, and *The Independent*, 8 July 1996, and by James Pettifer in the *Wall Street Journal*, 20 May 1996.

9

THE OTHER NATIONAL QUESTION: MACEDONIA AND MONTENEGRO

In the perception of Albania by the outside world from the end of the Axis occupation in 1944 to the collapse of the communist state in 1990-1, the national question as such hardly existed. Nor were ethnic minorities in the country seen as having any importance or even, in most cases, practical existence. Albanians living outside the state's boundaries in the Balkans and elsewhere were nearly always seen as the normal Balkan diaspora of a small and impoverished people, or as economic migrants of the traditional type, rather than as potential components of a wider nation, let alone a Greater Albania. Despite a few eruptions of militancy, as in Kosova in 1981 and 1989, which were briefly in the headlines, these people were mostly seen not as an important factor in international relations or even in regional Balkan politics, but as a vaguely perceived human rights problem internal to Yugoslavia. This prejudiced any serious consideration of their wider political and economic position.

The centrality of expansionism in Kosova to Milosević's political project for Yugoslavia generally was certainly not clearly understood; if it was, outside powers felt unwilling or unable to exert any effective influence on events there or in Belgrade itself. Furthermore, little was understood about either the history of repression of Albanian culture in the former Yugoslav Republic of Macedonia (FYROM), where techniques were tried out by the Titoist police before they were put into action on a wider scale in 1989 in Kosova, or the intimate link between the Kosovar and FYROM Albanians. The fate of the Albanians in FYROM, the most Islamic and often the most nationalist group, was thus totally neglected. It must be doubtful too whether the existence of important Albanian minorities in old Yugoslav Macedonia and Montenegro was even known to many Western analysts and diplomats.

At the level of cynical *Realpolitik*, once Western powers began to feel the danger of internal conflict in Yugoslavia, and that the break-up of the state was a real possibility, such serious repression of Albanian human rights as that instigated by Serbia in 1989 tended to be overlooked in the overriding concern to keep the Yugoslav state together, or seen as a separate issue subordinate to the central conflict between Croats and Serbs. Although this process was, and is, seen by many Albanian politicians, inside and outside the country, as a form of appeasement, with the predictable results that have been seen in ex-Yugoslavia, their views did not significantly influence political leaders or informed public opinion in the West. When, as long ago as the 1950s and 1960s, the Albanians of present-day FYROM were subjected to some of the worst abuses of the Ranković secret police, the fact was totally neglected by the West. In the era of superpower confrontation it did not suit Western interests to doubt the validity of the Tito regime's image as a 'democratic' or 'third way' to socialism or to draw attention to the human rights problems there when they occurred.

The collapse of Yugoslavia changed this situation fundamentally, and it came to be widely understood that there are two large groups of Albanians, totalling more than 2 million people, living outside the existing Albanian national borders in ex-Yugoslavia, and that the Albanians in Macedonia, like their Kosovar kin, aspire to a closer relationship with the Tirana-based state, or even unity with it, as part of the wider process of remaking the Balkans. The renewed Albanian national question is beginning to reach the international agenda just as the 'Macedonian' aspect of the question has been institutionalised in the new 'state' of FYROM, with its capital in Skopje. After a long period when Western political institutions hardly took account of the Albanians in FYROM at all, the leadership and orientation of this group became a matter of priority attention in the European Union and the United States.

The history of the Albanian national movement is complex, but it is clear that nationalism was an underlying prop for the communist regime. One of the main reasons why a regime of such arbitrary brutality, eccentricity and colossal inefficiency was able to survive for so long was that Hoxha had captured elements of the Albanian people's national consciousness while betraying vital elements of the national cause. The key period here is 1944-9, after the liberation from Axis occupation and the establishment of communism in Yugoslavia, when Hoxha and Tito, with their parties, evolved a 'solution' to the Albanian question in the context of the current turmoil in the Balkans and the developing split in the international communist movement between Tito and Stalin. The decisions taken then were intended to give renewed permanence and legitimacy to Albania's 1913 borders and independent existence. In essence this was done, at Tito's behest, by respecting the pattern of decisions by the nineteenth-century Great Powers, particularly on border problems, which originated with the Congress of Berlin. However, during the Axis occupation, another 'legitimacy' had been established by the Italians: of a different state, a Greater Albania including much of Kosova. The fascist occupiers had 'given' the Albanians something in terms of territory which they had never been able to achieve for themselves.

In the resistance struggle against the Axis occupation, a central problem for the Albanian communists was to be the new national question under a future socialist regime. The Party leadership was divided between those who saw the best hope for Albanian unity and prosperity in the country being part of Yugoslavia, and those favouring separatism. The split between Tito and Stalin in many ways safeguarded Albanian independence within the borders of the small state established in 1913; it enabled the Hoxha group to take unquestioned power and remove the nascent mechanisms and personnel of the Xoxe leadership group in the communist party, which was beginning to integrate the Albanian economy and political system with those of Yugoslavia. The close adherence of the Albanian communists to the figure of Stalin long after his eclipse elsewhere – which guaranteed Albanian national survival – originates in this period. Although these controversies may appear arcane and remote from the urgent problems of the 1990s, many of the post-Hoxha leaders of the state, such as Ramiz Alia, started their political careers in Kosova partisan groups during the war, and the views of the Tirana political élite on the national question have changed little since the end of communism. There is still entrenched and widespread prejudice in much of Tirana's intellectual and political class against the nationalist aspirations of both Kosovar and FYROM Albanians.

The history of the Partisans in the north and in 'Macedonia' and Kosova was essentially one of difficulties and sometimes failures; the impetus for Partisan victory in the liberation war came largely from the south of Albania proper. But the Albania legitimised by Hoxha was, in terms of actual territory, far from the dreams of the founding fathers of Albanian nationalism, and the underlying impetus behind the mythologisation of Partisan achievements during the resistance and popular revolution was the need to conceal this fact. Also mythologised was the conflict with Tito, so that 'the old renegade in Belgrade', as Hoxha liked to call him, could *de facto* be blamed, implicitly or sometimes explicitly, for the communist regime's failure to found a state to include all or most of the Albanians living in the Balkans. In this mind-set the future of the Albanians outside the borders, in Yugoslavia and elsewhere, could be largely forgotten, and for fifty years families in towns near the border, like Peshkopia, could not even visit relatives a few miles away in Yugoslavia.

Thus, where the national question is concerned, the communist state can be compared to someone living on a limited inheritance in a time of inflation. There was only so much 'good' history from the war for propaganda purposes to reinforce Hoxha's view of the national question in Albania, and as time passed and the Partisan campaign became more and more distant, the divergence of mythology and reality became ever clearer. Perhaps the crucial time when the Partisan heritage became utterly corrupted internally was after the Soviet invasion of Czechoslovakia in 1968. The communist leadership was worried (as it had been after the Soviet intervention in Hungary in 1956) that the same fate might befall Albania, and its response was to begin the bizarre and costly construction of over 400,000 pillboxes, the now notorious *bunkere,* throughout the country, a ludicrous expression of faith in the people's ability to resist the Soviets. There is thus an organic link between the decline and eventual collapse of the one-party state in 1990-1 and the reopening of the national question. Although they had been physically cut off from Albania proper for many years, the Albanians in adjoining 'Macedonia' and Kosova had never lost their sense of shared national consciousness, underlined by their understanding of what was still seen as an unjust allocation of borders by the Powers in the declining years of the Ottoman empire. Towns such as Diber, Gostivar and Tetovo, each with an overwhelming majority of Albanian inhabitants, were and are seen by Albanians as having been traded in 1913 by the Powers to Serbia in exchange for Serbian military support in a future war and to appease Russia, regardless of the ethnicity or aspirations of the inhabitants.

Like politicians everywhere, of all persuasions, the Albanian communist leaders were slow to realise the full gravity of the Yugoslav crisis, and to foresee the extent to which military criteria would begin to determine the future borders of the Balkan countries. By way of illustration Spiro Dede, a senior member of the Party of Labour Central Committee, said to one of the authors in January 1990 that the days of armed conflict in the Balkans over border issues had passed and that the looming Yugoslav crisis would be solved by the CSCE processes.[1] His views were certainly typical of people of most political persuasions in Tirana at that time. Hoxha and the Party had to define the existing Albanian homeland in terms of outside threats, whether from the West, from Yugoslavia or from elsewhere; and because the reality or appearance of some of these threats has declined, the existing borders of the Albanian state have inevitably become more and more open to question. It is ironic that under democracy and pluralism there is a genuine military threat to the country from Serbia, and that the Berisha government is therefore forced to resort to this traditional vocabulary again. The nationalist and royalist Right have always claimed that Hoxha was in some ways a betrayer of the nation, and point to the fact that the Albanian Party of Labour grew out of the Korca and Berat communist groups, in which Yugoslavs were influential. From this point of view socialism meant a strong Yugoslavia and a small and weak Albania. Although till recently these views were held by only a very small minority, mostly exiles, and were politically irrelevant, democracy and the demise of Yugoslavia have caused their proponents to resurface in Tirana. This is to suggest not that there is any significant measure of electoral support for an expansionist or irredentist regime, although two pro-Zogist parties and a Balli Kombetar organisation now exist, but that, as elsewhere in the general at-mosphere of nationalist revival in the Balkans, political ideas from

[1] Interview by James Pettifer, Tirana, 20 January 1990.

extreme and atavistic groups can substantially affect the main stream of political discourse.

It is increasingly likely that despite recurrent predictions of conflict between Serbia and Albania over Kosova, the resolution of the new national question will develop equally around the Albanians in western 'Macedonia'. Ethnic Albanians in FYROM make up about 25-30 per cent of the population of the state, living overwhelmingly in the western part adjoining Albania. Although the FYROM census of 1994 put the proportion at 23 per cent, this is likely to be an underestimate since some resident ethnic Albanians in political exile from Kosova were ineligible for inclusion. An additional obstacle to a fair census and subsequent election was widespread manipulation at the household level over residence requirements. In the referendum held in September 1991 by the ex-Yugoslav regional government in Skopje, many Albanians boycotted the polls, while the rest of those voting overwhelmingly supported 'Macedonian' independence. Relations between the Albanians and the Slav-speaking majority deteriorated sharply in the autumn of 1991, particularly after the two ethnic Albanian parties organised their own referendum, which showed that nearly all Albanians wanted a form of autonomy within what they believed would almost certainly become a Greater Albania. The town of Tetovo has become a regional capital for the Albanians. It is very difficult to imagine the Albanian border between Struga and the Šar mountains having any long-term reality in the event of Albanian autonomy in this region. The future of these people cannot be separated from many complex questions about FYROM itself or, increasingly, from the future of Kosova.

The ostensible policy of the Skopje government at the time of writing is for a non-sectarian multi-ethnic state in which the Albanians are able to play a full part. However, although there is no widespread physical oppression of the Albanians in FYROM as there is in Kosova, the reality is that severe human rights problems are developing under the Gligorov regime, in which very few leading positions are held by ethnic Albanians. Apart from the central problem of manipulated electoral districts, in the social and cultural sphere there is a complete absence of further and higher education in the Albanian language and little effective medical provision. This is in essence a continuation of many years of severe anti-Albanian discrimination under the communist regime in the Yugoslav Socialist Republic. In the 1970s and 1980s the Albanian communities lived a socially and culturally exclusive life, with little intermarriage at any level of society and little economic development. This was in contrast to the Slav-speaking villages where the people were leaving the land for urban jobs in Skopje and elsewhere.[2] In 1989 the former constitution was rewritten to exclude any mention of the Albanian or Turkish minorities as a legitimate component of the state. This process reflected the growing power of the Slav-nationalists, manifested by the re-establishment of the ultra-nationalist Internal Macedonian Revolutionary Organisation (IMRO) the following year. On 1 February 1990, 2,000 Albanians marched through the centre of Tetovo demanding that western FYROM be granted independence and absorbed into a Greater Albania. Though quickly dispersed by paramilitary police, the march indicated the rebirth of a radical nationalist tendency within the Albanian community which has since dominated the ethnic Albanian political agenda. An example of this was the victory of the PDP radicals in the inner-party struggle in 1994.

These serious and structural imbalances in the composition of the ruling élite have continued to the present, and FYROM has carried on many features of the political culture of the former Yugoslav Socialist Republic, especially in the attitudes of the ruling Slav-speakers, who are often closely linked by sentiment and economic interest to Serbia. In particular, the 10,000 strong FYROM army is almost entirely an ethnic 'Macedonian' body. In the autumn of 1994, only about 3.7 per cent of the officers were Albanian.[3] The senior ranks of the police and paramilitary forces are entirely Slav-speaking: only a single Albanian held the rank of Inspector or above in June 1994, and the Albanian political parties have organised a successful draft boycott. Most Albanians feel that in the period immediately after the founding of the state they strongly supported the aspirations of the Gligorov regime, postponing action over their own legitimate grievances inherited from the Tito years in the general interest of securing FYROM's future. They feel without exception that they have received little or nothing from

[2] Hugh Poulton, *Who are the Macedonians?*, London: Hurst, 1995, p. 132.

[3] See James Gow and James Pettifer, 'Macedonia – Handle with Care', *Jane's Intelligence Review*, September 1993.

Skopje in return, and that Gligorov has deferred unduly to the sensitivities of Slav-speakers on issues such as state jobs for Albanians and access to higher and further education. Many Slav-speakers in turn feel bitter over the original Albanian referendum boycott, and a climate of distrust of Albanians is spreading that precludes their full participation in the new state. By the summer of 1994 the number of Albanian-language classes in schools had dropped dramatically since the end of communism; only about 400 teachers remained, compared to nearly 2,500 in the autumn of 1991. The high Albanian-birth rate is a bone of contention among all other ethnic groups. The school curriculum is dominated by material drawn from Slav nationalist sources in the vital discipline of history, and there is virtually no Albanian content. This compares unfavourably with the situation of other much smaller minority groups in FYROM, such as the Roma (Gypsies) for whom provision is made.

The FYROM elections in November 1994 did not assist the integration of the Albanians into the state. The ex-communists in the Skopje PDP, such as Muhamet Halili, held on to their leading positions only with difficulty, and may have little political future if the general deterioration in inter-ethnic relations continues. There have been widespread and well-attested allegations of electoral manipulation against the Albanian leaders, particularly those from the 'radical' wing of the PDP, the main Albanian party. The electoral districts are largely unchanged from communist times, and have been gerrymandered ever since, but in themselves they were insufficient to prevent the election of the new Albanian radicals. The PDP leader Menduh Thaci won his Skopje seat on the first two ballots, but lost it by ten votes on the third ballot after it was claimed that large numbers of Roma were moved into the constituency and paid cash to vote against him.[4] A campaign was started at the same time to institute a new Albanian-language university, in reaction to the failure of the state to allow Albanian-language instruction in Skopje University or the entry of any significant number of ethnic Albanian students (currently

---

[4] See James Pettifer, 'Macedonia: Still the Apple of Discord', *The World Today*, March 1995; James Pettifer, 'The New Macedonia Question', *International Affairs*, July 1992; and Sophie Clement, 'FYROM: The Apparent Stability', *South East Europe Yearbook 1994/5*, Athens: ELIAMEP, March 1995. Most independent journalists who covered the 1994 election believe that the CSCE report was an apologia for ballot rigging.

only 2.7 per cent of the total). On 14 December the building designated for the University in Tetovo was attacked by the FYROM police and ransacked, while in Skopje some 2,000 Slav-speaking students demonstrated against the Albanians' aspirations. Even the most moderate Albanians have threatened to withdraw from the government over the university issue, a campaign that unites all Albanians irrespective of political loyalty. In an interview Arben Xhaferi, the chairman of the PDP(SH) in Tetovo, summed up the general feelings of alienation among the Macedonian Albanians after the election: 'I think the elections have brought a basic change to Macedonia. Despite the most unconstitutional pressure and electoral manipulation by the Interior Ministry, the new forces in the PDP polled many votes, a majority in most places. But our people are becoming ghettoised, there is no progress towards a democratic state. Instead Gligorov is returning Macedonia towards the Slav-Communist bloc dominated by Milosević. There is no future in that road for the Albanians.'[5]

Like several of the new PDP leaders in Tetovo, Xhaferi has strong Kosovar links and works closely with sympathetic friends and colleagues in the leadership of the Democratic League of Kosova in Priština. An important aspect of the contemporary national question is the growing convergence of the struggle with that of the Kosova Albanians. Many 'Macedonian' Albanians received their higher education before 1989 in Priština University, and some teachers in higher education played an important part in developing the underground educational struggle in Kosova after 1989. These include important PDP(SH) radical leaders, such as Nexhmije Palloshi. If education is going to become a key area of struggle for Albanians in FYROM, as it shows every sign of being, the impetus to join in a common struggle with the Kosovars will be that much greater. In 1989-90 2,794 out of 71,505 pupils in higher education in Macedonia were ethnic Albanians. By 1992, the first year of independence under the Gligorov regime, this already poor situation had deteriorated much further, with only 386 Albanians among 22,994 registered students. All classes continue to be held in 'Macedonian' only.[6]

In the first year after the referendum on independence, it was

---

[5] Interview by James Pettifer, Tetovo, 12 December 1994.

[6] Minority Rights Group report, 'The Southern Balkans', London, 1994, p. 27.

possible to feel that, while FYROM remained peaceful and relatively free from the general climate of xenophobia, inter-ethnic violence and militarism affecting so much of northern and central Yugoslavia, there was no reason why tensions between the Albanians and the other groups should not be contained, and that many Albanians might prefer the relative 'prosperity' of FYROM to unity with their poverty-stricken neighbours over the mountains. In western Macedonia, Albanian villages occupy some of the best agricultural land and could in theory attain a relatively high standard of living in the region, with particular opportunities for investment in wine production. But such an optimistic perspective depends on the establishment of a stable and economically viable 'Macedonian' state, and in particular on the restoration of traditional trading patterns with ex-Yugoslavia; in the old state over 60 per cent of Macedonian trade was with Serbia. It is obviously a matter of speculation whether this will be achieved.

The effects of United Nations sanctions have been particularly serious in FYROM. Because of the close integration of its economy with Serbia, most FYROM agricultural production was consumed in Serbia and Bosnia. The currencies of neighbouring states, even the Albanian lek, have established regional credibility and only infusions of capital from the World Bank and Western donor governments have kept the FYROM dinar a viable local currency. In 1994 industrial production collapsed to approximately 30 per cent or less of its 1991 level. Greece closed the border to the south, to the economic detriment of FYROM. There were particular problems with oil supplies, which hitherto had nearly all come through Greece, and with agricultural and timber exports for the same reason. The economy of FYROM has converged with that of Albania, where in 1994-6 rural living standards improved while those of FYROM declined rapidly. Albania received far more foreign aid in 1991-5 than FYROM. Although accurate statistics in this field are not available, it appears that the Albanian national annual income figure doubled in 1994-6 to $550, while that of FYROM fell by half to about $745. In Tirana and the adjacent region the figure is likely to be above $1,000. If this process continues, there will be economic convergence with FYROM in the later 1990s, and the traditional economic arguments used in FYROM against greater Albanian movement towards political unity will have little basis in reality.

The effect on this situation of Greece lifting the border blockade in 1995 remains to be seen. If there is a general Balkan peace agreement and traditional trade patterns in the southern Balkans are re-established, the FYROM economy would be likely to improve. There have been predictions of a great improvement in the position, even if the lifting of blockade is the only change in the current situation. Predictions of a dramatic economic improvement along these lines in FYROM should be treated with caution; there is no reason to suppose that many FYROM businesses will wish to trade with Greece, on political grounds, after all the difficulties since the country's independence. All the structural problems of the FYROM economy will remain, even if cross-border trade improves, and lack of real purchasing power will restrict FYROM's capacity to import Greek consumer goods. Up to the time of writing the main effect of the open border has been to benefit Greece rather than FYROM, giving it easier access to Serbian markets and transport routes and enabling it to import FYROM timber and minerals.

Already, against this dire economic background, there are signs of stronger trade and economic links being forged between Albania and the FYROM Albanians, and a greater radicalisation of the Tetovo leadership. The ex-communist leadership of the Party of Democratic Prosperity, the main Albanian party, was overthrown in a special congress in January 1994 in Tetovo and replaced by a new leadership group then headed by a lawyer of that city, Menduh Thaci. This final victory for the radicals had been prefigured by a long period of inner party turmoil during 1993. In June 1993 Mithat Emic, the chair of the Tetovo PDP municipal organisation, was purged and replaced by hardliners, and in August 1993 members from Tetovo called on the entire party leadership to resign. Although not openly committed to immediate separation and unity with Albania, the new PDP leadership has little real commitment to the ex-communist bureaucracy in Skopje, which is the main component of the current 'Macedonian identity' in FYROM.

The arrest of several prominent Albanians – including the Assistant Minister of Defence, Hisen Haskaj – by Ministry of the Interior police in November 1993 also contributed to this radicalisation. It was alleged against these individuals intended to start a revolution against the Skopje government and establish an Albanian

state called 'Illyridia'. However the allegations were not substantiated in court and accusations of involvement by Western intelligence agencies have been made in efforts to prop up the 'moderate'
PDP leadership. Ethnic Albanians held in goal in connection with
these offences have been subjected to serious beatings and other
human rights violations. Whatever the truth of the conspiracy
allegations, it is clear that the arms plot – whoever perpetrated it
– totally failed in its objectives and was a major factor in the
radicals' takeover of the PDP, three months later, during a winter
of internal turmoil for the party. It was difficult to avoid the
impression that the Interior Ministry made a conscious effort to
discredit the radicals when it appeared, correctly as it turned out,
that they would win control of the party at the January Congress.
Whether or not organisations such as the British MI6 were actively
involved, there is no doubt that their attitude and that of the
Skopje government entirely coincided.

The sentencing of the 'arms plot group' in June 1994 to prison
sentences of between five and eight years further exacerbated
inter-communal tensions: all Albanian members of Parliament
walked out, including PDP 'moderates', and Xelladin Murati
resigned as deputy parliamentary speaker. Four more Albanians
were arrested in March 1994 at Tetovo, in possession of what
was claimed to be 'a large quantity of automatic weapons and
ammunition', and another 'arms plot' was uncovered in Gostivar
in April. The Interior Ministry's *modus operandi* in these plots
strongly resembles that of the so-called IMRO arms plots, where
members of that organisation were implicated in similar seizures
in 1992 in Veles and Ohrid. It should also be noted that there
is a common pattern of activity with the Serbian paramilitary
forces in Kosova, where the Milosević regime continually alleged
the existence of an 'Albanian arsenal' to justify searches of domestic
property and arrests of individual Albanians. Although the alleged
conspirators were later released from prison, the wounds caused
by the 'arms plot' trial in the Albanian communities will take a
long time to heal.

It is uncertain whether the radicals will receive any active
support from Tirana. The Macedonian Albanians have never had
the high-profile, good-quality newspapers or the political and
economic influence in Tirana enjoyed by the Kosovars, or the
links with prominent historical figures in the Albanian nationalist

movement of the early twentieth century such as the Kosovars' Hasan Pristina and Isa Boletini. At the purely practical level they did not have a representative office in Tirana, let alone an embassy, till 1996. Most well-informed members of the Tirana élite only became aware of the leadership struggle within the PDP as a result of bulletins on Albanian television. Ordinary people in the provinces or countryside can have known almost nothing about what was happening, which is a measure of how important control of television was for Berisha: because it is seen as being controlled by his placemen, Albanians assumed from the presentation of the news that the new leadership was artificially installed by Tirana. Although many lowland Albanians would have had little active sympathy with the struggle in Kosova, almost everyone in the country understands its significance and sees clearly the threat from Serbia to the Albanians living there.

It is otherwise with the problems of the FYROM Albanians. They are seen in Albania as deeply Islamic – which is only a part of the truth, although Islam has made great inroads in some communities; as better-off than the Kosovars because of the lucrative tourist industry connected with Lake Ohrid in towns such as Struga; and as protected by the American troops in the UN's preventive peacekeeping force based near Tetovo. However, these assumptions have ceased to be correct. After 1991 the tourist industry in and around Ohrid virtually collapsed, with many hotels there and in Struga empty and bankrupt, and it was not generally understood in Albania that the US troops in FYROM were not mandated to intervene in internal quarrels there. In many of the cafés and markets of Ohrid a *de facto* state of apartheid exists, with a complete separation of Albanians from other ethnic groups, and widespread racist prejudice against them. In 1994-6 many Albanians, had to move – after threats against them from their minority areas in the town of Ohrid, which is an IMRO stronghold – to Struga, which became more or less a homogeneous Albanian town. The image of a harmonious multiracial and multicultural 'Macedonian' state, which the Skopje government has projected internationally with some success, has little reality for the Albanians in the western part of FYROM, but this is not widely appreciated in Albania itself or elsewhere. The violent demonstrations over the education issue in January 1995 seem to have come as a complete surprise to many members of the Tirana government.

President Berisha certainly lent his weight to the radicals in the power struggle within the PDP during the autumn of 1993 that led to the congress victory of the Thaci-Xhaferi faction, but he appeared later to moderate his FYROM policy under American pressure. He has a reasonable personal relationship with President Gligorov of FYROM, based in the classic Balkan manner, on having many common enemies, but it has been eroded by Gligorov's continuous and total failure to act on his numerous promises to bring about human rights improvements for the Albanians. Apart from the economic benefits, it is in the interests of any government in Tirana to encourage a stable and viable 'Macedonian' state as a buffer in its increasingly difficult relations with Greece and a hostile Serbia. As a sign of the importance of relations with FYROM, Berisha posted his government spokesman and key adviser Shaban Murati as Albanian ambassador to Skopje. Murati played a key role in Tirana backing the radicals in the struggle within the PDP in 1993.

Economic factors may also affect the calculations of the Berisha government. More hard currency circulates in Albania than formerly, and with many 'Macedonian' products unsaleable in their traditional markets because of difficulties with the Greek border and UN sanctions against Serbia, producers are prepared to sell them in Albania, even for much lower prices than they would like. There is a ready market there for all food products, and now that the Yugoslav border police have ceded control of the Quaf-e-Thane border crossing to FYROM, these links may grow. A new crossing-point was opened in the spring of 1993 on the southern border near Pogradec. There seems little doubt that Tirana policy continues to be based on the need to keep the FYROM state intact as the lesser evil, even if as the result the ethnic Albanians there endure increasing human rights violations and a restriction on their democratic rights to elect their chosen leaders to parliament. In the extreme case of economic and social collapse in FYROM and outside intervention by Bulgaria, Greece or Serbia, the Albanians would probably turn at once to Tirana. But that stage has not been reached, and a period of uncertainty and stagnation is more likely.

What is likely, for a number of reasons, is that the fate of the Macedonian Albanians will become inextricably linked to the Kosovars of whom there are perhaps as many as 40,000 living in FYROM. In the winter of 1994-5 a number of political initiatives were taken that strongly linked the Kosova cause with that of the Tetovo-based PDP, such as the attempted visit of a delegation of Kosovar parliamentarians to Skopje in December 1994. The delegation was turned back at the border by the FYROM paramilitary police, causing serious diplomatic ructions between the Kosovar leadership in Priština and the Skopje government. There is little doubt that the Kosova president Dr Ibrahim Rugova has worked more and more closely with the radicals in the Albanian leadership, while the Tetovo leaders have seen the extent of cultural repression engineered in FYROM. The question of higher education is likely to be critical in these struggles, since many PDP leaders have, or had, connections with the underground university for Albanians in Kosova. This is linked to the increasingly solid support received by the PDP radicals from young FYROM Albanians, who see qualifications as their only route out of an increasingly poverty-stricken and depressed local economy, and as something that may lead to further study and work abroad.[7]

In May 1994 one of the moving spirits of the Albanian university in Tetovo, Dr Fadil Suliemani, was sentenced to two-and-a-half years in prison for his part in this activity. This caused widespread protests in both FYROM and Albania. The 'liberal' face of FYROM in the international arena was seen to be particularly false and misleading since the penal code under which Dr Suliemani was convicted dated from the Ranković era. Although international human rights organisations made protests and succeeded in obtaining Dr Suliemani's release, there has been little sign of compromise in Skopje, where the government has been under extreme pressure from Slav nationalists over the university issue. It is clear that the Albanians in western FYROM are at the beginning of a long struggle for educational and political rights that may call into question the future of the FYROM state itself. In the autumn of 1995 teaching of about 1,500 students began, but in makeshift conditions and with the granting of any official status for the university seemingly as far away as ever. By the autumn of 1996, conditions had improved by the Albanians' own efforts.

[7] See article by Miranda Vickers in the *Times Higher Education Supplement*, 6 December 1996.

The Albanians of Montenegro

An additional dimension to the national question, albait a minor one, is provided by the Albanian community in Montenegro, which is concentrated in the south-east of the country, adjoining northern Albania. The predominantly Albanian-inhabited southern region was ceded to Montenegro following the Congress of Berlin in June 1878. The inhabitants of Ulcinj protested vigorously against the cession – as did those of Podgorica, which in 1880 had only some thirty Montenegrin inhabitants. The predominantly or wholly Albanian districts of Hoti, Gruda Plava and Gucia were at the centre of the crisis and were contested in fierce fighting. At the time, Albanians were to be found in considerable numbers in the towns of Ulcinj, Bar, Podgorica, Spuzh and Zhablyak in the valleys of the Moracha river and its tributary the Zeta, while the towns and districts of Plava and Gusinje were wholly Albanian. Throughout the region, however, there were many mixed villages comprising both Albanian and Montenegrin families.

In order to prevent a peace accord between the Albanians and the Ottomans which could have resulted in the creation of an autonomous Albania, the other Balkan states continued to keep conflict between them alive. On 8 October 1912 the Balkan Wars began, and the Ottoman army collapsed faster than had been anticipated as the Balkan allies marched deep into Albanian territory. Reluctantly the powers had to acknowledge that the empire was on the point of collapse and the *status quo* could not be maintained. The future of Albania was discussed at the hastily convened Conference of Ambassadors held in London in December 1912, and although the Conference agreed in principle to support the establishment of Albania as a new political entity, it nevertheless awarded the Balkan allies further areas of Albanian-inhabited territory, regardless of its ethnic composition. Large parts of northern and western Albania went to Serbia and Montenegro, Greece received the large southern region of Chameria, and the Albanian state was reduced to the central regions together with the town of Shkoder and its surrounding territory. More than half of the Albanian population was left outside the new Albanian state.

However, following the 1919 peace settlement and the subsequent creation of the Kingdom of Serbs, Croats and Slovenes (renamed Yugoslavia in 1928), tensions remained high between the Montenegrins and the thousands of Albanians remaining on their side of the border. In the former Yugoslavia, the Albanians of Montenegro escaped much of the harassment suffered by their ethnic kin in neighbouring Kosova; there was more tolerance towards them because their numbers were so small and because historically there had been a pattern of social interaction between Montenegrins and Albanians. The two peoples shared similar clan structures and traditions, and there was much intermarriage, especially in the border regions. There are today probably between 75,000 and 90,000 Albanians in Montenegro. According to the 1991 census, the total population of the Republic was 616,327 of whom 61.8 per cent were Montenegrin, 14.6 percent Sandjak Muslims, 9.3 per cent Serbs, 6.6 per cent Albanians, and 4.2 per cent who merely identified themselves as Yugoslavs. As elsewhere in former Yugoslavia the official census figures probably misrepresent and underestimate the number of Albanians, who have many Albanian-language schools and their own newspapers, magazines and cultural organisations. Radio Podgorica broadcasts in Albanian and there are plans for an Albanian TV station. Because they form a small population, Montenegro's Albanians tend to associate themselves politically with the more numerous Muslims, who comprise 13.45 per cent of the Republic's population.

In Montenegro's elections held in December 1990, the Democratic Coalition of Muslims and Albanians won thirteen seats out of a total of 125. However, although in Montenegro Albanians have had greater representation in the Republican government than they have elsewhere in former Yugoslavia, they are not immune to the events in Kosova, and the present Montenegrin government is as concerned about Albanian irredentist activity as are the goverments of Serbia and Macedonia. Cultural links with Albania are strong and Albanian state television is a dominant influence, but there do not appear to be a significant number of Albanians calling for unity with Albania, despite the political and social crisis in Montenegro caused by the war. To date they have been seriously affected by the social, political and economic crisis caused by the Yugoslav war, which has caused more than 75 per cent of Montenegrin GDP to be diverted to military purposes. The Albanians have allied themselves with the Liberal opposition in Montenegro and against the increasing integration of the country's politics with Serbia. But of greater general significance has been the Albanian role in sanctions-busting operations across the border with the Albanian state proper. This subject was the main item on the agenda when the Montenegrin President Momir Bulatovic visited Tirana officially in February 1994. Many Montenegrin Albanians have family links with the northern clans in the Hani-i-Hoti area, as with Kosovar Albanians, and have thus been able to play a key role in the substantial and growing trade across the border and across Lake Shkoder in such scarce and valuable commodities as diesel fuel. Montenegrin Albanians linked politically with the Kosova Democratic League are beginning to have a significant role in its leadership. Some evidence has emerged of attempts at ethnic cleansing by Serbs and Montenegrins in these communities. Montenegrin Albanian associations claimed in May 1995 that some villages – Genica and Pepaj were mentioned as examples – were losing most of their population.[8] There are also small Albanian communities in the south of Serbia itself, mainly centred on the *opstinas* of Presovo and Bujanovac, who are under threat from the local Serbian majority and unable to develop independent political organisations.

Albanian settlements here were artificially absorbed into Nis after 1878. In this context it should not be forgotten that Albania is a small, very weak country, emerging from fifty years of political and economic isolation and finding itself near the epicentre of the Balkan crisis. In the process of democratisation, the strain on the social fabric has been so severe that in the early 1990s society came close to breakdown. The new democratic leaders have widely different views on the possibility of integration with their Kosovar and Macedonian fellow-nationals, but whatever the difficulties and complexities of the situation, there is an underlying sense that a process of gradual Albanian integration will be on the agenda in the future. If the Balkans were a stable region without the political and ethnic conflicts that erupted with the break-up of Yugoslavia, it would be possible to foresee a process of developing economic links and the gradual abolition of border controls within the perspective of a gradually unifying Europe, of which Albania might eventually become a part. The now-defunct Balkan

[8] Voice of America, 5 May 1995.

Co-operation Process, which offered such a perspective, itself drew on some residual elements from the economic aspirations of the pre-war advocates of a Balkan Federation.

Few grounds for optimism remain. Social and economic decline in former Yugoslavia has spread southwards and, given the potential for violent conflict in Macedonia and Kosova, it seems likely that large number of ethnic Albanians there will be drawn into the crisis. Aspects of the Albanians' future are also tied up with the renewal of the Macedonian question, with all its potential for conflict. Although there are many differences of opinion in Tirana over what should be done if violence breaks out in FYROM or Kosova, or both, events would have their own momentum. There would be a large refugee problem, and Albanian military activity could result if only to defend what in those circumstances is likely to become an increasingly disputed and chaotic border with Serbia.

At a more basic human level, given the growth of Kosovar political and economic influence in Tirana, it is difficult to believe that any Tirana government could remain inactive if the Serbs attempted military repression in Kosova along the lines of 1989, or if the Gligorov regime increased repression in the Albanian areas of FYROM to levels last seen in the 1960s.[9] The best that can reasonably be hoped for towards resolving the situation is a process dominated by the formation of informal cultural, social and economic links between the different Albanian communities, unhindered by the external crisis in the Balkans. The developments in FYROM in the autumn of 1995 linked to the peace negotiations, the lifting of the border blockade with Greece, and the attempted assassination of President Gligorov do not fundamentally alter any of the factors in the national question affecting the FYROM ethnic Albanians.[10] The FYROM government has continued with

[9] In this context the public statements made by Dr Berisha on his visits to the United States in September 1995, and to Brussels in October were important. It appears that the Kosova question was not seriously considered in the Dayton, Ohio, peace talks. Because the United States was unwilling, or unable, to deliver any progress on the Kosova issue as part of its diplomatic efforts for a general settlement, the close political links between Albania and the United States under Berisha's government are likely to be modified. Following his election victory in May 1996, Berisha began again to take a noticeably more active and forward policy on Kosova, and he has distanced Albania from the United States.

[10] For an informed view on the significance of the car bomb and assassination attempt,

its divisive policies and on the key issue of education tension rose in the summer and autumn of 1996 after the re-arrest and imprisonment of Dr Suliemani, the Tetovo University rector. The local elections held in October 1996 were again conducted on gerrymandered boundaries, and although the Albanian parties took part, they do not indicate any serious attempt by the ex-communist regime in Skopje to develop democracy in the FYROM state. From the Albanian point of view, the recognition by Belgrade of FYROM under its preferred name of the 'Republic of Macedonia' is another retrograde step.

---

see 'The Birth of a Nation', a review article by Misha Glenny in the *New York Review of Books*, 17 October 1995. Also Hugh Poulton's survey *Who are the Macedonians?*, London: Hurst, 1994.

10

ETHNIC MINORITIES IN ALBANIA
AFTER COMMUNISM

The current position of ethnic minorities in Albania cannot be understood without some consideration of development during the communist period. Enver Hoxha and the Party of Labour promoted, through all the propaganda organs available to them, the view that the construction of socialism and the 'New Man' emerging in Albania had overcome the legacy of minority grievances and religious and ethnic division that had existed before the Second World War. In the Marxist-Leninist view these conflicts were a product of feudalism, capitalism and backwardness, and the new social conditions in Albania after the Liberation – in which, according to the official ideology, a united people had overcome the Fascist occupiers and their collaborators – provided no occasion for ethnic problems to arise. As in many areas of life under the one-party state, the reality was very different, despite the positive discrimination towards minorities pursued up to a certain point under communism. In practice most of the politically sensitive decisions taken by the PLA concerned the Greek minority, who lived predominantly in the south.

Unlike most Balkan states, Albania is to a large extent ethnically homogeneous. The Greek minority were, and are, the only minority in Albania large enough to have political, economic and social significance. This is augmented by their proximity to the neighbouring Greek state which in the past has claimed part of the territory they occupy. Elsewhere in Albania there are 15,000–20,000 Slav-speaking people, mostly in the east near Lake Ohrid and the Peshkopia region; c. 50,000 Roma (Gypsies); c. 80,000 Vlachs, and very small numbers of Jews, Armenians, Turks, Serbs and Montenegrins. Each of the latter communities amounts to no more than a few hundred people, and they have little wider political significance. In essence this has remained the same under pluralism and democracy, although the smaller minorities have tried taking advantage of democracy to organise themselves and assert their interests or, in the case of the Jews, to leave the country altogether.

At various times under communism significant numbers of Russians, Chinese and North Koreans lived in the country, mostly working on joint aid, industrial or military projects, but there is no evidence that any stayed on after the end of their contracts. Enver Hoxha himself was born in the southern town of Gjirokaster, which has a substantial Greek minority. He was thus well aware of the importance of the minorities issue in Albanian politics. During his childhood Greece was claiming much of the adjoining territory, known to Greek nationalists as 'Vorio Epirus', on the basis of decisions taken by the Ambassadors' Conference held by the great powers in December 1912-January 1913. Under the Protocol of Florence in December 1913 Albania had been given its present boundaries, within which at the time there was said to be a Greek minority of about 35,000 – a figure which Greek nationalists have always claimed to be an underestimate. In the years before that, there was bitter inter-ethnic conflict in the minority regions of Korça and Gjirokaster, as chronicled by the French war correspondent René Puaux in his book *The Sorrows of Epirus*.[1] This work, though very pro-Greek, gives a vivid and powerful description of the destruction caused by inter-communal conflict in Epirus during this period.

As early as 1944, Hoxha was careful to start building a constituency within the minority, some of whose members became involved in the Partisan struggle against the Germans alongside the ethnic Albanians. Subsequently a separate minority Partisan formation, the 'Thanos Ziko' battalion, was formed. Speaking in Korça in March 1944, Hoxha commented: 'The people of the Greek minority have proved themselves up to the mark, have fought loyally and have defended the interests of Albania against Greek reactionary circles.'[2] From his writings at the time it appears that Hoxha had little detailed knowledge of the divisions in the

[1] London: Hurst and Blackett, 1918. Puaux has some particularly useful records of events in villages with mixed populations.

[2] Enver Hohxa, *Two Friendly Peoples*, Tirana, 1985, p. 41. See also Basil Kondis, 'The Greek Minority in Albania', *Balkan Studies* (Thessaloniki), vol. 36, no. 1 (1995).

Greek resistance movement, or anticipated the outcome of the Greek civil war. In the latter context, his main concern was to limit any influence that the royalist and right-wing EDES movement of Napoleon Zervas, based nearby in Greek Epirus, might have on the Greek minority. Between 1944 and 1949 the Albanian communists assisted the Greek Left as best they could, but this consisted largely of allowing Albania to be used as a safe refuge for the Democratic Army forces. After the final defeat of the Left in 1949, some of these troops retreated over the border to safety in Albania, and were demobilised at Elbasan.

During these years, the existing Greek minority in Albania was augmented by a significant number of left-wing exiles who later provided a nucleus of trained professional and managerial cadres, especially in Tirana and Vlora; many became technocrats of relatively high status in the communist system, and provided an invaluable asset for Hoxha in his dealings with the culturally conservative majority in rural areas of the south. The 4,000-strong Greek minority population of Vlora was an especially promising recruiting ground for security police agents, and in other parts of the country some ethnic Greeks were generally believed to have had strong links with the *Sigurimi*. Hoxha's policies received wider backing in the south after 1945 than might at first have seemed likely, when the Chams, the ethnic Albanian minority in the Suli region of Epirus in northern Greece, were driven out, mostly by forces loyal to Zervas, and had to take refuge in Albania itself. Hoxha and the PLA leadership were able to claim that the Greek right represented disorder, violence and severe human rights violations for all Albanians, and used the events of the civil war to stop any EDES members from entering Albania, something that also effectively insulated the minority in Albania from the influence of contemporary Vorio Epirot activists. At the Paris Peace Conference in 1946, Hoxha successfully prevented the Greek government from reopening the Vorio Epirus issue, but the general sensitivity surrounding it can be seen from the way it reappeared with the Soviet Union during the Albanian breach with the international communist movement. Hoxha accused Khrushchev of falling under the influence of Greek Vorio Epirus militants, Sophocles Venizelos in particular.

These traumatic events of the 1940s must be considered in some detail, since they form the basis for the policy towards the minority as it evolved subsequently under communism and as in some ways it has continued under the government elected in March 1992. In a period of history when one form of identity is being rejected and a new one explored and constructed, the very existence of minorities has become a psychological threat to many Balkan peoples, as the tragic events to the north of Albania have shown. Although up to the time of writing the horrors of ethnic cleansing and the associated grave human rights violations have been avoided, there is no doubt that the conflicts between the Berisha government and the Greek minority have attained an importance out of proportion to the number of people involved because of the uncertainty over aspects of the new Albanian identity evolving after 1992.

Under communism any separate political organisation by the minority was not allowed, although officially-sponsored cultural and educational activity was possible at local level. Hoxha followed a policy of what amounted to tokenism, with a few favoured members of the minority taking prominent positions within the system, while the cultural and religious identity of the remainder was gradually eroded. Thus for many years after 1948 Spiro Koleka, a native of the southern coastal town of Himara, was a member of the PLA Central Committee and Hoxha's trusted henchman on minority issues. He survived the various purges of the Central Committee, remaining a member until 1976. But at the same time the status of the Orthodox Church was attacked, and in the view of most minority members educational provision in the Greek language fell far short of what was needed for cultural equality. Although some primary education in Greek was available in the minority areas, the actual content was identical to that taught to Albanian children, and whole areas of Greek history, literature and culture were excluded. All history was seen from an Albanian point of view, and in reality little Greek history of any kind was studied. The role of the Illyrians in the ancient history of the region was exaggerated, to the detriment of that of the Greek colonists from Corinth and elsewhere. The criteria used by the communists to classify a minority village were controversial, and in practice many villages with significant numbers of ethnic Greeks were unable to obtain minority classification because a few ethnic Albanians also lived there. This meant that some of the

Greek minority had no access to Greek-language education at all, even in primary schools.

Between the late 1940s and the 1960s this pattern continued. General local pressure on the Greek minority was intensified by occasional staged political trials, such as that, in 1947 of Shefqet Beja, who was accused of working with the CIA to overthrow the communists and reopen the border delineation issue with Greece. When ethnic Greeks were caught attempting to escape to Greece, penalties were severe: for the actual offender execution was common, and his whole family might be condemned to internal exile for many years, usually in the mining camps of northern and central Albania. But when the atheism campaign was launched by the Hoxha regime in 1967, the Greek minority were subjected to much more comprehensive repression, with the closure and subsequent demolition of many churches, burning of religious books, the removal of the last priests from their parishes, and widespread general human rights violations. Christians could not mention Orthodoxy even in their own homes, visit their parents' graves, light memorial candles or make the sign of the Cross. Any form of Easter celebration, such as colouring eggs red for the children, was banned. Many historic churches of great architectural value were vandalised in a way reminiscent of Ottoman attacks on Christian monuments. It was a time of wholesale, ruthless attacks on the very identity of the minority, and many of the intractable problems in minority relationships that have continued into the present are the legacy of the deep mistrust and communal hatred that resulted from the atheism campaigns. This has been handed down through families to people who were children or not even born in the late 1960s, and the adherence of many in the minority to extremist irredentist ideas coloured by revenge can be traced back to this time.

After Hoxha's death in 1985 there was little formal change in the position of the minority under his successor Ramiz Alia. But anecdotal evidence suggests that the attentions of the *Sigurimi* became gradually less pervasive and efficient, particularly in the larger and better organised minority centres such as Saranda and Gjirokaster. At the same time, relations with Greece itself, which have always been a vital factor in the atmosphere affecting the minority, had improved: the state of war between the two countries dating from the Greek Civil War period was ended in 1981, and in January 1985 a road crossing point was opened at Kakavia, north of Ioannina. The Tirana leadership went to some lengths to make this event a symbol of reconciliation; a large Greek-Albanian folkdancing competition was held at the crossing point, and a film of it was made for the television station in Tirana. Some leaders of the PASOK government in Athens, such as the old wartime EAM leader Manolis Glezos, were well acquainted with Hoxha personally and had been in touch with the Albanian leadership for some years.

As a basically secularist party PASOK was not much influenced by Vorio Epirus organisations with their traditionally clerical orientation, or the traditionally anti-Albanian northern Greek bishops such as Metropolitan Sevastianos of Drinoupolis, who were linked to the Greek extreme right and thus scorned by PASOK. Sevastianos was for many years leader of the anti-Hoxha cause in Greece and was seen by many Greek intellectuals as a figure of fun with his extreme views, eccentricity and strong sense of a personal messianic role in the destruction of Albanian communism. This led to President Sali Berisha calling him on one occasion an 'Orthodox Ayatollah'. He has remained since his death in 1994 what he was in life: a serious and important figure who contributed much to the political revival of Hellenism among the minority. His influence over the hearts and minds of the minority continued to grow even after the end of communism, and the new radio station he established in Konitsa has a considerable political following in northern Greece and Albania. The appointment of a successor to Sevastianos posed a problem for the Patriarch in Istanbul, who was under pressure from Athens to appoint a moderate to the post, while local people wanted a man in the Sevastianos mould. In the event local opinion prevailed.

Although obtaining exit visas to visit relations in Greece was extremely difficult, some tourism began to develop under Ramiz Alia; a very few 'politically sound' members of the minority went to Greece, and some reciprocal visits were made, mainly by Greek families with relations in Albania. Despite being closely controlled and supervised, these visits brought some practical improvements for the minority, with closer cross-border contacts and religious books and Greek newspapers beginning to circulate clandestinely in the minority areas. In 1988 it became possible for seriously ill Albanians to be treated in the modern hospitals at Ioannina, and this enabled some minority families to re-establish contact with members they had not seen for decades. By 1988, when the structure of the one-party state was coming under threat, there had been distinct advances in cultural self-awareness in the southern areas, although at the same time ethnic Greeks holding professional and managerial positions in Tirana still appeared content with their lot. Many remained in high Party positions, such as the last communist Defence Minister Simon Stefani and Alia's Deputy Foreign Minister Socrates Plaka, who were both partly of Greek origin, and any visit to the central courthouse or a hospital in Tirana would involve contact with Greek lawyers and doctors. The *Internationale,* in Greek, could occasionally be heard in Tirana being sung over the coffins of old KKE members as their bodies were laid to rest in soil they had no doubt believed would always remain socialist.

As in other areas of Albanian life, the self-organisation of the Greek minority was closely linked with the possibility of forming a democratic opposition to the PLA. Although the normal propaganda of the Albanian regime continued as before during 1989 and early 1990, in practice many of the restraints on cultural and religious activity began to disappear during this period. A key time was the last week of December 1989 and the first week of January 1990. After the founding of the opposition Democratic Party the previous month, the draconian border-security system that had prevailed along all Albanian borders for a generation broke down, with an immediate exodus of hundreds of refugees into Greece and other neighbouring countries. In the south many ethnic Greeks fled over the border as part of the wider pattern of population movement. It was in severe winter weather that the refugees moved into northern Greece without adequate clothing, shoes or food and were warmly welcomed. Ordinary Greeks were spurred to acts of charity in their horror at what the exodus revealed about conditions across their northern border. In small towns such as Filiates, near the Albanian village of Konispol but on the opposite side of the border, many family links remained to help bring the new arrivals closer in their moment of need. It was inevitable that the old prohibitions on independent organisation would soon collapse, and within three months of this time churches were being reclaimed by the general population, often with the assistance of Muslim Albanian neighbours, just as

Orthodox Greeks helped ethnic Albanians to repossess the central mosque in Korça in March 1990.

A human rights organisation to promote the interests of the Greek minority, Omonia, had been founded in February 1990, and received approval as a social organisation from the Ministry of Justice on 22 February in Tirana, under the name 'The Democratic Union of the Greek Minority'. An inaugural rally was held at Jergucat near Gjirokaster on 28 February, where both Greeks and Albanians spoke and stressed the contribution Omonia could make to a plural society. Omonia's formal origins in terms of the PLA are still not clear, but there seems to have been a close relationship between some of the founders and dissident members of the PLA of Greek origin who at various times had either left the Party voluntarily or been expelled. In turn, some of these people were from Greek Civil War exile families, and Marxist in their general orientation. A second much larger group was to emerge in later years, which did not have these links and whose politics and general cultural outlook were much closer to the traditional Greek hard right, but in 1990 they had yet to appear. These were days of hope and optimism in these communities; for outsiders it was enjoyable and often moving to visit the Drinos valley and find ethnic Greeks and Albanians working together in an atmosphere of progress and freedom, and reopening Bektashi *tekkes* and Orthodox churches without intercommunal prejudice or suspicion, let alone the open enmity that began to develop in the mid-1990s.

However, it soon became clear, despite Omonia's success in fulfilling its original aims, that much remained to be done before the Greek minority could have a secure and stable place in Albanian society. The church was quickly able to regain its surviving buildings, although many were in disrepair after being put to crude agricultural or industrial use; the principal church in the minority centre of Dervican, one of the most important ethnic Greek villages, was used for years as a store for agricultural machinery, and the eighteenth-century interior frescoes were vandalised beyond repair. As in other denominations, there were almost no indigenous priests available, and visiting clergy from Greece and elsewhere were required. For instance the first priest at Dervican, came to Albania from Sicily in 1991 and could speak hardly any Greek on his arrival. Other priests came from Cyprus and from distant areas of the Greek diaspora. This has led to one of the most difficult conflicts between the minority and the government when the Patriarch of the Orthodox Church in Istanbul appointed an ethnic Greek, Yannulatos, as head of the Albanian church.[3]

Yannulatos is a highly educated man, a born conciliator and diplomat, who had spent part of his previous career in high administrative posts in the Church. He was well suited to the difficult task of repairing and developing relations between the Muslim-dominated DP government and the Church hierarchy. He is free of the residual irredentist ideology which affects the thinking of many of the Greek bishops, especially those from northern Greece, and has made a priority of the education of locally-born ethnic Albanian priests. It remains to be seen whether these new priests will accept his authority fully; trouble in connection with a church in Elbasan declaring independence from his diocese in 1996 on nationalistic grounds suggests that there are still many difficulties to be resolved.

Unemployment rose rapidly in the ethnic Greek areas as elsewhere with the total collapse of the collective farm system in 1990-1, and consequently emigration remained high. Some areas populated by minorities, such as the coastal strip between Himara and Saranda, had been known as high emigration areas since before the Second World War; the coastal strip, though fertile, was narrow, and the adjacent interior land was poor, and thus the area could not support a large and growing population. Despite efforts by the PLA to improve the agricultural economy by large-scale fruit and olive plantations, such as the 'Terraces of Lukova' project in the 1960s and '70s, what amounted to mass emigration resumed with the demise of the communist state. In spite of being productive agriculturally and with a much better climate than most of Albania, and being near Corfu and potential markets, the Lukova project suffered particularly from the collapse of the

[3] For more on the Orthodox Church see Chapter 5, which deals with the religious aspects. Greek books and newspapers were able to circulate freely, and the informal use of Greek currency became common, but institutional change was much more difficult especially in education. This had been a difficult area for the minority ever since King Zog closed down all Greek-language education well before the Second World War. Under communism, primary schools and some secondary schools existed in the larger centres, but the lack of higher education in Greek and the exclusively Albanian nature of the curriculum with little opportunity to study Greek literature or philosophy, were recurrent grievances.

collective farm system and the communist state. Forced labour from criminals and youth pioneers had been used to construct it and associated complex irrigation works, which soon collapsed; there was not enough local free labour to pick the olives and fruit and look after the plantations. For the minority, being ethnic Greek and Orthodox, it was much easier to obtain visas and find work and a stable position in Greece than for their Muslim compatriots, and many villages in this region quickly lost almost all their young men and became refuges for the elderly, economically unviable and dependent on emigrant remittances. Large state fruit plantations reverted to nature, with only an occasional shepherd to be seen grazing sheep under the decaying vines and peach trees.

The highly sensitive position of the Greek minority led to many political tensions in addition to the existing conflicts between the central authorities in Tirana and Omonia as a political organisation. Although the regular granting of visas issued by the Greek embassy in Tirana in 1992 meant the flow of emigration could proceed, social tension remained at a tolerable level, the flow increased considerably in the winter of 1992–3, mainly because of the Berisha government's programme of land privatisation. This involved what many ethnic Albanians in the south considered excessively favourable treatment of the Greek villages. The generally accepted reason for this was the fact that the ethnic Albanians from the minority areas lacked political influence in Tirana; as southerners and Tosks they were seen as having nearly all been closely linked with the communist regime while the Greeks were largely anti-communist. Berisha may have felt that generous treatment of the Greeks' claims would not only settle some local political scores but help bring visas and investment from Greece. However, the reality was that land-hungry Albanian villages were confronted with a redistribution that gave fertile acres to ethnic Greeks who did not cultivate them because they were absent working in Greece.

Meanwhile Albanians, often with much larger families if they were Muslim, did not have enough land to feed their families adequately, or enough capital or skills to invest in non subsistence forms of agriculture, even assuming that markets for their goods might have been found. A common feature of life in this region was the gradual impoverishment of the Muslim villages since the end of communism, particularly in the area south of the Butrint archaeological site on the coast. Life here is as primitive as in many of the more remote parts of northern Albania, although with the redeeming features of a good climate and more fertile soil. The little villages perched on hummocks above the drained marshlands have become prisons, from which the young are unable to emigrate because visas to work in Greece are unobtainable unless they renounce their religion, at least nominally, and all there is for them to do locally is scratch a living from the marshlands and try to breed horses to sell in Greece for a little hard currency. These conditions have led resentment against Greece and the Greek minority.

On the opposite side of the political divide, similar forces are at work, although the ethnic Greek communities are divided politically rather than economically. In November 1992 the mayor of Dervican was sentenced to six months in prison for raising the Greek flag in the village on '*Ochi*' ('no') day, which celebrates the beginning of Greek participation in the struggle against the Axis invasion of the Balkans. He had also renamed a street in the village after Antonis Samaras, the former Greek Foreign Minister, who had strongly defended the rights of the minority under the previous government. Vorio Epirus organisations in Greece, together with some more mainstream politicians and newspapers, began to express concern publicly about the deteriorating relations between the two communities. Religion provided, as always in the region, a regular supply of conflicts. Followers of Sevastianos and other extreme right-wing clerics had begun to work among the minority villages, putting out Vorio Epirus propaganda calling for border revision and the union of most of Albania south of the Shkumbi river with Greece. In some villages they were beginning to win followers, so that by the spring and summer of 1993 surveillance of the population by the security police was noticeably on the increase. In August 1993, the authors found that the unwanted attentions of these people caused them considerable difficulty in conducting their research work in the Vjoses valley.

As far back as April 1992, Sorit Qiriazati, then chairman of Omonia, wrote an open letter to the Greek Prime Minister, Constantine Mitsotakis, calling for an autonomous region to be established in Vorio Epirus, and for substantial Greek government help in the economic and social development of the region. The Omonia leaders understood better than the Athens government

the precarious nature of their present freedoms and the need for
greater constitutional rights than the old Albanian constitution
gave them. The rejection of these proposals by the Athens government, understandable as it was, passed the political initiative
generated by Omonia to the radicals who were beginning to
argue that only *Enosis* – union with Greece – would bring the
necessary central government commitment to the area.[4]

In the spring of 1993 the atmosphere worsened with the arrest
and expulsion from Albania of a Greek priest, Archimandrite
Chrysostomos, for alleged subversive, anti-Albanian activities;
Tirana accused him of abusing his ministry by preaching *Enosis*. In
August Greek-owned shops in Saranda were attacked, and in
September some Greek-language schools in the town were closed
by central government decree, an irony in view of the size of
the Greek minority population and the large Greek church being
built in the centre of the town near the seafront. In October,
Amnesty International published a report in London condemning
the pattern of abuses committed by the Albanian police against
the Greek minority, and in November tension rose further following the expulsion of 2,100 ethnic Albanians from Greece.
The Berisha government claimed that in Albania ethnic minority
members were allowed to stay, even if they lacked documentation.

After the return of Andreas Papandreou's PASOK to power
in Greece, some effort was made by both governments to improve
relations. PASOK had always had much more cordial relations
with the Albanian leaders than any other Greek government: this
went back to the early 1980s and the beginning of greater trade
and cultural exchanges. Berisha himself had seen the ex-Foreign
Minister of New Democracy, Antonis Samaras, as personally
responsible for many of the problems in bilateral relations since
1991. In December 1993 Berisha commented:

> 'There will be better relations with Greece. The visit of Papoulias
> [the Greek Foreign Minister] was of great value to us. It will
> be of great benefit to Greek-Albanian relations. We will stick
> to the values of the Copenhagen Charter [the Helsinki Final
> Accord] as regards the rights of the minority. Samaras has created
> all the problems here, and with Skopje. Mitsotakis was very
> willing to be flexible but Samaras had much more influence

[4]. Minority Rights Group Report, *The Southern Balkans*, London, 1994, pp. 34-5.

over New Democracy.[...] It is Greek policy to keep the Vorio Epirus question alive so that it can be used to take pressure off any number of problems the Greeks have internally.'[5]

In 1994 relations between the Greek and Albanian governments deteriorated sharply, with rhetoric of a type that recalled the days of Hoxha beginning to dominate the media in both countries. The Berisha government accused Greece of working with Serbia to undermine the Albanian state, while Albania was seen in the Greek popular press as little more than part of a covert Islamic conspiracy to encircle Greece. In April 1994 the first armed violence broke out, when ethnic Greek paramilitaries, allegedly based on Greek soil, attacked a small military post near Gjirokaster, killing two Albanian soldiers. In April five of Omonia's leaders were arrested and tried for complicity in the attack, while Greece vetoed a loan to Albania by the European Union of 35 million ECU in protest.

At the same time, the Tirana government began to move landless Muslim peasants from the north of the country into empty Greek land and Greek villages in the extreme south of Albania near Konispol, which the minority saw as the beginning of 'ethnic cleansing' in the area. A purge of ethnic Greeks in the professions in Albania continued in 1994, with particular emphasis on the law and the military. But by far the most serious event for the minority was the opening in September of the Omonia trial in which the five defendants were charged with treason and spying charges and convicted. The trial was popular with most Albanians but caused outrage in Greece. International observers regarded it as deeply flawed in its procedure, a particular focus of criticism being the use of secretly-filmed SHIK videotapes of Omonia meetings, alleged by the prosecution to show treasonable activities but which the defence claimed were faked. For Greeks right across the political spectrum the whole event was little more than a traditional totalitarian show-trial.

In October 1994 President Berisha announced a provision in his new constitution that would restrict the right of Greek nationals to hold positions in the Albanian Orthodox Church, but it did not come into force because the constitutional proposals were defeated in the November referendum. At the end of 1995, the

[5] Interview by Miranda Vickers with President Sali Berisha, 6 December 1993.

position of the minority remained insecure and fraught with many dangers. Although relations with Greece improved somewhat from the nadir reached at the time of the Omonia trial, they remain essentially poor, even though the defendants were released in February 1995. Another visit to Tirana by the Greek Foreign Minister, Kostas Papoulias, in April 1995 was a success; the diplomatic atmosphere improved and an agreement was signed to set up joint working parties to address a number of contentious issues. American diplomatic influence appears to have been decisive in this rapprochment. However, the economic issues of visas, land use, investment and illegal immigration remain as difficult as ever. The expulsion from Greece of hundreds of thousands of Albanians in the aftermath of the Omonia trial verdict is likely to have serious long-term effects on the Albanian economy, with remittances from migrant workers in Greece contributing perhaps as much as one-third of Albania's foreign currency income. In Greece there are many different views on the correct policy to pursue over this issue. Some special interest groups in the Greek business community, such as the citrus growers of the north-west and the building industry employers, would welcome a generous visa policy for Albanian migrant workers, since the cheap and docile labour they provide gives a considerable boost to their profits, but many lower-paid Greek workers, e.g. in the catering industry, are bitterly opposed to any Albanian immigration at all.

Although an individual ethnic Greek may prosper in Albania, the future of the whole community is unclear and will depend on the state of bilateral relations. With the general improvement in the Balkan atmosphere in the autumn of 1995 following the Dayton peace agreements, both governments accelerated negotiations over outstanding issues. The United States used its dominant influence in the region to press for a continued rapprochement between Athens and Tirana. This resulted in a new 'Friendship and Cooperation Agreement' that was signed in March 1996 by the Greek President Kostas Stephanopoulos while on an official visit to President Berisha in Tirana. It included some advances on previous documents of its kind, with the Albanians giving written guarantees about the educational and human rights of the Greek minority in Albania, while the Greek side agreed to state its intention to legalise Albanian workers in Greece. Various procedures were agreed for regular military contacts, and both sides proclaimed the inviolability of existing borders.

The Greek government rejected the pleas of the Albanian opposition for support in the May 1996 elections, and gave vigorous support to Berisha's re-election campaign. President Stephanopoulos was sent to Tirana again on an official visit just before polling day, with promises of visa agreements. Given the importance of Greek remittances to many Albanian family economies, this may have been a significant factor in voting decisions. Another little-known issue is the need of the Orthodox Church for good relations with Tirana in negotiations over the return of pre-1939 Church-owned land from the state.

It remains to be seen what the outcome of these policy changes in Athens will be. The undemocratic way the May election was conducted made the open support it had given to President Berisha an embarrassment for the Simitis government, which was widely criticised in the Greek press for appearing to endorse a nascent one-party state. There is little sign up till the time of writing of any practical activity on the ground to boost Greek-language education in Albania, although the Greek minority representatives in parliament are almost the only Opposition members to have taken their seats.[6] It is difficult to imagine what formula any Greek government could devise that would make large-scale Albanian immigration acceptable to public opinion. In general, it may well be that this agreement will turn out to be yet one more diplomatic product of the period of post-Dayton optimism that has little long-term practical significance or effect.

Other minority groups in Albania

Other minorities in Albania generally fared well under communism, much as the Greeks did in the early years, but without the ferocity of repression that accompanied the conflict with the Greek Orthodox Church after the pro-atheism campaigns began in 1967. After the Greeks the Vlachs are the largest minority, comprising perhaps 80,000 people – exact figures are uncertain. The Vlachs are predominantly transhumant shepherds living in the Pindus

---

[6] There were allegations in the Tirana press in July 1996 of coercive state pressure on the individuals concerned.

mountains of Greece, the Lake Prespa region and areas of southern Albania. Their Latin-based language is akin to modern Romanian.[7] Most Albanian Vlachs live in two well-defined areas, one around the town of Korça and the village of Voskopoja, and the south-east highlands between Korça and Polican, and the other near Vlora. The destruction of their traditional patterns of pastoral life by collectivisation caused them to be relatively assimilated under communism. The agriculture of the Vlora hinterland underwent great changes, since the draining of the Myzeqi marshes provided large new areas of fertile land. There was an influx of settlers from other regions, many originally northerners brought to the area as part of the forced labour system. Almost everybody working in such labour camps as Maliqi near Korça and Tepelena near Gjirokaster was a Zogist or Ballist northerner. When they were released from the labour camps they were often forced to work and reside in the Myzeqi village settlements. Settlement patterns had already been disrupted there before the Second World War by refugees from Kosova and Chameria. As the result of changes to traditional Vlach agricultural and social patterns during this process, many Vlachs had to find work in the new industrial centres being established in Vlora itself. Likewise, the Sarakatsan transhumant pastoralists – a colourful feature of Vlora life in the 1930s – have been completely assimilated.

However, more of Vlach life and culture has survived in the south-eastern highlands, where the language withstood the enforced standardisation of the communist period, at least as a means of domestic communication. The Vlachs, having no irredentist backers in a neighbouring state, did not pose the same threat to established Albanian culture and national identity as the Greek minority and they had no particularly strong religious identity to be destroyed during the atheist period. In the south-eastern mountains they had been only marginally and inefficiently integrated into the collectivised system, and in practice PLA officials could not easily control their activities. They suffered the same cultural repression as other small minorities, in so far as their language had no official status and their tradition of travelling to Bucharest for higher education had been closed to them. With the end of communism

---

[7] For a detailed study of the Vlachs see T. Winnifrith, *The Vlachs*, London: Duckworth, 1981, and *Balkan Fragments*, London: Duckworth, 1995; see also an article on the Vlachs by Miranda Vickers in *The European*, 4-10 April 1996..

the Vlachs began to reassert their identity: a Vlach association was formed in 1990 and a Vlach Congress was held in Tirana in 1992. Although there was some depopulation from the south-eastern highlands after 1990, it was on nothing like the scale suffered by the northern mountain areas, and Vlach life and culture seem secure there for the time being.

The Roma or Gypsies, are a minority of similar size to the Vlachs, and are not localised. Most Albanian towns have a traditional Gypsy quarter – in Tirana near the railway station, in Korça encompassing the heart of the old town, and in Shkoder near the Rosafat castle river-bridge. In the Ottoman period certain trades, particularly metalworking, became Gypsy specialities and have remained so till the present. As in many countries, Gypsies suffer various forms of discrimination and tend to be at the lowest economic level, although with the return of capitalism this has not been a straightforward process; there are some Gypsies in Albania with considerable wealth although this is not always reflected in their living conditions. Albanian Gypsies speak a dialect of the Gypsy language Rom, with many unique words; they call mainstream Albanians the *Gaxhie,* while the Albanians refer to them as *Yevgjet* or, less politely, *Lapse.* There has been no easily identifiable change in the position of the Roma since the end of communism, except that the collapse of the planned economy has tended to encourage traditional Gypsy trades. Gypsies are beginning to make their presence felt in the nascent recycling industry in Albanian cities – they collect metal cans and bottles for sale in Greece – and in the booming motor-car trade.

Albania's Jewish community has never numbered more than 1,000 during the twentieth century. It was centred on Vlora, where there had been Jewish settlement since late antiquity and where the only Albanian synagogue, destroyed during the First World War, was to be found. The community was granted official recognition only in 1937. Just before the Second World War King Zog granted political asylum to nearly 200 Jews fleeing from Nazi Germany and Austria, and Serbian and Croatian Jews also found sanctuary in Albania later. During the German occupation, the Jews went into hiding, sheltered by Albanian families, and thus the community survived almost intact. Under the communist regime they suffered the same religious persecution as Muslim, Catholic and Orthodox when religion was officially abolished in 1967. Nearly the whole Jewish population migrated to Israel in 1991; this was for economic reasons and not because they had suffered any persecution or prejudice from their Albanian neighbours. At a time when many Albanians were desperate to leave their homeland and seek a better life abroad, the Jews were fortunate to have in Israel a country that would welcome them.[8] It is said that a very small number of families have returned to Tirana, although it seems unlikely that they will ever become a community again.

The Slav minorities – the Serbs, Montenegrins and Bulgarian/ Macedonians – are among the most isolated inhabitants of the country, living mainly in the remote mountainous north-west, in the Diber region around Peshkopia, and near the shores of Lakes Ohrid and Prespa. About 2,000 Serbs and Montenegrins have traditionally lived in and around Shkoder, with settlement centred on the remote village of Vraka, east of the Shkoder-Koplik road. Most of this community arrived in Albania only in the Zogist period after 1926 and between 1938 and 1948. Relations with Serbia and Montenegro were much better under Zog than at other periods, and cross-border population movement was possible. The Vraka land is poor and had hitherto been underdeveloped, and probably the colonists from Montenegro were welcome there because, unlike local Albanians, they were able to use motor vehicles and the iron plough to help work the difficult land.

One of Albania's greatest poets, Migjeni (1911-38), was an ethnic Serb from Shkoder who, despite being sent by his parents to study at the Serbian Academy in Monastir (present-day Bitola), returned to Shkoder where he devoted his short life to the study and writing of Albanian literature. Despite its small size, this Slav-speaking minority has produced other important figures in Albanian life, including some of the early communist leaders such as Koçi Xoxe. After freedom of movement across the border became possible, the Shkoder community began to leave Albania for Montenegro, and between March and December 1991 Vraka, Borici and the surrounding area were more or less abandoned. The Slavs near Macedonia, known as the *Gorani,* remained in their traditional homes, and have continued to live there. The ethnic balance of

[8] For further reading see Harvey Sarner, *The Jews of Albania,* New York: Brunswick Press, 1992.

the Shkoder districts was disturbed by the Hoxha land programme, with mountain villages near the borders subsidised and over-populated for national defence reasons. Some villages near Vraka received newcomers evicted from the Tropoja region as the communist regime disintegrated. These were people who had originally been moved to Tropoja and other border regions as part of Hoxha's policy of boosting local population levels for defence and security reasons. The Yugoslav authorities attempted to settle them in Kosova, but this was resisted by the people themselves, who believed they would be sent to Belgrade. They were made welcome in Montenegro but the authorities there were unable to find them suitable land. Some family members usually remained behind to preserve land rights. Many of these people returned to Vraka after the outbreak of war in Bosnia in 1992, having discovered that they were unable to secure either land or jobs.

Although the community has not been restored to its former size, it possesses an independent identity, and in 1991 a Montenegrin Association was formed in Shkoder. Many members of the community have been active in smuggling across the border into Montenegro and Serbia, since they can easily obtain visas for former Yugoslavia; this has not contributed to their popularity locally. Their long-term future remains to be seen but meanwhile there have been repeated accusations of human rights violations and police violence against this minority. It is difficult to know whether they have any substance, but they have been taken up by Belgrade in anti-Albanian propaganda, and may indeed have stemmed from there originally.

A Dutch human rights activist interviewing a senior Shkoder police officer as part of an inquiry into the situation said to him that many members of the Slav minority were alleged to have been beaten in the Shkoder police station. The policeman replied cheerfully that beatings were common for anyone arrested and taken to his police station, and suggested breaking off the interview and going to the café for a *raki*. The high-minded interviewer then claimed that these people had been beaten twice. The policeman then surmised gently that they must have been slow to answer questions, and left for the café on his own. In May 1995 a new organisation to represent the rights of the Slav-speakers was set up, but almost immediately the houses of its two main leaders in Shkoder were attacked with firebombs. There is an obvious danger that the fate of this small group of people will be manipulated by extremist nationalist politicians in Belgrade and Tirana for their own ends.

The *Gorani* group of Slav-speakers in Albania numbers about 15,000 people, thinly spread in border regions between Korça and Peshkopia. In some places the population is perhaps 60 per cent Albanian and 40 per cent self-styled 'Macedonians'. They are also known by the Albanians as *Bulgareci*, and for some, like the people living around Shishtaveci, this is particularly appropriate since they speak what is in essence a dialect of Bulgarian. The same is true of some people around Lake Ohrid, although others speak a dialect more akin to Serbian. Both groups are residual elements of populations dating back to the medieval Bulgarian and Serbian empires in the Balkans and, in common with other minorities, had no independent organisation under communism and suffered cultural discrimination. Like the Serbs and Montenegrins, some *Bulgareci* eventually crossed into FYROM to find work after the collapse of communism in Albania. In the summer of 1991 Radio Korça began broadcasting in 'Macedonian' for several hours a day, and in September the Minister of Justice approved the creation of a political association for the Slav-speaking community, at first called Bratska (Brotherhood) and later renamed Prespa. The Association mounts campaigns for more educational provision in the Slav language and more local control for the community over its own affairs.

By 1996 Prespa had grown into an organisation of seventeen branches. These included members from large cities such as Berat, Tirana and Korca, as well as the Prespa villages and the traditional Slav-speaking areas further north along the border with FYROM. A conference was held in February 1996 at Dolna Gorica in Albania, which was notable for the attendance of various high-level FYROM officials, who clearly see the promotion of a 'Macedonian' minority in Albania as a counterpart to Greek influence based on a resident minority. It appears that hitherto few of the educational and cultural ambitions of the Slav-speakers have been realised. The Albanian government claims that this is a result of resource constraints, while Prespa has accused the government of lack of commitment to multicultural education. It appears that in the Prespa villages at least some Slav-language education takes place though this is mostly at primary level, much as it was under communism.

Before 1939, some of the *Gorani* villages were strongholds of support for the Internal Macedonian Revolutionary Organisation (IMRO), which may prejudice Tirana government officials against the emergence of much independent 'Macedonian' political organisation in Albania. The *Gorani* wartime history also presents difficulties; the Albanian partisans under Haxhi Lleshi actually ruled part of modern FYROM around Diber in 1944, and encountered opposition from pro-Bulgarian IMRO supporters in some villages. The degree to which many Albanians think of communism as a Slav phenomenon cannot be over-emphasised, and may always restrict Prespa's political standing and influence.

There are about 800 Armenians in Albania, in Tirana and Vlora. Most came to Albania after the genocide in Anatolia during the First World War, although a few claim descent from administrators in the Ottoman Empire. Most Armenians supported the partisans during the Second World War, and Hoxha had good personal relations with some of the community's leaders. One example, Dr Asdurian from Vlora, became Hoxha's personal dentist (his son, Dr Emil Asdurian, founded the new 'Armenians of Albania Association' in 1991). The community was consequently spared some of the rigours of the government's Albanianisation campaigns – being allowed, for instance, to keep the characteristic '-*ian*' name ending. Most Albanian Armenians are highly educated, and a significant number are in the legal and medical professions. King Zog's personal physician, Mokin Poturljan, was Armenian. Because of its small size, the community, whose historic church belongs to the Orthodox tradition, have tended to marry into mainstream Albanian society, choosing Orthodox Albanians as partners rather than Muslims or Catholics because of their doctrinal compatibility. The travel and cultural restrictions imposed by the communist state were highly irksome to this naturally cosmopolitan people. In early 1990 the Armenians had formed close links with the energetic and wealthy Armenian community in Thessaloniki, which provided gifts of educational materials. In 1993-5 many leading members of the community emigrated, but those who went abroad to take courses of advanced study mostly said that they would eventually return to Albania. It remains to be seen how many will actually do so, given their generally marketable skills and the serious decline in employment opportunities offered by the state medical system. In these or similar circumstances the remaining members of the minority could become absorbed, since there are too few of them to support a church or a school, even in Tirana, although some education in the hitherto banned Armenian language has been attempted.

The Cham question

The region of Chameria extends from the Ionian coast to the Ioannina mountains in the east, and in the south almost as far as the Preveza gulf. Only seven Cham villages, centred on the village of Konispol, are in Albania itself. The name is believed to come from the ancient Illyrian term for the Thyamis river, which traversed the territory of the tribe of Tesprotes. Chameria was part of the Roman empire before being conquered by the Byzantines, and in the thirteenth century it became part of the Epirus despotate. In the second half of the fourteenth century it was included in the Albanian despotate of Arta. After the Ottoman invasion in the fifteenth century it was first in the *sandjak* (municipality) of Delvina, then in that of Ioannina. In the seventeenth and eighteenth centuries the mostly Albanian population of northern Chameria, from Konispol to the Gliqi river, was forcibly converted to Islam, while the people living south of the Gliqi down to Preveza bay remained Orthodox Christians.

During the Albanian independence struggle spanning the end of the nineteenth and beginning of the twentieth century, the Chami fought with the other Albanian regions against the Ottomans. In 1913 the London Conference of Ambassadors allotted the region to Greece, and in the 1920s the Greek government set about trying to deport Albanian Muslims from it in order to give their lands to Greeks deported from Asia Minor after the war of 1922. In 1941 the Cham leader Daout Hoxha was murdered, allegedly by Greek police, and his head was displayed in various border villages.[9] In 1944, in an attempt to establish an ethnically pure border region, the Greek government unleashed a reign of terror in Chameria, as the result of which some 35,000 Chams

---

[9] *Eastern Europe Newsletter*, vol. 8, no. 8, 13 April 1994. See also *Blue Guide to Albania*, p. 154, and the novel *Captain Corelli's Mandolin* by Louis de Bernières, London: Secker and Warburg, 1984.

fled to Albania and others to Turkey. Greek governments have always claimed that the Chams were active collaborators with the German occupation forces, but whatever the truth of this allegation, which has been partly supported by some of the British liaison officers seconded to the Greek Resistance movements, the forced movement of the entire population has left a lingering sense of injustice in an entire Albanian community. In a minor way this has contributed to poor bilateral relations between the Albanian and Greek states.[10]

After the collapse of communism, the Chams in Albania set up the 'Chameria Association', dedicated to the return of their expropriated lands in north-western Greece. The then Greek Foreign Minister, Karolas Papoulias, said in the summer of 1991 that these demands should be settled by a bilateral commission, but there is no chance of forming one because under current Greek law legal means of challenging requisition (or expropriation) of land by the Greek state do not exist.[11] Meanwhile the issue has been taken by the Tirana government to the International Court of Justice, in an effort to secure financial compensation at least for lost Cham property and land. There has been little progress to date.

---

[10] See *Australian Macedonian Newsletter*, 6 February 1996.

[11] See Nigel Clive, *A Greek Experience, 1943-45*, London, 1985, and Arthur Foss, *Epirus*, London, 1978. Also Manda and Kondis (ed.), *The Greek Minority in Albania – A Documentary Record*, Thessaloniki: Institute of Balkan Studies, 1994, and James Pettifer, 'Albania, Greece and the Vorio Epirus Question', *The World Today*, London, August 1994.

11

INTERNATIONAL RELATIONS
AND DEFENCE

In all states, whatever their political or economic system, foreign and defence policy have a close, organic relationship. However, in Albania under communism this relationship was much closer than in many other rigidly organised communist states. After the dispute and then the break with the Soviet Union in 1960-1 and the similar process with China a decade later, isolation was the keynote of Albanian foreign policy, and security policy was formed by it, at times almost exclusively. The 1976 socialist constitution formally forbade the establishment of foreign bases or the stationing of foreign troops on Albanian soil.

In many of their aspects these processes were rooted in the immediate post-war period, when the break with Tito's Yugoslavia and the subsequent quarrel between the latter and the Soviet Union meant that Albanian communism had a distorted and artificial series of foreign policy priorities. This followed what had seemed to be stable relationships between a small client state and a larger patron such as had existed with Italy before the Second World War, and after the establishment of communism of Albania with the Soviet Union and later China. For the Soviets in these years the main strategic element in the relationship was its ability use Albanian ports on the Adriatic coast for naval purposes, culminating in the construction of the large submarine base at Sazan island in the Bay of Vlora in 1957. Albania thus provided valuable refuelling and naval service facilities in a period when naval confrontation in the Mediterranean was an important element of superpower rivalry, and when the break with the Soviet Union finally came, Nikita Khrushchev threatened to occupy the facilities with Soviet troops; had the Cuban missile crisis not intervened,

209

Soviet troops could possibly have been involved in military operations on Albanian soil at that time.

In earlier times the link had seemed to be Albania's principal guarantee of international security. The communist regime in Albania had secured Soviet protection at a time when it was still subject to covert attempts to overthrow it by Western intelligence agencies; the state was militarily weak and relations with neighbouring Yugoslavia were poor. Albania had joined the Warsaw Pact in 1955 but left it in 1968, and with the split in the world communist movement it moved into a close relationship with China. After Mao Tse-tung died in 1976, Chinese aid was progressively reduced.

The period of isolation

When these client relationships with superpowers ended, it was necessary to rely for defence on the country's own resources and in consequence an arbitrary pattern of international relations developed. Little military aid was received from any source after 1978, and the country had to maintain itself in isolation from both NATO and the countries of the Warsaw Pact. Links within the Non-Aligned movement were in practice restricted because of the movement's domination by Yugoslavia. The solution was found in a mixture of Marxist notions of people's war; hence defence was limited to the concept of an armed people and the construction of hundreds of thousands of bunkers all over the country, coupled with the ideological mythologisation of the wartime Partisan struggle in resistance to the Nazis. In many East European countries this mythologising process had taken place to some extent, with 'good' history being a representation of the people and the communists seemingly united together in a common struggle against an evil occupier from outside. This helped to legitimise the communist present. In this, however, few states went to such lengths as Albania: for example, the leading Albanian cigarette was called Partisan, shock workers in industry were known as 'Partisan Industrial Brigades', and a whole artificial history of Enver Hoxha's role in the struggle was invented as part of the cult of his personality. A particular aspect of this was the appropriation by Hoxha of many of the achievements of Mehmet

Shehu, his deputy in the Partisan war and a man of undoubted military ability.

After Hoxha's death in 1985, the Party made vigorous efforts to keep this key aspect of his heritage alive. This was reflected in the overall distribution of resources between different branches of armed forces. In 1986, out of a total of 42,000 regular troops, 31,500 were in the infantry, only 3,300 in the navy and 7,200 in the air force, of whom many served in what in other countries would be regarded as an infantry role. In addition, 12,000 men and women were employed in the paramilitary forces, 5,000 in internal security and 7,000 in frontier security. Of the 155,000 reserves, only 5,000 were not in infantry units. Given the small size of the population and the long compulsory conscription period, the notion of military service as an infantry foot soldier and the image of an armed and hence independent mountain people assumed a vital part in the formation of Albanian national identity under communism. However, in practice this conflicted with any rational discussion or analysis of defence priorities. The organisation of these forces, even in terms of this false defence doctrine, seems to have been colossally inefficient. Military training was minimal, fuel and ammunition were frequently in short supply, uniforms and personal equipment were of low quality, and the military leadership was scattered across the whole country without a proper command system.

One cannot avoid the sense that an important reason for this was Hoxha's desire to avoid the military becoming an equivalent or rival centre of power to the Party. As late as 1974, there was a major conflict between the Party and military leadership: General Beqir Ballaku, the Defence Minister and a Politburo member, was arrested and executed, and a number of senior officers were purged. It was the most serious challenge to Hoxha since the break with Tito in 1949. Ballaku had differed from Hoxha and Shehu on a number of important foreign and defence policy issues but in particular on whether it was safe for Albania to isolate itself in Europe and engage in a simultaneous struggle against Soviet revisionism and American imperialism and, by implication, whether the link with China was of any genuinely defensive value to Albania. Contemporary editorials in the Albanian press, seeking to justify the action against Ballaku and the turmoil in the armed forces' leadership, revealed serious disciplinary and organisational problems in the army, including absenteeism, low morale and the absence of basic operational efficiency in many spheres. Hoxha's writings were not being studied, a key sign of political dissent at the time. Hoxha himself seems to have feared that Ballaku could play a role in Albania analogous to that the Marshal Zhukov, the Soviet Defence Minister, in the intrigues surrounding Nikita Khrushchev.

There is little reason to believe that the purges improved the situation, and by the time communism ended fifteen years later a great part of the armed forces was operating in unbelievably primitive and backward conditions. A large proportion of the infantry were employed in nominal, and generally pointless guard duties, and some soldiers spent much of their time tending cows and sheep.[1] Perhaps partly to disguise the real situation and to discourage any public or rational discussion of defence problems, enormous emphasis was placed on secrecy. Even ordinary maps were classified as top secret. In early 1990, the 200 soldiers based at the key border post of Lin, near Lake Ohrid and thus near the sensitive frontiers with Yugoslavia and Greece, spent all their time growing vegetables because the central military food supply system had broken down. The flock of sheep which the soldiers had appropriated from a nearby collective farm was in turn stolen by the Lin villagers for their own winter meat supply. Although the long lines of conscripts hoeing near the beautiful lake made an evocative rural scene, they were also a sad and living testimony to the collapse of Albania's defences. In Tirana itself the military academy was attempting to train new officers largely without books, typewriters or modern communications equipment, and during much of 1991 and 1992 all military publications failed to appear.

Nevertheless, until the final demise of the one-party state the whole military service and conditioning process became an important weapon for the regime in enforcing national feeling and ideological conformity. It also provided employment for a useful network of trusted henchmen from wartime days who were strong supporters of Hoxha's regime. The people's army concept also took hundreds of thousands of young men off the overcrowded

---

[1] See S. Marx, 'Reforms under the Double Headed Eagle', *Jane's Intelligence Review*, September 1994.

labour market, something that seemed relatively unimportant under communism, but became a major problem in the period of anarchy immediately following its demise. In addition it helped, through mass participation in infantry units, to provide the illusion of effective national defence as practised by certain small but otherwise very dissimilar states such as Israel and Switzerland. Hoxha and the PLA claimed during this period that the government could, within twenty-four hours, mobilise 600,000 men and women (women had been enlisted in the army since 1967 and allowed to become officers since 1969) for the defence of the country. After the Warsaw Pact invasion of Czechoslovakia in 1968, Hoxha believed that Albania might suffer a similar fate, which was the cause of thousands of concrete bunkers being hurriedly built all over Albania. These were complemented, at the height of the 'Cultural Revolution' phase, by a bizarre 'do-it-yourself' air defence system against airborne invasion: units of Young Pioneers were taught how to fix long pointed spikes at the tops of trees to impale foreign parachutists as they descended on to the soil of Albania.

Thus the defence doctrine depended largely for its 'reality' on the existence of sealed borders and totalitarian controls on freedom of movement and information. This applied to those within the system as well as to the people as whole. The political and ideological alliance with China was particularly harmful to Albania in the military sphere, since the merging of Maoist notions of people's war with the mythologisation of the Partisan struggle in Albania meant that vital technical modernisation problems were never faced. China was not a naval power in the Mediterranean, and thus could not use the Sazan base and Adriatic ports which were Albania's only marketable asset if a military confrontation were to break out between the superpowers. Thus the pro-China period was not as useful economically as the Soviet alliance had been, and only caused the military problems that would await the first non-communist rulers to accumulate. Accurate information on the equipment position during these years is difficult to obtain, but Chinese aid appears to have been limited to military transport vehicles, hydrofoils to assist coastal patrol work and a number of MiG-19 fighters and Shenyang J-7 trainers.[2] Chinese leaders had

[2] *The Military Balance 1986*, London: Brassey's, 1986.

tried to discourage some of the wilder fantasies of the Albanian leadership about the actual security offered by the link, and there seems little doubt that only during the years of the Cultural Revolution (1967-72) was there any substance to the alliance as a military reality, and that for the Chinese it had little more than sentimental value after 1973-4.[3]

In the period of total international isolation, after the break with China in 1976, the structure of Party authority in the armed forces was reinforced, with the Minister of Defence always in the Politburo and often head of the Military General Staff. This continued when Hoxha died, and remained substantially unchanged till 1990, when the important Party of Labour military committee ceased to meet. Reformist soldiers such as General Kostas Karolli, in 1985 head of the military training academy, began to discuss possible reforms after Hoxha's death, but could make little progress, against entrenched Party conservatives who were resistant to change – these included Ramiz Alia himself. The prestige of the PLA General Secretary stood relatively high among the old army leadership, and he was thought to understand military problems, although it is not clear on what evidence this view is based. Perhaps, as with so much else in Albanian history, this was a sentiment partly related to the critical wartime period, when Alia's Partisan activities acquired their own legendary mystique. In reality he had been a political rather than a military figure during the resistance, and anyway he had at that time been a very young man who, for someone playing a minor role, had been fortunate enough to attract the attention of Hoxha's wife, Nexhimje. However, this was not how his work was presented in PLA propaganda for internal Albanian consumption, in which the all-encompassing 'Partisan' designation was used to glamorise and exaggerate his achievements. Alia's conservative views on military issues may also have held sway among uncommitted officers because of the continuing Cold War atmosphere and the hostility of most neighbouring countries, although relations with Yugoslavia had improved after Hoxha's death. Internal propaganda focused for many years on external threats, particularly from the United States and British intelligence agencies. A siege mentality therefore became so much

---

[3] For further details of this period see E. Hoxha, *Reflections on China* (2 vols), Tirana, 1979.

part of the culture of the senior military staff that many aspects of PLA propaganda, however, obviously irrational, were never questioned even by the most reformist-minded officers till the late 1980s. As late as March 1990, a major military exercise of a highly traditional type was held along the Adriatic coast, designed to test Albanian readiness to resist a NATO seaborne invasion, but the effective power of the PLA collapsed during that year throughout Albanian society. Reform in the military began under the National Unity government.

At the beginning of 1991 a law was pushed through the People's Assembly calling for the depoliticisation of the armed forces, and debate began over how the army could adjust itself to the process of political change. During the transition period all parties tried for their own ends to put pressure on the military, with conservatives in the armed forces under pressure to organise military intervention or a coup to protect the one-party state, while reformers urged officers to keep out of politics and accept the end of communism. However, the long years of material neglect and over-politicisation by the communists took their toll, and only a small minority of officers showed any inclination to act unconstitutionally to protect the regime. Most officers seem to have understood that the loyalty of conscripts could not be relied on if they were ordered to fire on demonstrators. An intimidatory massacre in the manner of Tiananmen Square was not a safe option militarily or politically during the crucial months of January and February 1991, when political tension in Tirana was at its height and the visible symbols of communist rule were being physically attacked. There were various skirmishes between demonstrators and the authorities during this period, and on a number of occasions soldiers fired shots into the air, without being ordered to do so, and military officers have made various claims about the role of the PLA leadership in these events. However, there is no evidence that the military leadership had any appetite for confrontation. The absence of ranks in the army and of any stratum of competent non-commissioned officers may also have been a deterrent to violence in that there was often no clear chain of command on the ground that would have enabled the demonstrators to be dispersed efficiently.

In this sense the hardest internal military issues resolved themselves peacefully and did not have to be faced, but the same cannot be said of border defence and the country's relationship with the looming Yugoslav conflict and all its myriad effects and dangers. As soon as the structure of the one-party state began to crumble in 1990, Albania was left virtually defenceless and unable to control its borders. The mass attempts at emigration, with thousands of refugees fleeing to Greece in the winter of 1990-1, and the seizures of ships the following summer, were a direct consequence, and showed that the internal security units were no longer an effective military force. The state had relied on military border units and internal police controls to make it effective, and this was an integral element in the way it functioned. In alliance with this was the system of permits for internal movement and the widespread use of internal exile. This was both a method of political coercion against opposition forces and a part of the forced labour system.

The country has remained all but defenceless in terms of modern military capacity since the end of communism, and it has been an urgent priority for all governments holding office after 1989 to proceed with the modernisation and reorganisation of the armed forces. The equipment position varied. Factories established for small arms and ammunition production at Polican near Berat were still able to function after they were modernised through the purchase of Swedish machine tools in early 1980s, but their production was, and is, limited to a copy of the ubiquitous Kalashnikov rifle, pistols and other small arms, and a mortar. Ammunition production has been reported as irregular in quality. The motorised element in defence equipment reflects many of the general problems besetting Albanian industry, with a dependence on outdated Chinese technology and widespread shortages of spare parts. Particularly weak areas were military communications, which in some areas still depended on the public telephone system, transport, anti-aircraft artillery and radar. The obvious vulnerability of Tirana to an air strike was to preoccupy Albanian military planners in the early months of the Yugoslav war in 1991-2.

In 1991 some of these problems were addressed by the National Unity government, at least in theory, but in the chaotic political and economic conditions of that year little progress could be made on the underlying problems. In 1992 a priority for the newly-elected Democratic Party government was a rapid reduction in the size of the 6,000-strong officer corps. This was for two interlinked reasons: first, many of the officers were believed, justifiably, to have had strong links with communism, and secondly many of them too were the offspring of Tosk Partisan families and consequently seen by President Berisha as a potential threat to his government. Soon after the DP election victory, there began a series of sackings and early retirements with the aim of reducing the numbers of the officer corps by about half. The military academy was closed for almost two years; no students were admitted and the training curriculum was comprehensively reviewed. This was organically linked to a second main process whereby military units were regrouped into a small number of large bases, and at the same time many small infantry bases around the country, originally designed as command and control centres for a people's war involving the bunker defence system, were closed. This new deployment coincided with the government's political objectives and with the technical and operational demands of modernisation. By 1994 numbers had been reduced by 40 per cent and the average age of officers had fallen to thirty-five. The Minister of Defence Safet Zhulali and his deputy Baskim Shehi were civilians. Foreign assistance with these major changes was obviously required. As early as December 1990 a military agreement, mainly for officer training and military education, was signed with Turkey, which became, in 1991 the first foreign state to appoint a full-time resident military attaché in Tirana. In August 1992 the Turkish destroyer *Fevzi Cakmak* visited the port of Durres, the first Turkish warship to visit Albania since the end of the Ottoman empire. By early 1995 about 200 Albanian officers had attended training courses in Turkey.

The ultra-egalitarian system dating from the Cultural Revolution years was gradually abolished during 1991 under the National Unity government. Laws were passed in June abolishing the system of political commissars in the armed forces and in August for the return of military ranks. The first contacts with NATO were made in July 1991 through the Italian army, which provided troops for the food-aid programme Operation Pelican. The Albanian government contacted NATO ambassadors in Tirana shortly afterwards and requested military contacts. In September some officers attended a NATO training exercise in Germany as observers, and General Karolli met all NATO chiefs of staff in October 1991. Marxism-Leninism was dropped from the curriculum of the military academy, and the *Sigurimi* were rooted out of the armed forces and replaced by an Armed Forces Information Service. The start of the war in Yugoslavia led to a re-examination of priorities during the autumn: troops were moved to reinforce the northern sector, and senior officers discussed defence policy at a round table meeting in December. The principal issues under review were the possibility of a military relationship with Croatia against Serbia, the defence of Kosova, and arrangements to control the movement of refugees in the event of a conflict there. But the decisive problems of military re-equipment were not addressed, and the Berisha government sought assistance from the United States for this soon after taking office. As a result, a number of military advisers were appointed to the Albanian Ministry of Defence; most were specialists in communications, logistics and military transport. There is reason to believe that the army's reluctance to take any practical steps to assist Croatia against Serbia was because of the equipment and organisational crises, and that this factor strongly influenced Berisha's thinking. However this issue turned out to be irrelevant because of the Croatian President's reservations about political co-operation.

Help in officer training and logistical attachments was forthcoming from Germany and in other aspects of modernisation from Italy and Britain. However, there have been no major deliveries of equipment, although in May 1994 the United States government, under considerable pressure from Tirana, signed a second military agreement which included a provision for equipment transfer, though not of any specified nature. The country's economic difficulties have so far prevented significant purchases of equipment on the open market. It remains to be seen whether the renewed links between Albania and the Islamic world will lead to any significant offer of military assistance; there has been little sign of it up till the time of writing. In the mean time border defences have been strengthened as far as equipment allows, with a number of tanks being dug in as fixed artillery pieces to guard the road approaches from Serbia, and modern telecommunications and radar equipment being purchased. Some major foreign companies have been called in to plan the modernisation of the Vlora harbour complex for the navy. In the spring of 1993 the US Central Intelligence Agency took over the largely disused border military airfield near Lezha as a base for unmanned observation flights over Serbia, Montenegro and Bosnia, and there have been reliable reports that the advisory personnel from the Pentagon working in the Albanian Ministry of Defence on various issues have been augmented by experts at the Sazan island base. If confirmed, these would be important developments for the future and the possible precursor to wider US assistance for Albania if there is a resumption of the Balkan war. The uniformed US advisers have mainly confined their activity to expert technical advice in the spheres of telecommunications, road transport and broad logistics and modernisation. However, it is questionable whether the Albanians will be prepared for these arrangements to continue in the absence of any serious US commitment to a comprehensive military re-equipment programme. Joint land and naval exercises with US forces were held in the summer of 1995, coupled with visits by the NATO military leadership. In 1996 Albanian forces participated alongside a US force in 'Operation Peaceful Eagle', a major multinational exercise.

Since 1983 there have been warm relations with NATO. The late NATO Secretary General, Manfred Wörner, took a particularly close and sympathetic interest in Albanian military and security problems, but tangible security guarantees for the Albanians have hitherto been wanting. Involvement in the Partnership for Peace programme began in late 1994, but it offers Albania little beyond the opportunity for dialogue with NATO, and does not affect the long-running equipment crisis.

In 1995 US commitment appeared to strengthen with the first joint exercise between the two navies in the Adriatic. The United States provided the Albanians with uniforms, military vehicles and other equipment, and a commitment was made for further teams of US advisers to work in Albania on defence planning and civil aviation control. Intelligence reports on some matters are said to be passed from the CIA to the Albanian leadership. The US Assistant Secretary of Defense, Joseph Nye, was in Tirana during the exercise and told a press conference that the Pentagon believed Albania to be a pillar of stability in the Balkans.[4] How far the key question of offensive equipment will be faced in the future is impossible to foretell, but increasingly the US must be seen as one aspect of the reappearance of traditional great power

---

[4] *The Guardian*, 2 February 1995.

rivalries in the Balkans. Just as Russia has given increasing material support to Serbia, the United States, has done the same with Albania. Albanian officers and Ministry of Defence Staff were heartened by the US commitment to the Croatian army in 1995, and hope to receive similar assistance themselves in the future.

International relations

Because of the dominant parameters of superpower protection and international isolation, Albania has usually been seen as having little internal evolution or organic development in its international orientation, and therefore capable of no independent diplomatic activity. In reality this is not so, nor was it even under communism when the intractable conflict that arose with the Soviet Union in the Khrushchev years led to new alliances and directions. Furthermore, under Hoxha some consistent elements remained, of which the major one was hostility to Yugoslavia and Tito, although this was mitigated by the closer economic links of the early 1980s and the construction of the Titograd-Shkoder rail link. But suspicion of most Western countries remained, and in particular deep hostility to the United States and its close ally, Britain.[5] After Hoxha's death in 1985 Albania's maverick course continued, but it came to be gradually modified under the pressure of events, and with significant openings to some Western countries and to the secular and left-wing Islamic countries.

Nevertheless, links with China remained closer than the formal break in and after 1976 might have indicated, probably not due to the Tirana government's choice but because the central development of the economy had been linked to a number of massive industrial projects developed with Chinese assistance; of these the best known is the ferro-nickel reduction plant and metallurgical combine at Elbasan. This was the key element in Hoxha's strategy to make Albania an advanced industrial power rather than an exporter of raw materials. Called by Hoxha 'the second national liberation of Albania', it had the tallest chimneys in the Balkans and emitted clouds of dangerous pollutants. The Chinese were the most important customers for Albanian chromite ore. Chinese

---

[5] See Enver Hoxha, *The Anglo-American Threat to Albania*, Tirana, 1982. It contains amusing pen-portraits of British SOE officers in Albania in the Second World War.

influence in the Tirana Foreign Ministry seems to have remained considerable right up till the end of communism. Many Albanian diplomats received their higher education in China, and informal links with some Chinese officials remained close for many years. However, Foreign Ministry staff went on strike in 1990 in protest at the decision of Alia's Foreign Minister, Reis Malile, to make what had become a regular annual visit to the People's Republic. The Chinese link affected Albanian diplomatic links in other ways during this period, for example with the apparently arbitrary pattern of relations with sub-Saharan Africa that was actually determined largely by Chinese interests. Up till 1989 Albania had a substantial presence in an internationally insignificant country such as Tanzania, while it had no mission in Nigeria, a wealthy oil producer. Small but politically sympathetic countries like Cuba and North Korea had large missions in Tirana, while many important countries had no representation there at all.

There were also diplomatic links with countries where Albanians had played an important role in the Ottoman past. Of these Egypt had the highest profile in Tirana, but as communism ended it was supplanted by Turkey. The old monarchy in Egypt which Nasser overthrew had been of Albanian origin. Egypt, also, was seen as progressive and non-aligned. After that time its relations with Albania remained fairly close, but they deteriorated after the break with the Soviet Union. Longstanding cultural and religious links also exist between Egypt and the Albanians in FYROM. Turkey had a strong presence in Albania even under communism, but political relations were always limited by its being a NATO member and firmly in the Western camp. In spite of this there were many cultural exchanges, such as folk-dancing competitions, linked to the large number of Turkish citizens of Albanian origin (as many as half a million in the area of Istanbul alone) and the large Albanian communities in Turkish cities such as Bursa. During 1989 and 1990, before Operation Pelican was established, Turkish food aid was important for Albania. Military contacts soon followed, as mentioned above, and Turkish government finance was the first major foreign source of assistance for the restoration of mosques and religious buildings. The close co-operation between the two countries in education suggests that the Turks have a long-term strategy for Albania. Scholarships have been granted to Albanian students for higher education in Turkey, both civilian and military.

In November 1992 a Turkish military delegation visited Albania. It was headed by Defence Minister Ayaz, who stressed during the talks between the two sides that Turkey would help its 'sister and friend Albania', adding that it considered such help to be 'an obligation'.[6] This referred to the 500 years of Ottoman rule in the country. Less conspicuous but still important links were kept up with Libya, Tunisia and Syria, where an identifiable Albanian community still exists in Damascus. Cultural links with these isolated diaspora communities benefited from the end of communism.

Among Western industrial countries France was by far the most important partner. A tradition of left-wing Albanological studies was established there by professors sympathetic to Enver Hoxha's system and there was thus a history of independent Albanian cultural activity that enabled some prominent Albanians – including ironically, Dr Sali Berisha – to pursue expert specialisations at French universities. This in turn was built on a francophile tradition in élite education in Albania, and a well educated and often politically radical Albanian diaspora before the Second World War centred in Lyon. Enver Hoxha himself attended the French *lycée* at Korça and later studied at the University of Montpellier, receiving his basic Marxist indoctrination in the 1930s from the French Communist Party, then ultra-Stalinist in orientation. He may have owed some aspects of his political thought and general psychology to that experience. His memoirs of his youth indicate a marked respect for French culture, and France was later seen as an opponent of Anglo-American domination of Europe through NATO, and as such a 'progressive' capitalist country. In turn French heavy industry benefited in the late Hoxha and Alia period– such as the turbine machinery used in the River Drin hydro-electric schemes. A French joint-venture company, ADA, was one of the first companies of its type established by Ramiz Alia to run duty-free shops.

The same relatively sympathetic framework was applied to a small number of other Western countries, ostensibly with little or no connection with Albanian interests. In the late 1970s and early '80s Switzerland was always taken seriously as a neutral state and as the home of thousands of Kosova refugees with a good

[6] *Radio Free Europe*, vol. 2, no. 11, 12 March 1993.

record where political asylum applications were concern. Austria always had a mission of respectable size in Tirana, and was viewed favourably as a neutral country which historically had generally backed Albanian national aspirations against Serbia and Russia in the late Ottoman period. These links provided discreet methods by which the Albanian leaders could, if they wished, take part in international discussions and use the capitalist system – with the traditional benefits, in efficiency and discretion, of the Swiss banking system. In 1991 the opposition in Tirana accused the Hoxha family and other communist leaders of having deposited large amounts of embezzled public funds in Switzerland, but to date no evidence has been produced to support these allegations.

Relations with the Soviet Union remained virtually non-existent in the early 1980s under Ramiz Alia, as they had been for many years, but a few trading agreements negotiated when Albania was a member of Comecon and had a resident representative, Shahin Ruka, in Moscow remained in force. This was not the case with all Warsaw Pact and Comecon countries, although Bulgaria, East Germany (the GDR), Romania and Czechoslovakia all had functioning embassies in Tirana. In practice the GDR ambassador, a relatively high-level functionary who had been posted in Tirana for the extraordinary period of twenty-one years, handled all Soviet concerns in the country. Trade interests with Bulgaria were most important in the late communist period since the entire Albanian supply of important commodities, such as newsprint, came from there. Yugoslavia had a substantial mission in Tirana, consisting mainly of a large consular section dealing with the visa applications of Albanians wanting to visit their relations. Albanians with links to countries such as Canada, where there was significant Albanian emigration in the early twentieth century, had to use this embassy to contact the appropriate foreign embassy in Belgrade.

The most important foreign embassy in Tirana during the Alia years and often since has been that of Greece, with the Albanian ambassadorship in Athens being one of the Tirana government's most important posts; its impressive ambassadorial residence adjoins the American embassy in the fashionable Kolonaki quarter. When the 1976 economic agreement was negotiated, a trade representative office was opened in Tirana, which was later upgraded to full diplomatic status. After 1991 the Greek embassy building became the target for a wide range of political demonstrations, and with

armed riot police often present and high walls and fences surrounding it, it has often resembled a building under siege. Long
queues seeking entry visas are always waiting outside, and the
visitor is impressed by the long tables piled high with hundreds
of passports, and by irritable chain-smoking staff attempting to
process applications. Telephones never cease ringing, and angry
Albanians wait for interviews with equally stressed-out consular
officials who often never materialise. In these circumstances much
pressing trade and political work cannot be done and the normal
diplomatic interchanges in Tirana have virtually ceased to exist
– this has been a significant factor in the worsening relations
between the two countries since 1992. The Greek government
has argued that if local consulates were provided in Korça, Saranda
and Gjirokaster this situation would improve. Violent incidents
led to the closing of the Gjirokaster office, and soon afterwards,
in April 1994, the other offices were closed as well. An attempt
was made in July 1994 to burn down the Sarande office; it re-opened
in 1996.

Early in 1990, discussions began with both the United States
and Britain on the long-outstanding issue of the Albanian gold
held in the Bank of England after the Corfu Channel incident.
This inevitably involved diplomatic contact, and officials of the
British Foreign Office were able to meet their Albanian counterparts
in Italy for the first time in fifty years. The talks went smoothly,
and after resolution of the outstanding problems concerning the
gold issue, both countries opened missions in Tirana in 1991.
The British office has been situated in the French embassy, in
rather cramped and unsatisfactory conditions, and then in other
premises pending the return of British property seized by the
communists after the war. These negotiations are expected at the
time of writing to be completed in late 1997, after which a new
British embassy will be built, or an existing building modified.
The US embassy recovered large premises occupied by the Italian
government mission for many years.

During the period in office of the National Unity government
and the late Alia period before it, foreign relationships were chaotic,
with conservatives in the Foreign Ministry attempting to continue
arrangements with communist and Third World governments laid
down many years before, and Western countries attempting to
establish normal relations with Tirana. Italy was the first to do

so, and after the ship and embassy seizures of July/August 1991, was chosen by the European Community to organise the food aid programme it had already started. The Craxi Socialist government formed a close relationship with some of the reformist communists, and later attracted serious criticism, particularly from the Democratic Party in Albania, for corruption and trying to prop up the communist system. Italian influence was very strong between July 1991 and March 1992, but disappeared almost immediately after the Berisha government was elected, after which the views of United States held unchallenged sway with the President and the DP's senior echelons. It remains to be seen if this will continue, given the President's defeat in the constitutional referendum of November 1994 in which US influence on the new constitution was noticeable, and given also the retirement of Ambassador Ryerson, and US concerns over human rights in Albania after the May 1996 elections.

An equally important issue is the role of the Islamic countries. Despite attempts by the Islamic republic of Iran to open a mission in Tirana, full diplomatic relations had not been established at the time of writing, largely due to US pressure on Berisha. But a trade and economic aid office does exist, and similar pressures have come from a variety of Islamic states, some in the form of official missions, others by more informal routes. It is likely to be a key issue for Albanian governments in the next few years; economic aid from these quarters would be very welcome but it may have unacceptable military and strategic implications.[7]

Developments in Turkey are likely to be important in Albania. A reorientation of Turkish security policy is taking place at the time of writing, and a more nationalist foreign policy is emerging, even under the Islamic coalition government formed in 1996. This tendency was set to become more marked with increased Islamic influence in Turkey following the election of an Islamist Welfare Party government. In these conditions it is possible that Albania will become a more important potential ally with far-

---

[7] An informative survey of the Albanian military equipment position is to be found in Andres de Lionis, 'The remains of Albania's defences', *Jane's Intelligence Review*, vol. 7, no. 7 (April 1995). The writer concludes that not only does Albania still lack the basic military equipment to cope with external threats, but the government would be unable to suppress major internal disorder if it ever took place, and cannot control illegal population movements.

reaching implications for security and foreign policy. Developments in the Albanian government will in turn be affected in equally fundamental ways by the rapprochement between the Berisha government and Athens in the spring of 1995, which is clearly linked to the worsening climate of Greek-Turkish relations, and the simultaneous realisation in Tirana that Greece has an effective stranglehold on the Albanian economy. Greece has a clear and defined interest in the future of the government in Tirana, linked to the crisis in the Berisha modernisation project which was emerging after its first three years in government.

In this period the United States had a stabilising effect and was the dominant influence, followed by Greece and Turkey.[8] The assistance given to President Berisha from Germany before the 1996 election caused a marked increase in German influence. A key figure is the German leader of the Council of Europe, Mrs Leni Fischer, an admirer of Berisha. Albanian ministers had talks with German defence experts in the time following the election, and it must be assumed that equipment issues were discussed.[9] A major German investment in the chrome industry is also planned. It would appear, from the scale and content of these initiatives that the Berisha government's confidence in the United States has sharply declined. If this is the case, it would conform to the classic pattern of previous Albanian breaches with superpower backers such as China.

---

[8] For information on the strengthening of US bases and the arrival of 'Predator' aircraft at the Gjader air base in Albania in mid-July 1995, see *Balkan News* (Athens), 2 July, 1995. The United States experienced various practical difficulties in establishing the base, see the article 'Tense Situation at Gjader Air Base' in *Koha Jone* (Tirana), 13 July 1995, and BBC/SWB, 15 July 1995. The best general statement in English of the Albanian view of the defence issue is in an article in *NATO Review*, March 1996, by Major-General Adem Copani, the President's defence adviser. He concentrates on technical and equipment matters.

[9] See *Albanian Daily News*, 10–12 October 1996.

12

THE END OF PARTY POLITICS? – DEMOCRACY UNDER THREAT

Although the difficulties of the Berisha government only attracted widespread international attention after the failure of the referendum vote in the autumn of 1994, the Democratic Party government was in crisis as early as the end of 1992, with an ever-widening gulf between most of the founders of the party on one side and President Berisha and his immediate personal circle on the other. It had become clear that there would be endless splits and breakaways between the different groups, often related less to policy differences than to the over-dominant personality of Berisha. This in turn reflected the intractable structural problems of the state machine itself, where the President was central to almost all decision-making processes.

After the destruction of the traditional communist structures scarcely any effective executive processes remained in Tirana, and Berisha's apologists have claimed that in Albanian conditions his increasing reliance on a network of kin links and placemen was inevitable. He has also faced the central problem of post-communist Tirana governments, namely that the people are impatient for results and quickly lose patience if leaders do not deliver. In practice this has meant the exclusion from the serious decision-making process of all who are not Berisha acolytes. This absolute centralisation of government around the Presidency, has alienated the more liberal and European-minded elements of the original DP leadership, and has also led to bad decisions being taken. A similar process took place in the winter of 1991, when the Ceka-Pashko group were defeated by Berisha and decided to pull out of the National Unity government and create the movement that led to the Democratic Alliance being formalised as an opposition party to the DP. That process was to be a political paradigm for a continuous process of loyal and trusted supporters breaking away from Berisha, so that his political base became ever narrower.

This process was seen by some of those involved as a product of Berisha's communist background, his political culture having grown from a national tradition that polarised conflicts, encouraged intolerance and stigmatised the very idea of constructive opposition. The DA leader Neritan Ceka said in May 1994:

'In communist times in Albania, no opposition was allowed. The students and intellectuals in 1989 and 1990 created the idea and then the reality of opposition on the streets and in the University, but Berisha was not among them. He was sent by Alia as the right personality to control the movement. He had not only been a communist, he was a hard-line communist, a double communist. When he argued with Kadare, he said he was not for political pluralism but only for the pluralism of ideas.

That was the problem with Berisha and it accounts for what has happened in 1992 and last year. The only way he understands politics is for there to be discussion within the party, then the party carries it out without opposition. That is how he has made the DP a party like the PLA used to be. And he understands about controlling the media – he learned that from Alia and about the need to work through other people, people of no importance. That is why Selami is important now. When the party was created, Selami was unimportant. Now he is important because he says what Berisha does not wish to say.'[1]

Another important difficulty was the personality of the President, where his strong Tropoja roots and traditional Gheg qualities embody strength, courage and steadfastness but also a tendency to dogmatic authoritarianism and a deep suspicion of opposition.

This and similar perceptions were not confined to the political élite, as perhaps they had been in 1991 and 1992 when for the majority of the population Berisha could do no wrong, but spread widely outside it. So 1993 began as it was to continue, with ever-increasing strikes and demonstrations organised by the many disaffected groups throughout the country. An increasingly weak

[1] Interview with Neritan Ceka by James Pettifer, Tirana, 8 May 1994. See also *War Report*, June/July 1994, p. 22. For background on Eduard Selami see p. 244.

and isolated President was facing political, social and economic reality, but to foreign states, and in particular, Berisha's close friends in the US State Department it did not appear that way. The good figures for economic growth and currency stability were seen in those quarters as completely validating the Berisha project along with the government's willingness to collaborate closely with the United States over defence and intelligence matters. To many Albanians with widely differing political viewpoints the personality and power of the President personally had become a focus for opposition. One of the most demonstrative of these groups of opponents was that representing the former political prisoners, some fifty of whom ended a hunger-strike in Shkoder on 15 January. They did so only on learning that the People's Assembly had adopted the draft law 'On innocence, amnesty and rehabilitation of the former political prisoners and persecuted'. This group presented the government with a dilemma because its members continued to live in abject poverty despite being hailed as 'the martyrs against communism', and bore witness in their own persons to the horrors of the forced labour system in places such as the pyrites mine at Spaç, in Mirdita, where inmates lived on starvation rations before its closure in 1990 and were literally worked to death. Despite the Berisha government's rhetoric about justice, the former prisoners felt keenly the irony of their poverty-stricken situation and the fact that not even one of their tormentors had been put on trial for human rights offences. Their hunger-strike was organised to protest against the miserable conditions in which they continue to live and the lack of governmental initiative to pay them compensation.

In a quite different area of society other conflicts were developing. A new class of private landowners, created by the land privatisation laws hurriedly passed in the autumn of 1991 by the Socialist-led coalition government, now found themselves under attack from the country's pre-war landowning families. These families had the strong support of increasingly vocal and powerful right-wing groups such as Balli Kombetar, Legaliteti, the National Unity Party and the Republican Party, and the far right of the DP, which was dominated by members of these families who had fought against the Partisans during the war. This became known as the 'Dosti' group, after one of its leaders Tomor Dosti, also a former political prisoner. The land reform and the associated rises in agricultural productivity had been one of the success stories of the early Berisha period, and the conflict is an indicator of the growing political difficulties facing the government and the President.

The country's most urgent task was to advance the process of economic reform and establish law and order. With around 400,000, (38 per cent) of the workforce unemployed, the domestic situation remained volatile. Poverty in the north was extreme, especially around towns such as Kukes where people felt totally ignored by the government and far removed from events in Tirana. In 1976 the old town of Kukes had been flooded to make way for a hydro-electric project and the population rehoused in a soulless cluster of shoddily-built concrete apartment blocks on the shores of the new lake which now covered their old homes. In this remote and inaccessible area there are people who have rarely met Albanians from other regions, let alone foreigners. The population exists at subsistence level due partly to the division of the collective farms in 1992, which left them with plots too small to be of any economic benefit in such mountainous terrain. Almost everyone was unemployed in 1992-3, especially after the escalation of the war in Bosnia and consequent decline in the cross-border trade with Serbia, which had helped to provide some income. UN sanctions had become increasingly discredited in northern Albania. Also men often supplement the family diet by hunting, and small groups of them can be seen going to and from the mountains with their guns.[2]

The difficulties of the north-east can be exemplified in a single funeral. At the end of 1992 Albania's greatest contemporary poet, Martin Camaj, died in Munich, where he had taught Balkan studies at the University. His funeral, poignantly reflecting the abject poverty of the north, was described by an English writer:

> This was the day that Martin Camaj came home. They laid him out on the terrace outside the family home in his best clothes and with a book of his poems at his head. The women tore their hair and ululated, the men groaned and chanted and thumped their chests. It was just like the old days. Only the body was missing. The Dukagjin, a Catholic clan in the mountains east of Shkoder, survived five centuries of Ottoman

[2] See article by James Pettifer in *The Times*, London, 12 June 1995.

rule by discretion and cunning, keeping their religious practices and clan laws safe among the sheep and goats and stony hills. But Enver Hoxha succeeded where the Ottomans had failed by replacing the authority of both clan and religion with communism. And when the clan's most gifted son Martin Camaj fled to Belgrade in 1946, all the Dukagjins were made social pariahs as punishment. Their life grew harder and harder. Though his elder brother Zeff dresses in rags and children are visibly malnourished, things have begun to improve since international food aid finally reached the mountains last year. Amid such poverty, bringing Martin Camaj's body home was out of the question. Instead they laid out his clothes. Or at least clothes such as he might have worn, borrowed from around the village. And they didn't actually bury them, which would have been a reckless extravagance. Once the mourners had exhausted themselves with their chest-thumping, the clothes were quietly returned to their owners.[3]

The death of the political past was more difficult to achieve than that of an individual. In February Nexhijme Hoxha was sentenced to an eleven-year gaol term, in effect the rest of her natural life, for offences committed under the dictatorship. She admitted that 'perhaps we went too far, too idealistic, too romantic...but the collapse of the old system has brought only chaos to Albania. Why? Because where there is no community there can be no law. And it is quite shocking to think that my people could ever be so barbarous [Nexhijme was referring to the day when the crowds pulled down the 12-metre-high statue of her husband in Tirana]. That was more painful to me than his actual death.'[4] Although few would shed tears for the dictator's wife, till the very end a stern opponent of reform who had undoubtedly been connected with many serious human rights violations over the years, the actual conduct of the trial gave rise to some concern. Almost no hard evidence of corruption was produced apart from such trivia as the number of television sets and bunches of plastic flowers that were found in the Hoxha residence. Observers claimed that the rules of evidence had been flouted. Although this was academic in the special case of Nexhijme Hoxha because her

---

[3] Peter Popham, *The Independent Magazine*, 20 February 1993.

[4] *The European*, 17 December 1993.

conviction was a foregone conclusion, it proved later in the year to have set an unfortunate precedent for the Berisha government: the trial in September 1994 of the Omonia Greek minority defendants also left much to be desired from a procedural point of view, and the highly charged atmosphere in which it was conducted damaged the government's international standing.

Whatever their reservations about the opposition, Albanians had lived for fifty years under a system where respect for the law by the executive organs was extremely low if it existed at all. They therefore had no wish to provide the Berisha presidency with so much as a basic framework for the experience to be repeated. In March the Socialist Party called on the government to resign on the grounds that it was incompetent. A month later, on 6 April, Berisha announced Cabinet changes, which were designed to engender some confidence in what was seen as a wholly inexperienced and weak Cabinet. Although the Ministers of Tourism and Education were replaced by political independents, Xhazair Teliti and Edmund Spaho, the more important posts of Agriculture and the Interior were given to hardline right-wing DP members, Petrit Kalakula and Agron Musaraj. In May the DP chairman, Eduard Selami, called on the Socialist Party to dissociate itself from its corrupt leadership. In a press conference he described its chairman, Fatos Nano, as 'the leader of the red Albanian Mafia', and said that 'the Mafia chiefs had been carefully selected by Nexhijme Hoxha and Ramiz Alia'.[5]

In the first week of May, secret PLA documents were put at the disposal of the central state archives, and the revelations from them shocked the country. A special fund, called the 'Fund for Solidarity', was found to have paid a New Zealand citizen to work in Albania for twenty-three years as the official translator of Hoxha's works into English, and he apparently pocketed US $10,000 of Party money when he left Albania finally in April 1991. It seems that the fund made payments to various Marxist-Leninist parties throughout the world. According to Decision no. 190 of the Central Committee of the Party of Labour of Albania, issued in 1964: 'The aim of the fund is to further the interest of the work for the international Communist movement, for the fight against imperialism and revisionism, and for the propagation

[5] BBC, *SWB*, EE/1695 B/1, 22 May 1993.

of Marxism-Leninism.' The fund was not intended to provide the expenses for the endless receptions held for foreign guests. The ultimate aim of the fund was probably to propagate the cult of Enver Hoxha outside Albania, and for this the people would have had to pay 'Marxist-Leninist friends' abroad for almost thirty years. The paperwork for these payments has yet to be found.

The government-controlled television continued to broadcast the amazing details of the wasteful years of communism to an unbelieving population, so acutely aware of their own poverty, and as each day passed Albanians became ever more surprised to learn of what the PLA had paid out at their expense. A mood of indignation set in, which was exactly what the DP government hoped for during these difficult times. The more attention and anger that could be focused on the Hoxha and Alia regimes the better. Equally shocking was the announcement that Enver Hoxha had also helped foreign guerrilla units. From 1966 till 1970 such units from several Third World countries were given military training and financed by the PLA; there was even documentation which testified that in May 1969 an Italian left-wing group requested to be trained in Albania for the triumph of the proletarian revolution.[6] A continual diet of these and similar revelations, however irrelevant to the all-important problems of economic and social renewal facing Albania, helped to maintain some support for the government.

On 15 May thousands of people gathered at a rally organised by the Socialist Party in Berat's central square to protest at the government's anti-democratic and repressive measures. Representatives from other towns and from Tirana joined the predominantly unemployed protesters – Berat alone had 15,000 out of work. Some veterans also attended the rally, anxious over their low pensions and sudden loss of status. Control of this demonstration was among the first tasks of the new Public Order Minister, Agron Musaraj. He arrived in Berat half an hour before the crowd gathered, as did hundreds of his policemen – thus adding superficial credibility to the speaker's claim that Albania was once again a police state. A few days later the National Association of Owners of Expropriated Property (one of a number of such

[6] Radio Tirana in English, 1430 gmt, 20 May 1993.

organisations) held a rally in Tirana, and its chairman, Rrapo Danushi, told the crowd that former property owners had decided to resort to all democratic measures, including a hunger-strike, necessary to secure the return of their property. Danushi reiterated the stand of the All-National Movement for the Return of Property, which had resolutely rejected compensation and demanded instead the return of all property. Representatives from the Republican Party, Balli Kombetar and the Tirana Association also took part in the rally. The Legality movement, represented by its chairman, Nderim Kupi, expressed full support for the demands for the return of property.

Protests by disaffected groups continued. On 22 May the Tirana branch of the Association of Former Owners of Property for Justice staged a hunger-strike in a private building in the city centre. This organisation was made up of ex-labour camp and prison inmates incarcerated for political reasons over the communist years. An estimated forty-two strikers demanded the unconditional restitution of all property to the former owners or their legitimate heirs, and the abolition of artificial co-ownership implemented in 1945, which had been a source of conflict and resulted in non-recognition of the title deeds. The following day, the Socialist Party organised yet another anti-government rally, this time in the north-eastern town of Peshkopia, with Fatos Nano and other leaders of the Party taking part. Following this, an impracticable land compensation law was hurriedly pushed through Parliament whereby rural landowners were to be allotted up to 10 per cent compensation for their land, and those who had once owned property in urban areas could 'share' their former properties with the current owners. The former owners had expected, quite un-realistically, that they would receive up to 95 per cent compensation. This demonstrates how the government failed to inform the popula-tion of its actual and real economic dilemma, and as a result how far the waning of support for Berisha came from the right – from the Ballists and Legaliteti.

Legaliteti actually consists of two separate organisations. One is the Legality Movement, which claims to be the only Albanian political group genuinely uncontaminated by communism. It is headed by Nderim Kupi, son of the movement's wartime founder, Abas Kupi, and professes to have gathered the signatures of 100,000 supporters throughout the country. One of its campaign documents was a copy of the 1929 constitution which gave King Zog almost absolute power. The smaller monarchist party, the National Organisation of the Legality Movement, headed by Ibrahim Sokoli, was also set up during the war and campaigns for a constitutional monarchy under King Leka. The headquarters of the Legality Movement in Tirana, occupying part of the building used by the Democratic Party when it first operated legally in 1991, conjures up the atmosphere of Albania's distant past. In a tiny room painted a shade of yellow, very old men in worn-out suits crowd around the daily newspaper on the table under a picture of the long-dead king. It is noticeable, in conversation with them, how some of them refer to Zog almost as though he were still alive. Many have a strong sentimental attachment to Britain as the country whose Special Operations Executive (SOE) officers worked most closely in the war with Kupi in the north. Some of them, such as 'Amery' (Julian Amery) and 'Hilly' (Darrel Oakley Hill, of the pre-war British-officered Albanian gendarmerie) are held in almost as high regard as Zog himself.

In Albania, as in many Balkan countries, the politics of war-time resistance movements are still very current. For as long as some members of that generation remain alive, these issues will continue to excite controversy. A feature of Legaliteti's genuine, if limited appeal is that it can offer understanding and sympathy to people who suffered from the victories of the Partisans and whose family prospects have been blighted ever since, often as the result of a minor decision taken by a father or grandfather more or less by chance over fifty years ago. Some of these people lived for many years in the United States, and have been sustained over the years by a commitment to a royalist Albania they are now free to strive for. For many it is not an entirely comfortable experience. Young Albanians generally do not take the idea of a monarchy seriously, and support for either Legaliteti party is scattered, only existing in any real sense in pockets of the north especially in the Mati region, traditionally the Zogist heartland – and in the far south.

Legaliteti also has a strong presence in some of the ethnic Albanian villages in the Greek minority areas of the south, where royalism constitutes a bulwark of Albanian identity against Hellenism, and in some areas of the ultra-conservative north. There royalism is linked to the traditional clan culture, even though Zog actually did more than any other twentieth-century Albanian leader other than Hoxha to attack it. However, the pretender Leka is viewed primarily as an object of curiosity. He is thought to be considerably less able than his father Zog, and his colourful past, with allegations of involvement in arms-smuggling in the Far East and unsavoury political associations with neo-fascists, has not helped him to establish a foothold in public esteem. It has been difficult for the royalist émigrés to establish a political base in contemporary circumstances, although Leka attracted some sympathy as part of the considerable anti-Berisha mood when he attempted to visit Albania briefly in November 1993. He was humiliated by immigration officers, and after twenty-four hours in the country, was asked to leave because his passport gave his occupation as 'King of Albania'. He was bluntly told that he would only be re-admitted to Albania if he was in possession of an ordinary citizen's passport. On present evidence, among the Balkan ex-monarchs he is one of the least likely to return. The Zogist political operation outside Albania, which is based in Paris, claims that a constitutional monarchy would help attract investment to Albania and stabilise the political scene. In this scenario Leka's role is modelled on that of King Juan Carlos in Spain after Franco.

Attempts by émigrés to collect hundreds of thousands of signatures to a petition calling for a return to the 1929 constitution have come to nothing: Any hopes of success have arisen more from a temporary upsurge in émigré influence in Albanian life generally than from any genuine royalist support. Those calling for a constitutional version of the pre-war monarchy have suffered from the absence of any constitutionalist tradition, from the excesses of the Zog period linked to Leka's own eccentricities, and from the lack of a serious programme for the present day. Leka, whose wife is a former Australian schoolteacher, lives in Johannesburg, and from 1989 he made repeated calls for Albanians to follow the example of other East Europeans who overthrew their communist governments. Leka's claim to his royal inheritance seems tenuous. He left Albania in 1939 aged only two days when his parents fled to Greece following the Italian invasion. Zog had proclaimed himself king only in 1928. Leka maintains that when his father died in Paris in 1961 he succeeded legally to the throne. He claims that his government in exile organised guerilla operations inside Albania while Hoxha was alive, but to date there has been no evidence that this is true. He lived in Spain with his mother

Geraldine, daughter of a Hungarian aristocratic family, until he was expelled in 1979 for plotting armed action against the Albanian government, and it is certainly true that he devoted his life to bringing about the overthrow of Hoxha's regime. In 1980 his anti-communist sentiments caused him to be expelled from Zimbabwe after the downfall of Ian Smith's government. Moving to Johannesburg, he remained confident that the Albanian people needed him to act as the arbiter between the country's different regions and factions. His personality has been an object of ridicule by his opponents, who have seen him as a comic opera figure, obsessed with his own image and with his personal arsenal. He was not allowed to enter Belgium in 1992 because he was carrying numerous weapons, and has been changed several times with gun-running.

In a discussion Leka comes across as a quiet and serious, but insecure man who finds difficulty in coming to terms with his new role in the post-communist era. Of towering height (he is nearly seven feet tall), he is nervous in conversation and ill at ease with people he does not know well. It was easy for him during the communist period to pose as a romantic Bonnie Prince Charlie type of figure of a monarch driven into exile by evil forces, but as other Balkan pretenders like the undoubtedly more able, responsible and moderate Simeon of Bulgaria have found, it is difficult to articulate a convincing role within a newly democratic country which endured fifty years of communism and has little memory of a monarchical tradition. Leka has argued that a return of the monarchy would help to ensure the continuation of the democratic process. However, his greatest difficulty is the pressing need for a clear political programme on the land issue; most of his influential émigré supporters are from the old landowning class, and wish to see the restitution of their original estates, a political impossibility for any democratic regime in Albania today. Whatever else the Berisha government has or has not achieved, it has created a large class of small peasant proprietors who are implacably opposed to any return of pre-war land-tenure arrangements. Leka has some support among the diaspora Kosovars, but the Kosova Democratic League leadership have been careful to keep their distance from his entourage, except on an informal and personal basis. Leka speaks of the need for foreign investment, but without any indication of how he would be any more successful in attracting it than anyone else. The monarchical idea has virtually no support among the older Tirana professional élite, who are still firmly modernist, secular and technocratic in their orientation. Any growth in support for Legaliteti, as for the Socialists and the centrist Alliance Party, only indicates the depth of the crisis facing Berisha's government and his failure to satisfy even those on the hard right of the spectrum.[7]

By the early summer of 1993, the Berisha administration was coming under threat from an opposition increasingly vocal and restive at the lack of progress towards drafting the country's new constitution. Almost all the opposition parties had dismissed the DP's first draft constitution, which was designed without any parliamentary approval. The DP responded by setting up a parliamentary drafting commission to work out another constitution, while at the same time stridently denouncing all oppositionists in official reports, using language that recalled the days of Hoxha. The general response among the population was to ignore the incomprehensible political slanging-matches in Tirana. They were too busy getting on with their own lives, and hoping to be left alone while they built up their smallholdings. The peasants could still glance up and read, high on the mountain sides, the words *'Rroft Enver'* or *'Enver Parti'*, an inescapable reminder of their so recent lives under the Hoxha dictatorship and their not so very different lives under the 'new' regime. They knew that the words would eventually fade because no one was sent up any longer to re-paint them. Many also suspected that they would be abandoned by the Mercedes-driving bureaucrats in Tirana too.

The general mood on the streets was that the country was now verging on yet another dictatorship since Berisha had established what amounted to exclusive presidential rule. Oppositionists were intimidated by gangs of DP thugs, threatened with the still-unopened files of the *Sigurimi,* and denounced by the state media as 'Serbian or Greek agents', 'communists' or simply 'enemies of the state'. Thus the very principle of parliamentary opposition was dismissed. In June a minor Tirana politician, the leader of the National Unity Party (membership 21,000), Idajet Beqiri, was put under house arrest for insulting the President in an article in the Unity Party's newspaper *Kombi.*

---

[7] Interview with Leka by James Pettifer, London, 6 December 1991.

He had called Berisha the 'murderer of all Albanians' for not pressing strongly enough for a 'Unified Albania'. However exaggerated his rhetoric, in no other European country would it have brought an immediate gaol sentence. Beqiri drafted an angry letter to the Council of Europe, Amnesty International, the European Parliament and the Helsinki Federation for Human Rights. In it he complained: 'Freedom of speech and of the press in Albania is still subjected to severe censorship and the voice of the opposition is not taken into account and is being fought to its annihilation. The process of political purges has already started on all who think differently from the President and the other power-holders of the Democratic Party.'[8]

The political polarisation led Berisha to give his first series of major speeches in the south of the country rather than around his usual stamping-ground in the north. Perhaps he now realised that his support-base had to be widened. He made a point of addressing all the main institutions in the city of Korça, including the military and farmers' representatives. However, his optimism about the country's economic situation fell on deaf ears. The predominantly middle-aged and elderly audience appeared to lack the President's enthusiasm as they stood in the once lively town, now denuded of its young men almost all of whom had left to find work in Greece. Here, as in the rest of the country, people still heavily dependent upon foreign aid had to queue daily for bread and milk. Across on the other side of the country was the antithesis of 'intellectual' Korça: the city of Vlora, long the regular recruiting-ground for the *Sigurimi*. Here were the wide-boys from the Liab slums in and around Vlora, with long straggly hair, open-neck shirts and medallions hanging on their hairy chests. They had expected immediate wealth from the new capitalism, but even life as a footsoldier in the Mafia, while it may have a tawdry glamour for the young men, does not produce wealth except for few.

At the same time Berisha unleashed the legal process on his most serious opponents. Revenge for real or alleged past misdeeds had always been a potent factor in Albania, and so it remained. On 29 July the Socialist Party leader, Fatos Nano, was arrested

---

[8] I. Beqiri, *National Unity Party to the Named International Organisations*, Tirana, 1 July 1993.

and charged with 'the abuse of duty and falsification of official documents in connection with Italian aid'. He was also accused of authorising the purchase of food, as part of the 'Operation Pelican' food-aid arrangements, using Italian credits from the Bari-based Levante company at three times the market price. It was indisputably true that the Italian food-aid was mismanaged, and that large quantities of rice and flour that had been accounted for in Italy disappeared before it reached the intended recipients in Albania.[9] However, there was little evidence that Nano had diverted an alleged $9 million for his own use. On 30 July the Socialist Party announced a rally in support of Nano, and between 5,000 and 7,000 demonstrators marched to Skenderbeg Square. They were confronted there by a DP counter-demonstration and the police, who had been told that the security of the state was under severe threat; they promptly intervened, arresting thirty-two SP demonstrators. On the television news that evening the Ministry of Public Order condemned the SP demonstrators as 'criminals'.[10]

The arrests continued with the detention and summary trial of the former Prime Minister Vilson Ahmeti, who had headed the four-month transitional government in 1991-2. He was convicted of wasting $1.6 million in a failed effort to reschedule Albania's $450 million foreign debt, and sentenced to two years in prison. In his defence Ahmeti claimed that he was inexperienced and unaccustomed to dealing with complicated financial regulations. Convicted with him in what became known as the Arsidi Scandal were two senior bank officials who had ordered payments to be made to Nicola Arsidi, a Frenchman hired to help reschedule the debt. The susceptibility of the government and of all Albania's post-communist governments to corruption is clear. The officials in the ministries often were (and continued to be) inexperienced and badly paid, and naturally were very unfamiliar with high-technology international finance. At this time there was no effective supervision of the banking system, and some of the small banks from Italy that were the first to open could have been used by their owners for money-laundering before some controls were introduced. These convictions in 1993 gave rise to little protest

[9] A useful of speculative survey of the influence of organised crime in Albania in this period is found in 'The Albanian Cartel filling the crime void', *Jane's Intelligence Review*, November 1995.

[10] *Eastern Europe Newsletter*, vol. 7, no. 16, 10 August 1993.

or outcry from human rights organisations. It could certainly be argued the the Nano conviction was justified by the proximity of the Socialist leader to the Italian Mafia involved with the Craxi government in Rome, but it is difficult to avoid the impression that Ahmeti was gaoled in a simple act of revenge against a Socialist politician.

Amnesty International at once became more active in Albania after receiving a deluge of material from individuals and organisations following these trials, but kept a low profile and attempted to secure good legal practice by informal pressure on the government rather than by open protest. Local human rights activists were able to monitor developments in their localities, but were closely followed and observed by informers from the SHIK intelligence agency and thus could not organise any resistance to what was happening. The media were indifferent to the views of dissenters. Thus it appeared that the Berisha grouping had *carte-blanche* to follow whatever policies it liked. However, this was not the whole truth.

The Berisha project suffered from one serious weakness: the alienation and discontent of the Greek minority. As already described, in the summer of 1993 the authors of this book found research work difficult in the Greek villages of the Vjoses valley, where they were followed by SHIK agents in a way that made normal contact with the community and open discussion of political life almost impossible. The repression was also causing concern in Athens, where the government did not wish to see an authoritarian, nationalist regime in Tirana. Within the following twelve months the consequences of this were to become serious for the Berisha government. The effective economic stranglehold which Athens exerted over the Albanian economy, with as much as one-third of Albanian GDP dependent on remittances from Greece, was not widely appreciated in the wider international community. On the contrary Albania was considered in many ways to be quite successful. Its austere and bleak social conditions did not prevent a European Union sampling of social attitudes across the former Soviet and East European countries from finding Albanians consistently ahead of their post-communist peers in their tolerance of the pain of transformation. 'Albanians often reveal the most positive attitudes of all Central and Eastern Europeans concerning their economic and political conditions,' declared one poll analysis. While in sixteen of the eighteen countries surveyed less than half of those questioned expected the economic situation to improve over the next year, this was the belief of seven out of ten Albanians.[11] It was not surprising that Albanians held such a view since they started from a lower base than any other former communist state. But the relative improvement in Albania's economy proved fragile. In 1994 Gramoz Pashko, the one Albanian leader whose economic expertise was genuinely respected by international financial institutions, cast doubt on what has been achieved:

> The economic success is very superficial. What you must remember is that when Berisha took power GDP had dropped by about 45% from the last year of communism, and it was impossible that things could not get any better. There has been no real investment or growth, except from the Kosovars who are very unpopular. The fiscal police are used against them – some of them are leaving because of it. There is a kind of anti-capitalist ethos growing up – wealth is starting to get unpopular because the wealthy pay almost more or less no tax. The peasants pay no tax either. And Berisha has lost out because of the failure of the US link, economically. Two years were wasted in inner-party battles because the US wanted a strong man with whom to play Balkan politics. But there have been no real US investments to show for it.'[12]

By the autumn of 1993 Berisha had clearly outlived his role as Albania's deliverer from communism. His influence over right-wing elements was diminishing, particularly the traditional nationalist right who resented his dependence on the United States. Berisha badly needed to restore to the DP its sense of political direction by trying above all to eliminate factionalism in its ranks, but it was already too late for this. The party's right wing – led by Petrit Kalakula, a former agriculture minister, and Abdi Baleta, who had been Ambassador at the UN under Hoxha – were preparing to organise a split from the DP. But Berisha was having most trouble from the so-called 'Dosti' group, named after Tomor

---

[11] *The Guardian*, 24 July 1993.

[12] Interview with Gramoz Pashko by James Pettifer and Miranda Vickers, Tirana, 6 May 1994.

Dosti, who had spent thirty-seven years in internal exile. Its hold over Berisha lay in its lack of contamination by communism and its ability constantly to reminded him of his communist past. On 4-5 December the Democratic Party held its second national convention in Tirana. Berisha tried to foster party unity by attacking the usual communist scapegoats, now termed the 'red pashas and the blockmen',[13] but this all sounded a little hollow and irrelevant more than two years on from the last days of communism. President Berisha, in his fiery address, squarely blamed the red pashas for the country's chaotic state in the 'winter of anarchy' (1991-2):

'The First Convention of the DP was called at a time when the red *nomenklatura* with their collaborators were preparing to deal the finishing blows to the Albanian democratic movement. They decided to replace the gallows, the camps and the prisons with treacherous murders, exodus burnings, destructions and corruption. With this they wanted us to forget the catastrophe in which they had plunged Albania. The red pashas, who up till yesterday masterminded the camps, the prisons and the isolation and plight of Albania, tried to justify their macabre strategy of criminalising, humiliating and disfiguring the Albanian people and link it to the emergence of the new democratic forces.'

He continued: 'To realise their wicked purposes they used the Stability Government, which for numerous reasons turned into a political shield for the old regime and a dangerous instrument in its hands, against the opposition and the democratic process in Albania.'[14]

The language of this speech provides insight into Berisha's mentality at the time. The inevitable disorder and anarchy of the popular movement, which many observers thought modest compared to what accompanied the demise of similar regimes such as that in Romania, is blamed on outside agitators. The 'new democratic forces' are seen as separate from the popular movement;

[13] The term 'Blockmen' refers to the infamous 'Block', a protected area of Tirana where leading communists such as Hoxha and Shehu lived.

[14] President Sali Berisha's address to the Democratic Party's convention in Tirana, 4-5 December 1993. See also statement by the US State Department, *Judicial Independence in Albania*, 6 October 1995, for expressions of American concern over developments. The EU countries such as Germany and Britain made no comments.

there is no sense of the people's need to feel they had destroyed a hated and oppressive government. It is thus profoundly élitist in its psychology, and far removed from the actual reality of the transition. Perhaps it was a symptom of the growing political isolation of the President. A figure who emerged with advanced power at the Congress was the party chairman, Eduard Selami. Trained as a philosopher and educated in France, Selami had been an acceptable young intellectual in the PLA, and was accused by some of belonging to the team who ghost-wrote Hoxha's final works when the old dictator had become too senile to work on them himself. He distanced himself from the PLA in 1989, and moved on to become Berisha's vital link with the DP cadres. However, he cut a lonely figure in the Congress as one of the few educated men among the Mafiosi, wideboys and unsophisticated rural leaders who comprised most of the delegates. He was seen as the man through whom the views of the US Ambassador were channelled to the assembly.

Berisha's origins in the north-eastern highland Tropoja district, where his family is well established over a large area including western Kosova, dictate his approach to politics; there highland clans are firmly bonded together, and absolute loyalty to blood relations is unquestioned. However, nobody could have anticipated the scale of nepotism in Berisha administration. Every ministry and institution was loaded with northerners and professed DP loyalists, and their appointment to ministerial office and other positions was accompanied by a vast migration from the north to Tirana as families sought to capitalise on relations who were now holding high office in the capital.

All civil servants had their biographies scrutinised so that grounds could be found for dismissing them in favour of DP loyalists or northern clansmen. Competence and merit were displaced by considerations of loyalty – which must partly explain the poor calibre of the entire administration. A case in point is the Defence Minister Safet Zhulali, previously an undistinguished mathematics teacher. Many of his family were ensconced in various state jobs after he was catapulted into his ministerial post in 1993. His brother became dean of Tirana University's faculty of economics; one of his sisters was secretary to Blerim Cela, the somewhat ruthless and apparently wealthy head of 'state control'; Cela's sister became Zhulali's secretary; Zhulali's other sister, Zymbyle

Hasani, was made director of the country's foremost hotel, the Dajti in Tirana; his brother-in-law Ivzi Cipuri was a departmental director in the Ministry of Education; the first cousin of Zhulali's wife, Bashkim Gazidede, was made head of SHIK (the secret service); and Ndue Gjika, the DP parliamentarian and party chairman in the Mirdita region, had the good fortune to be married to Zhulali's cousin.[15]

These and similar patterns of appointments caused the DP government to be seen by many Albanians, even those sympathetic to its aims, as intrinsically dangerous and needing to be controlled and resisted. Otherwise there might be a new ruling élite who might be less feared than Hoxha's regime but who would have the same exclusive control of the country. It should be remembered that when the DP government was elected in April 1992, Albania was seen as having reached a watershed; in the eyes of the outside world the transition to pluralism appeared complete. Berisha, with a large majority of the votes, was secure in power, and this was reflected in his parliamentary majority. The programme of his government promised 'shock therapy', with a quick transition to capitalism, full privatisation of all industries and state-owned assets, and strong central monetary control. The ex-communist Socialist Party was a shadow of its former self, and had only succeeded in getting its MPs elected in any strength in such traditional southern strongholds of communism as Fier and Berat. Other opposition parties had fared little better. Yet within three months of the national election, the Socialist Party had so revived in the local and regional government elections that it had a majority of mayors of major towns.

Although the Albanian people showed an overwhelming desire to put a final end to the one-party state in the elections of 1992, the Democratic Party and President never had an effective majority of popular support except for that short period after those elections. This reality determined many different aspects of social and political developments thereafter, especially the increasing difficulties of the presidency in 1993. It seems likely that many voters who may not have seen themselves as natural DP supporters nevertheless voted for the party because they believed Berisha's promises of immediate and massive outside help for Albania if he took power.

[15] *Eastern Europe Newsletter,* vol. 7, no. 9, 27 April 1993.

These did not materialise although wages and salaries rose in the more favoured areas. Opinion-polling techniques were at an early stage of development and results varied over time, but there seems little doubt that for most of the period between April 1992 and 1994 effective voter support for the DP was between 25 and 35 per cent, with the centrist Democratic Alliance varying between 5 and 15 per cent. In the absence of a new constitution, power was still effectively concentrated in the Presidency, following on from the pattern established by Ramiz Alia.

The most important foreign backers of Berisha and the DP, particularly the United States, considered a strong central government a vital ingredient in the transition to democracy. In these circumstances, power was increasingly devolved to the President and away from Parliament or the executive. The judiciary was heavily purged after 1992, and most senior judges were now Berisha appointees. The opposition, as well as many independent observers, viewed these developments with concern, seeing in them the potential for a return to authoritarianism and centralism. Supporters of the government justified them as necessary measures in view of the anarchy in large parts of the country throughout 1991 and 1992. It was also claimed that most of the old professional strata in the law and the civil service were either personally sympathetic to communism or unduly influenced by its values.[16] Further justification for the general orientation of the DP government was found in the economic growth that followed its election, the stability of the currency, and the improvement in public order. Although in this period Parliament passed a mass of legislation affecting every area of Albanian life, much of it did not pass into popular culture or understanding, and therefore had little effect on the life of ordinary Albanians. The first opportunity the Albanian people had to express their opposition to these centralist and authoritarian trends was in the 1994 constitutional referendum campaign, and they had no hesitation in seizing it.

---

[16] For an objective and non-political view of the problems with the bureaucracy, as seen by British experts in a specialised field, see article by Peter Leonard and Allen Davis in *Prison Service Journal*, London, no. 98 (September 1994). Both were prison governors, and went to Albania to write a report for the Foreign and Commonwealth Office in London on prison reform.

13

RENEWED POLITICAL TENSION AND THE CONSTITUTIONAL CRISIS

Albanian politics took an ominous term at the beginning of 1994 as the Democratic Party government became increasingly involved in confrontational and undemocratic methods of ruling, dominated by a heavy-handed approach to opposition forces. The year was marked by four events which significantly weakened the Berisha government. These were the assassination in Shkoder in January of a member of the Democratic Alliance Party (DA), the Nano trial, the rapidly worsening relations with Greece and, most crucially, the Democratic Party's defeat in the November referendum on Albania's first post-communist constitution. Politically-motivated crime became an increasingly important factor in the atmosphere of social instability. Both the Shkoder assassination and other political violence and intimidation were linked to the government, and international human rights organisations and European Union bodies began to take an interest.

The Shkoder victim was Gjovalin Cekini, aged twenty-six, who was gunned down in the street in a classic Mafia-style killing at the end of a DA meeting held at the Migjeni theatre in the city centre. The killing was claimed as the first open act of political terrorism in Albania after the fall of communism. Conflicting accounts of the incident followed. According to an implausible report issued by the Ministry of Public Order, the DA leadership had been responsible for Cekini's murder by issuing unpatriotic and leftist statements which angered the crowd and led to the shooting. The Ministry report virtually exonerated the killers from any real responsibility:

> Leaders of the Democratic Alliance Party had a meeting in which they made a number of irresponsible statements, among them pro-Serbian ones, such as 'We have not killed Serbs

nor have they killed us', thus forgetting the blood of hundreds of Albanians killed by the hands of Serbs in Kosova. The statements caused indignation among participants in the meeting who considered it a provocation. Threatening reactions then followed, which led to the presidium requesting help from the police who joined with local government representatives in adopting the necessary measures. Then most of the participants left the hall. After the meeting, supporters of the DA leaders behaved violently and shouted insults outside the hall. At this moment a citizen, Selami Cela, who was passing in his 'Benz', got out of the car and exchanged a replica [i.e. gun] with the group. Immediately a group of five people attacked Selami with punches and kicks, and during the clash Gjovalin Cekini was killed.[1]

The DA secretary-general, Arben Imami, replied to the official statement in an interview in *Zeri-i-Popullit:*

While we were holding our meeting, about twenty-five members of the Democratic Party who work in the local DP presidium entered. Not receiving the support they had hoped for to break up the meeting, they left, shouting insults and slanders. It was when they were leaving the hall that the murder took place. According to eyewitnesses, a car arrived and stopped in front of the Migjeni theatre. Its engine was left running and someone got out to meet someone else in a Toyota with an official number-plate. At this moment, people from the hall arrived, and this person turned to the meeting's participants saying 'Whoever insults Sali Berisha is a so-and-so and does such-and-such [obviously obscenities]'. A minor conflict ensued; the person in question had the revolver he used for the attack constantly drawn. Other people tried to hold him back and calm him and then he committed his crime against a member of our party. The plan was very clear. They entered the meeting in order to disrupt it, failed, went outside, organised themselves, decided to do something, came with the car, left the engine running and committed the crime. The car drove off and the murderer escaped on foot.[2]

---

[1] Albanian Telegraphic Agency, Tirana, 1808 gmt, 17 January 1994, and BBC, *SWB*, EE/1901 B/1, 21 January 1994.

[2] *Zeri-i-Popullit*, 16 January 1994.

For several days after Cekini's death the police in Shkoder could not be contacted by journalists and public telephone lines were cut off. The killer, Selami Cela, was the brother of Shkoder's former police chief and a notorious bully-boy. The murder was linked to a complex world of local intrigue and extortion, where lucrative rackets in the smuggling of diesel fuel and petrol to Montenegro and Serbia across the Buna (Bojana) river nearby were being contested by rival Mafia gangs. The Shkoder and other regional police were alleged to be heavily involved in this trade, and the majority of the Mafiosi are strong government supporters. Whatever the precise details, the crime created the general impression that Albania was sinking into a state where criminals and their associates were in the ascendant. The desperation of the people in the streets of Shkoder, misty in the mid-winter cold, with half-starved horses pulling heavily-laden carts into the town from surrounding villages, seemed sadly apposite. The ambience was reminiscent of late Ottoman times.

The DA accused the DP deputy chairman Ali Spahia of being the direct organiser of the group of DP supporters who entered the meeting and of organising the escalating violence against members of the DA. Spahia argued that the government was so unpopular that it was forced to work with criminals in order to maintain support for its rule. The DA called on the European Union to ask Berisha to respect democratic standards in Albania. According to the President of the DA, Neritan Ceka:

> The most worrying precedent now is the link between the government and the Mafia, particularly around Shkoder, which is breaking the UN sanctions against Yugoslavia. We believe this connection was used to engineer the murder of a Democratic Alliance member on January 14. According to our information, the Shkoder Democratic Party arranged for 25 party members to attend our meeting. We believe that the assassin was among this group. No arrests have been made, and the government has refused repeated requests to meet with DA members.[3] The next day, following Cekini's funeral, more than 2,000 people gathered to hear a mass for the victim in Shkoder cathedral. That Shkoder had been the scene of the killing was significant because the city is an important political barometer; it was

[3] Neritan Ceka, *War Report*, February 1994, p. 13.

where active dissent against the communist regime resulted in the killing of four demonstrators on 2 April 1991 by Alia's police. Thus the DP, aware that it had lost its monopoly of support in the rest of Albania, wanted to preserve its influence at least in Shkoder. In 1993 an attempt by the Socialist Party to hold a large public meeting in the city had ended in a pitched battle outside the cinema where the meeting was supposed to be held, between hundreds of supporters and opponents of the SP; the Party's supporters from surrounding villages were later chased down the main street by gangs of men firing guns into the air and brandishing pickaxe handles.'

The city's tradition of political intolerance and Mafia-type activity dates back a long time: the inhabitants were condemned by the local communists as early as 1942 for 'their scheming behaviour, lack of communist discipline and lack of a clear-cut political line'.[4]

Many factors besides the UN embargo conspired to make the government unpopular in the north and in the provinces generally. Promised investment from Italy had not materialised except for a small Benetton shoe factory. While DP largesse benefited a minority of favoured individuals in Tirana, the government had done little to raise general living standards. Without aid from Catholic charities, there would have been little or no education or health care. By mid-January the Democratic Party was in a state of siege. Official statements accused all opposition groups of being hijacked by extremists. The DP leader Eduard Selami said at the national meeting of the Democratic Party in Tirana on 17 January that the opposition block was headed by leftist extremists who had usurped the leadership of the Socialist Party and the alliances of different extremist trends (i.e. the DA) which had joined the struggle against the Democratic Party.[5] The killing in Shkoder made DA members and other opposition activists throughout Albania concerned for their personal safety. On 2 March 1994 the deputy editor of the DA newspaper *Alieanca* was attacked in the street and left unconscious, and another DA par-

---

[4] Enver Hoxha, *Vepra*, vol. 1.

[5] Albanian Telegraphic Agency, Tirana, 1914 gmt, 18 January 1994, and BBC *SWEB*, EE/1901 B/4, 21 January 1994.

liamentarian, Theodor Keko, was violently assaulted by three men near his home in Tirana.

The discrediting of the DP outside the ranks of its most committed supporters led to a level of intolerance bordering on paranoia. The principle of parliamentary opposition had completely ceased to be respected as armed thugs were increasingly used to intimidate opposition figures. In April 1994 the DA leader Neritan Ceka said in an interview that he was under pressure from his family to leave politics because of the recurrent threats to his personal safety;[6] and Ceka is a centrist who was once a close ally of Berisha's and has never been a left-wing radical. Because of the events in Shkoder political rallies of opposition parties were now effectively banned throughout the country, but at the same time these parties gained credibility despite an ever more apathetic populace. The DP was ceasing to be a cohesive party as it found itself deserted by almost all its former allies, and suspicion of the government among nationalist and anti-communists intensified. The Albanian Democratic Party of the Right (DPR) was established after Petrit Kalakula was expelled from the DP at the end of 1993 and the staunch nationalist Abdi Baleta also withdrew his support. Baleta had never been a member of the DP, but was belonged to its parliamentary group.

The DPR argued strenuously for land to be returned to its former owners and for the eventual formation of a Greater Albania which would include the Albanians living in former Yugoslavia, as well as the remaining Chams in Greece. It believed that the DP had been far too lenient towards those who had actively supported the communist regime. The aim in mid-1994 was to form a unified coalition of the right, which would try to incorporate the Republican Party, Legaliteti, Balli Kombetar and the ex-political prisoners' organisations, all of which agreed on the restoration of land to its former owners and a far more aggressive policy in support of the right of Albanians in the former Yugoslavia to self-determination. (Balli Kombetar, primarily an émigré party with little support inside Albania, was trying hard to live down its tarnished image of wartime collaboration with Axis forces.) The new forces on the right began to draw some support from Kosovars who were disillusioned with what they saw as the vacil-

---

[6] Interview by both the authors with Neritan Ceka, Cambridge, 27 April 1994.

lation and compromises of Berisha. Although they understood on a rational level that the President's position over Kosova was weak and restrained by many outside factors, the new party had a strong emotional appeal. This gave the right more financial support than was usual for a small party, the kind of support that enabled the Republican Party to have prestigious offices in central Tirana. In this connection Kosovar business interests were beginning to use their economic muscle to influence Tirana politics for the first time. Similar forces also influenced the right-wing parties themselves. One of the authors visited the office of the RP's newspaper in April 1994, and every employee without exception was a Kosovar, whereas a year earlier there had been none there at all.

Thus the right-wing anti-communist parties and organisations continued to erode DP support. Baleta and Kalakula both repeatedly criticised Berisha's hesitant policy on the national question and his deals with those active in the former communist regime, and they now openly drew attention to his twelve-year-long commitment to the PLA, when he was a candidate for membership of the Central Committee. The government was repeatedly accused of patriarchal authoritarianism, corruption and neo-communism, and of adopting a casual and excessively moderate stance on the Kosova issue. Anyone disagreeing with the DP line now faced the possibility of arrest. In February 1994 Martin Leka, a young journalist working for the popular independent daily *Koha Jone,* was sentenced to eighteen months in prison for revealing military secrets under a new law that in practice forbade comment on almost any military or national security issue. The unfortunate Leka had reported that officers in Tirana would cease to be allowed to carry their weapons while on duty. This was a trivial procedural matter with no bearing on national security, but it was enough to secure his conviction. The paper had published a photocopy of the internal government document which made this ruling. As part of the same clampdown on the media, the United States personnel attached to the Ministry of Defence were forbidden to talk to the press. The previous government attack on press freedom, involving the arrest of Alexander Frangi (who went into exile in Switzerland), had at least involved a matter of substance – the reporting of movements of military equipment towards the border with Serbia. Similar concerns were evident when the government attempted to charge one of the authors of this volume with espionage in December 1992 for reporting on normal military matters already discussed on the BBC World Service.[7]

On 5 March the former Prime Minister and opposition leader Fatos Nano, a reform-minded economist who had not been among the communist leadership before 1990, was put on trial. The prosecution case was that when in office he had favoured an Italian company that sent food aid to Albania in 1991, and another firm owned by an Albanian expatriate which had transported the aid. According to the judge, only one-third of the aid ever arrived. There is little doubt that this is true, but it is difficult to be clear what happened to the bulk of the shipments. It is possible that it was stolen by the Mafia before it ever left Italy. The same fate befell EU food aid shipments that were supposed to be sent to Ethiopia and Somalia at this time, but after an investigation ordered by the EU commission in December 1992,[8] it was found that the criminal activity was organised exclusively in Italy. Thus there was no *prima facie* reason to assume that this had not also happened with the Albanian aid programme. However, the consideration of evidence was of diminishing importance in the judicial process, where the over-riding factor was that the government required the opposition leaders to be convicted, as in the Omonia trial later the same year.

The refreshing atmosphere of genuine press freedom and freedom of thought in Albania after 1991 was fast disappearing as the state-controlled television relayed only the prosecution side of the Nano case. Right-wing organisations called for a severe sentence, while Socialist supporters alleged that the government was only staging the trial to discredit the Socialist Party. However, it seems likely that the Berisha group had subtler motives. Socialist Party support had stabilised at about 30 per cent of the electorate, and the government could do nothing to shake the loyalty of its traditional southern strongholds or the support of dispossessed urban workers who could not find jobs or emigration opportunities. Nevertheless the trial could deprive the SP of its most effective leader, a man who had gained respect in international bodies while in government in 1991, and could strengthen the vital

---

[7] See article by James Pettifer in *The Times*, 12 December 1992.

[8] *Financial Times*, 11 December 1992.

American commitment to Berisha as the only available leader of Albania capable of effective government. This was the view of key State Department officials such as Chris Hill and Ambassador Ryerson. They felt, and said in Washington, that Berisha was the only man who could stop the country sliding back into chaos. This was also the view of influential Britons such as the parliamentarians Lord Bethell and Geoffrey Pattie, who advised the government (led by John Major) on Albanian matters within the upper echelons of the Conservative Party .

Nano's defence lawyers argued that they had very little time to prepare an adequate defence; and, above all, that Levante, the company involved in the aid programme and allegedly the main conduit for Mafia influence, had been chosen by the Italians and not by Nano or any one else in Tirana. In Italy several former ministers, including the former Foreign Minister Gianni de Michelis, were now on trial in connection with the same affair. Nano himself refused to co-operate in what he declared was purely a political trial. In retrospect, this may be seen as something of an error of judgement, for however true his general contention, a good lawyer could have exposed the weakness of the government's case. The Nano trial further damaged the democratic credentials of the government because two of the trial judges subsequently resigned, and it excited widespread adverse comment on the judicial procedures.

Even though the economy was gradually improving, pulled along as it was by private agricultural growth, the DP's popularity was manifestly declining in the spring of 1994. Despite better supplies of consumer goods, it was clear that without infrastructural improvements the government could not satisfy essential needs such as adequate water for new washing-machines. The DP now began to take increasingly desperate measures to discredit the opposition, using the security service SHIK to gather incriminating material on its personalities and selectively publishing old *Sigurimi* files. In June a conference was organised by Kujtim Cashku, vice-chairman of the Helsinki Albania Committee, to discuss the highly sensitive matter of opening up Albania's secret archives. Even former political prisoners were reluctant to see the files opened, saying that they were full of lies and therefore should not be taken seriously. Still all the country knew that they were being used by DP politicians to discredit certain targeted individuals.

A decision therefore had to be taken at some stage. According to the Helsinki Committee, some 4,800 political prisoners were executed under the communist regime between 1946 and 1991, but it is likely that when the full history of the forced labour system is written, all these figures will turn out to be underestimates. For example, hundreds of northern Ballists and monarchists evidently disappeared or died at the Tepelena forced labour camp in the Vjoses valley between 1945 and 1949. Many also died in a major cholera epidemic in 1947.[9]

The Tepelena camp, known as 'the Albanian Belsen', was only one of several operating at the time. Others were opened later such as the huge land-drainage work camps at Maliqi near Korça and Gradishta near Fier; both held thousands of inmates for much longer than Tepelena. An important reason for the apparently irrational intransigence of the DP government, faced with the claims of the hunger-striking ex-prisoners, may have been that many thousands of families in Albania, especially in the north, had one member or more who had suffered, often severely, in forced labour camps under the Hoxha regime. Both Fier and Maliqi were situated in notorious malarial swamps, and the death-rate from disease and malnutrition must have been high. They remained in operation till the 1960s but in addition thousands of political prisoners, or people who could claim to be considered as such, passed through the forced labour system in mining settlements like Puka or Spaç. A generous settlement with the ex-prisoners would have encouraged many more claimants to come forward, placing a heavy burden on the economy and the Finance Ministry.

For as long as these claims remain feasible, the *Sigurimi* files will be important in order to verify them. Perhaps the most illuminating aspect of the whole issue is the extent to which the DP administration had become isolated from its northern anti-communist roots. The element of popular justice in the ex-prisoners' claims, however exaggerated they may have been, seems at first to have been, completely overlooked by the government, which emphasised only the administrative and practical difficulties in coming to an accommodation with the ex-prisoners' leaders, most of whom were originally strong DP supporters. It also il-

[9] Author's interview with Gjon Marka Gjoni and family, Shkoder, 12 December 1993.

lustrates, in a more general sense, the DP government's problem
in coming to terms with the communist past and 'cleansing the
Augean Stables' where this was manifestly necessary. Among
Berisha's entourage there were still people who had held senior
positions in the one-party state. Here, as elsewhere in Eastern
Europe, the need to protect the interests of these people, some
of whom were of genuine integrity and had taken no part in
human rights violations, resulted in little or no action being taken
against the genuinely guilty. Independently documented accounts
of life in some of the Albanian camps reveal conditions as bad
as in any Gulag in the ex-communist world, and there appears
to be no practical reason why at least some of the camp com-
mandants and guards, who were undoubtedly responsible for the
torture and murder of inmates should not be identified, arrested
and tried.[10]

Apparently only about one-third of the original *Sigurimi* files
still remain in the archives of the SHIK national information
service, the rest having mysteriously disappeared. The exact status
and orientation of the remaining files has proved difficult to
establish with any certainty. It was generally believed that under
communism each individual's file or '*biographi*' was held in tripli-
cate, with one copy in the central *Sigurimi* register in Tirana,
another in a secret underground archive in Berat and another at
a similar establishment in Korça. This has never been proved,
but if it is true, what has happened to the duplicate copies of
these records? The more important records of most ex-communist
East European security agencies are said to have been purchased
by the CIA, MI6 and other Western intelligence agencies, and
Albanian records could have been subject to a similar transaction.
Ex-*Sigurimi* employees and members of the old PLA leadership
have certainly tried to sell such documents.[11] Opposition parties
persistently ask for all the files to be opened, and the majority
of Albanian citizens share this view when asked, but doing so
would deprive the DP of a valuable weapon to use against its
opponents.

---

[10] *Human Rights in the People's Republic of Albania*, report by Minnesota Lawyers International
Human Rights Committee, Minneapolis, 1990.
[11] James Pettifer's interview with Spiro Dede, Tirana 22 April 1994. See also article in
The World Today, April 1991.

Throughout the country different groups were increasingly demanding compensation for the damage their interests suffered under communist rule. At the beginning of May, police were brought in to evict 200 hunger-striking protesters in the northern town of Kukes who had occupied the town-council building and blocked all the approach roads. The protesters demanded compensation for property they lost when the Fierze hydro-electric dam (on the Drin river in the north) flooded the old town of Kukes some twenty years before. The Interior Ministry blamed the protest on communist provocateurs and there may be some truth in this accusation; Kukes was, and is, one of the few places in Albania where there is any real support for a return to the planned economy. An emergency meeting was called by Berisha in Tirana, after which Premier Alexander Meksi stated that the government would try to honour its commitment to deal with all the problems of displaced families and that it would meet reasonable demands, although some were 'absurd and unaffordable'.

Many former political prisoners were given jobs in the chronically over-manned government ministries, but the majority did not regain the property and status they had enjoyed before being interned. Their hunger-strikes continued despite the government's insistence that under the existing economic circumstances no one could realistically expect full compensation for loss of livelihood and property. Nevertheless, the government announced at the end of May a hastily assembled compensation package for former political prisoners. This envisaged compensation of $1,200 a year *per capita* – equivalent to 75 per cent of the annual wage of a miner.

In July the former President Ramiz Alia, who had been on trial accused of conspiring to abuse of his position, and so causing violations of the basic freedoms and rights of citizens, was found guilty of these charges and sentenced to nine years in prison. The former Premier Adil Carcani was sentenced with Alia on the same charges, but because of his age and poor health his five-year sentence was suspended. A host of other former communist officials were also imprisoned, including the one-time Interior Minister, Hekuran Isai, and chairman of the State Control Commission, Simon Stefani, who were sentenced to respectively five and eight years in prison.

However, the judicial procedures in the trial were chaotic and many eye-witnesses felt pity for the aged defendants who looked tired and frail as they were humiliated by the twenty-eight year-old judge. The prosecutor's staff were also all in their twenties, and as with Hoxha's widow, they found great difficulty in bringing forward hard evidence to secure convictions. People were crammed into the stiflingly hot courtroom, and the whole event lacked order or dignity. Like any communist show-trial, it was presented on television, but many Albanians viewed the proceedings with indifference. A correspondent covering the trial for the London *Daily Telegraph* found people more preoccupied with the IMF-imposed price rises, and whether they could afford basic goods like an electric heater for the winter.[12] Alia now seemed to belong in a political museum, and if Albanians felt anything about his sentence, it was that he had been fortunate to avoid a longer one. There is no reason to believe that the Alia sentence had any wider effect on the Socialist Party and the political scene generally, unlike the conviction of Fatos Nano. In August, police broke up a week-long countrywide hunger-strike by some 2,500 former political prisoners demanding compensation in a continuation of the frequent strike policy they had pursued through the previous year. The government rejected the hunger-strikers' compensation claims on the grounds that it could not afford the equivalent of millions of dollars which they demanded, and accused the strikers of destabilising the country's fragile democracy.

The Constitution defeat, November 1994

Following the March 1991 elections, which were won by the PLA, an interim constitution was approved until an entirely new one could be drafted. Under Article 16 of the interim document a referendum could only be called by parliament. Work on drafting a new constitution was supposed to begin immediately after the DP victory in the 1992 elections. Progress on the constitutional reform bill was incredibly slow but it received a jolt when it was believed that Albania stood a realistic chance of admission to the Council of Europe once an acceptable constitution had been decided upon. It was necessary to meet a European deadline of 30 December 1994 for its approval. For Berisha this problem was

---

[12] *The Daily Telegraph*, 5 June 1994.

linked to the critical need to gain admission to the conservative group of European right-wing parties, a move vigorously opposed on human rights grounds by the centre-right Democratic Alliance. Some European governments, particularly the British, had attempted to help the DP, and a British ex-minister and Conservative, MP, Geoffrey Pattie, played a leading role in the matter with the British government. However, progress was slow. The European Union and various foreign governments had taken note of the unfavourable reports emerging from Albania about the lack of democracy, and the flood of critical comments from various human rights organisations, notably Amnesty International. The Democratic Alliance leaders, who were the most vigorous opponents of the DP, were well-thought-of and influential in many EU foreign ministries. Greek protests over the treatment of the minority were beginning to be taken more seriously with the emergence of independent verified evidence of the arrest of the Omonia defendants, the bitter rows involving the Orthodox Church, and the disturbed state of the minority areas in the south.

In these circumstances it became an urgent priority for the President to break the political deadlock and the spiral of declining support for the DP by resolving the constitutional problem. American academic lawyers were employed by the government to draw up a final version of the draft document that had been discussed in the inter-party working groups over such a long period. The stamp of US influence on the final document, with its effort to create a strong central presidency along the lines of that already developing around Berisha, was unmistakable. In order to by-pass Parliament, the President would have a constituent assembly, chosen by himself, to endorse his decrees. This gave him a level of personal power unequalled in any supposedly democratic state. The constitution was designed to increase the President's influence over appointments to all important ministerial, ambassadorial and judicial posts without the prior approval of Parliament; he could use the institutions of justice to eliminate his political rivals. Another undemocratic clause stated that public gatherings could only take place after a permit had been obtained from the government. A highly controversial point in the constitution was the granting of powers to the President to halt criminal investigations into government corruption.

Just before the referendum, three judges from the constitutional court resigned in protest at the matter being put to the people in this way rather than by the parliamentary route of amending the constitution. Berisha, who was blatantly amassing power at the expense of Parliament, needed to acquire a two-thirds parliamentary majority to pass any constitutional amendments. However, this was not possible because the DP had a majority of only eight seats in the 140-seat Parliament. The support of seven coalition members would have been needed to enable the 140-seat parliament to amend the constitution. However, the seven Social Democrat members had resigned from Parliament in protest at the government's blocking of investigations into official corruption. The opposition was solidly opposed to the draft constitution, and many called for a boycott on the grounds that it was illegal. Even many DP parliamentarians abstained from voting to show their opposition to the referendum. The main issue was how power was to be split between the President and Parliament, with most opponents concerned at the lack of firm guarantees safeguarding the independence of the judiciary. The referendum was the first big test for the DP government since its election in March 1992. A DP poll in advance of it predicted a 70 per cent 'yes' vote, and optimistic DP spokespersons continually referred to the exercise as 'an expression of advanced political culture.'

President Berisha has counted on his draft law being swiftly approved. A key provision, in view of the developing crisis with Greece, was that by which all religious leaders had to be Albanian citizens who had lived in the country for at least twenty years. This would automatically have ruled out the Greek Orthodox Bishop Yannulatos, who (despite the official annulment mentioned above) had come in 1991 to re-build the Orthodox Church in Albania; most ethnic Greeks, along with the Greek government in Athens, saw the clause as specifically directed against them and designed to limit their religious freedom. However, following the drafting of the proposed constitution, Berisha announced that the controversy over the leader of the Orthodox Church in Albania would soon be resolved. He said to reporters: 'Anastas Yannulatos should be leaving Albania the day the new constitution is in place.'[13] In reality, Yannulatos is a man of moderation who attempted to build good intercommunal relations between all

---

[13] *Illyria*, 14–15 October 1994, p. 2.

Orthodox believers and mainstream Muslim communities. However, it was not too difficult to associate him in the public mind with the irredentist extremist, Metropolitan Sevastianos of Konitsa, whose activities in the southern minority areas inevitably caused conflict with all Tirana governments, communist and post-communist.

The gulf between rich Tirana and the rest of the country was apparent during the build-up to the referendum, as fleets of black limousines left the capital and sped through impoverished villages on their way to the towns, where Berisha's glitzy campaign message drummed home to sceptical listeners the benefits that all Albanians could expect if they voted 'yes'. All the presidential rallies were accompanied by about 100 DP fanatics who were bussed from one place to another carrying the same placards and shouting 'Sali Berisha!'. During the meetings the fanatics tended to stand in front of the bemused locals so that Albanian television cameras, trying to capture the image of crowds of eager DP supporters, instead merely relayed pictures of the same familiar faces and placards at one meeting after another.[14] In the latter stages of the campaign, Berisha played the Kosova card with the appearance of Kosovar leaders Dr Ibrahim Rugova and Adam Demaci at rallies supporting the Berisha line. This seems to have been another serious misjudgement, because the Kosovars, most of whom would have supported Berisha anyway despite widespread disappointment with his performance on the national question, may have alienated many Albanian voters.

The final result of the referendum was an overwhelming anti-government vote, with 55 per cent against the new constitution and just over 40 per cent for it. This was undeniably a vote of no-confidence on the first occasion which the people had openly shown their dissatisfaction with the DP government. On the following day a visibly shaken Berisha conceded defeat on television. Just before the poll he had said it would be 'the greatest day in the history of Albania'; he had clearly anticipated approval for a constitution that would have ensured his personal rule indefinitely. It was almost two days after the poll that the government finally announced the official results.[15] The defeat seriously weakened Berisha's position, so confident had his inner circle been of victory.

---

[14] *Eastern Europe Newsletter*, vol. 8, no. 22, 2 November 1994.

[15] 'Berisha Broken', *The Economist*, 12 November 1994.

The opposition immediately called for his resignation and demanded that the general election scheduled for April 1996 be brought forward. It was said that Berisha hastily offered his resignation at a closed meeting of the DP but was advised against it; it was widely believed in Tirana that the German and US governments in particular were alarmed at this possibility and instructed their ambassadors to persuade Berisha to remain in office. In protest at Berisha's refusal to resign over the referendum defeat, the Minister of Culture, Dhimiter Anagnosti, himself resigned and wrote in a letter to the Prime Minister, Alexander Meksi, that the President should have had the courage to view the referendum defeat as a personal failure.

There followed the ousting of nearly half of the Cabinet – nine ministers out of nineteen – as part of what the DP chairman Eduard Selami described as 'sweeping changes in the composition of the government'. Berisha's beleaguered administration then lost the last of its parliamentary support as the Republican Party pulled out of its coalition partnership with the DP on the grounds that the government was incapable of fighting corruption and inefficiency. There was general public awareness that the issue of safeguarding parliamentary democracy was at stake. Only two-and-a-half years after the introduction of the democratic process in Albania, the people were extremely suspicious of anything that might threaten it. They were not going to accept a draft constitution thrust upon them by a single party without the full consent of parliament. A new all-party constitutional commission promptly set about redrafting the proposed constitution so that this time it could obtain that consent. Berisha had seen the referendum as a test of his government's popularity, and the 'no' vote solely as a protest against harsh market reforms and not as one against himself and his party. His defeat gave a much-needed boost to the waning fortunes of the DA, whose leadership, though generally respected as comprising sincere intellectuals, were not considered capable of seriously challenging the government. The vocal and coherent arguments pitted against the proposed constitution thrust the DA into a new arena as the rallying voice for the country-wide opposition to the DP government.

In another important sign that the centre of gravity of Albanian politics was moving away from the entrenched prejudices of the previous two years, the commemoration ceremonies for the fiftieth anniversary of the 'Liberation' in November were dominated by the rehabilitation of at least some of the Partisan leaders who fought with Enver Hoxha, and by the participation of British liaison officers from the Special Operations Executive who had fought in Albania with the Partisans during the war, such as Sir Reginald Hibbert. This prominent former diplomat had been ostracised by the Berisha government and attacked in the government newspaper *Rilindja Demokratike* in 1992 for his account of the Partisan campaign. Two years on, however, he was able, as a sign of reconciliation, to play a leading part in the ceremony organised near the monument to the Frasheri brothers in Tirana's central park, where the British war cemetery was officially opened on 27 November (see page 291, below).

On the wider political canvas, the Socialist Party was still the largest political party in Albania, with an estimated 100,000 members in 1992 – about 5,000 more joined in 1993 and a similar number in 1994. These, however, were mostly the sons and daughters of former PLA members. Yet the new SP could no longer be labelled as the PLA by a different name. The majority of new members were young people who, though coming mainly from communist backgrounds, had a comparatively fresh, moderate approach to socialist politics which helped to temper the undoubted conservatism of many older members who had been members of the PLA. The basic principles of SP economic policy centred around building a market economy and at the same time safeguarding social welfare. However attractive this policy appeared to a sceptical Albanian population, the fact remained that the SP would be tainted for a least another generation by association with its forerunner the PLA and the terrors of the Hoxha years. This duly proved to be an important factor in the May 1996 election. In a country where personal and family histories are handed down from one generation to the next the memories of how a every family fared during the Hoxha and Alia years will play an important role in determining its political affiliations for years to come.

The question of land reform still dogged Albania as late as the winter of 1994 and seems likely to remain largely unsettled for the foreseeable future. The land issue opened deep rifts in Albanian society and halted many foreign investment schemes. The division of property formerly owned solely by the state into that owned by the 'old owner' and by the 'new owner' has created much bitterness and resentment. The 'new' property-owners cannot feel secure in their ownership, fearing as they do that any change in government may deprive them of their ownership rights. According to the law in force at the time of writing, all physically-existing property is to be returned to the former owners. But those who have lived and worked in many of the shops and studios in urban areas have been recognised by a presidential decree as the legal owners. Whereas rural dwellers acquired a plot of land as their own under the new law, together with the ownership of their houses, urban residents gained only the flats or houses they lived in. This confused situation has led to endless intractable disputes, major and minor, as long-time users of a property and its previous owners have attempted to assert their rights.

The general condition of many parts of the countryside is also causing great concern. In northern and southern Albania there has been considerable population movement away from the land, so that entire state farms have been abandoned and most of the land lies uncultivated. In the south this is exacerbated by emigration of the young to work in Greece. In the region inland from Albania's so-called 'Riviera coast' lie scores of abandoned settlements. Deserted groves of trees with rotten unpicked fruit are all that remains of the once richly-peopled countryside, now empty except for a few elderly women dressed in black sitting outside their dilapidated cottages.[16] As Albanians struggle to find enough cash to buy imported Greek fruit and olives, hundreds of thousands of olive and citrus trees have been abandoned. Terraces that were cut into the flanks of the rugged coastal hillsides by thousands of work parties in the 1950s are now crumbling away. The once all-important chrome mines, potent symbols of an industrialised Albania, now operate at only part capacity. In these conditions the confidence which the Tirana government seems to display in its success and in the future seems hollow to many Albanians, just as the wrecked factories and high unemployment of the in-

[16] For a comprehensive overview of the migration position in 1993/4, see report published by the International Organisation for Migration: 'Profiles and Motives of Potential Migrants from Albania', IOM, Geneva, 1995. In political terms the IOM research is important in demonstrating that the popular desire to leave Albania has not been reduced at all by the economic developments of the Berisha years. In this, as in other ways, the 'stability' which the West has seen the DP administration as creating is quite illusory.

dustrial towns symbolise the end of Albania as an industrial country. The consumerist boom in Tirana and the more prosperous parts of the coast is manifestly artificial, and for the people reality is all too apparent. The Croatian writer Slavenka Drakulić has noted: 'What Albanians are enjoying now is the theoretical possibility of buying a bottle of whisky or a good perfume, when you don't have enough money even to smell it. In a way, they are living in an illusion of a capitalist society, as well as with the illusion of freedom or democracy. The extreme poverty of the country makes this all still a dream.'[17]

[17]   Slavenka Drakulić , *Café Europa* London, 1996, p. 58-9.

14

THE MAY 1996 ELECTIONS
AND THE FUTURE

Albania has always been a country where it is easy for outsiders to indulge in personal political fantasies. In the 1920s its very throne was something that could be offered to such an unlikely person as the famous English gentleman cricketer, C.B. Fry. In the contemporary period the journalist Misha Glenny has written of the sense of a 'wacky little country' that had somehow been taken up as an American protectorate in the Balkans.[1]

Despite its small size, Albania matters much more to the international community in the post-communist era than it did previously. However, most of those who visit the country for official reasons such as diplomats, politicians or heads of international organisations know little about the history of the curious place they are visiting. As a result the DP government has had a unique opportunity in ex-communist Eastern Europe to practise the politics of public relations illusions. The images of disorder in the 'Years of Anarchy' were so strong that any form of 'stability' has seemed preferable. The overwhelming view of Western diplomats is strongly favourable to President Berisha and his government on the grounds of what is perceived as the economic miracle and social transformation achieved during his administration, combined with the end of 'disorder'. Most see Berisha, absurdly in view of his actual 'biography', as a leader untainted by past communist associations or mentality. In reality the whole evolution of the Democratic Party has been closely linked to that political tradition, and Albania is now a classic contemporary Balkan state, with an over-powerful president, little or no effective parliamentary op-

[1] *Foreign Affairs*, Washington, DC, May 1995, p. 62.

position, and an over-large, privileged and highly politicised police and security apparatus.

The real and genuine achievements of the Albanian people, or lack of them, during the transition period and the rich but contradictory nature of the country's contemporary development is thus largely obscured. The information about Albania that reached European capitals was consistently manipulated by some Western missions and intelligence agencies in the interests of boosting the Berisha government. For example, the release of Ramiz Alia from prison on 7 July 1995 was greeted with great surprise by most Western foreign ministries, although the subject had been widely discussed in Tirana for the previous three months.

We have attempted in our earlier chapters to explore more critically what has and has not been achieved since 1991. We have seen how many of the failings manifested by the DP government have stemmed from the intolerant and anti-pluralistic mentality of many DP politicians, who received their political education during the most intellectually bankrupt and arid period of Albanian communism. This has been combined with the objective difficulties resulting from the absence of a modern constitution, the lack of any tradition of parliamentary democracy, and the difficulties which have been caused by the wider Balkan crisis. Top DP officials, including the President, have successfully managed to disguise their own communist past in the international arena, but they have been far less adept at changing their personal psychology and methods of political operation at home. In the early days of the DP's political honeymoon with the Albanian people, it is arguable that much of this did not greatly matter since most people were so glad to see the end of the communist system that they could have forgiven the new leaders almost anything. But that situation has since changed. The reality of lack of progress in so many areas of life, particularly for those living far from Tirana, has come home to the government if not always to its international backers. Much of the DP project has always depended on propaganda coupled with large flows of international aid and émigré remittances to underpin the value of the currency. But all propaganda suffers from the law of diminishing returns.

The strong backing that Berisha received from the United States in the power struggle for the leadership of the opposition in 1990–1 was largely dependent on his charismatic public image.

However, within two years many Albanians had become aware of the threat of authoritarianism from Berisha personally, and this was demonstrated in the rejection of his proposed constitution in November 1994. The artificial status accorded to the DP regime has actually diminished the great achievement of the 1990-2 democratic revolution, where all those who took part in the struggle for democracy have seen their achievements appropriated by the 'Democratic Party' and legitimised internationally.

By 1995 the heady days of 1991 with images of Illyria Holdings, Sejdia's red taxis and the later discredited Italian Foreign Minister Gianni de Michelis's motorcade speeding through Skenderbeg Square, had been replaced by a tacky veneer of commercialism – pizza restaurants, ice cream stalls, cheap furniture shops, piles of rubbish, streets choked with petrol fumes, and Tirana's once tranquil, rose-filled parks lined with rows of unhygienic cafés. People had certainly become far better dressed during the 1990s and there was a proliferation of domestic appliances, with more than half of Tirana's families now owning a colour television. There was also a building boom in the capital's environs. Nevertheless, despite the horrendous morning traffic jams in the city centre, still only 5 per cent of Tirana families owned a car in the spring of 1995, and the percentage of car ownership in the rest of the country was then only about 2 per cent of families (not of individuals). Back in 1992, desperately hungry people were clamouring for bread in the windowless hole-in-the-wall state kiosks. By 1995 these same streets had shops selling solid gold jewellery, luxury package holidays and very expensive Italian designer clothes; but in the winter of 1994-5 there were still chronic bread shortages caused by electricity breakdowns at the bakeries, and the same old queues reappeared throughout Tirana. The bread shortage that winter, which nearly brought down the government, led at first to official threats to imprison any baker who did not buy a generator. By the summer of 1996 there were still many hours in the day when there was no water supply, and thousands of villages were still without telephones because people had stolen the wires in order to enclose their newly-acquired land.

Albania had become, as one French journalist was told, 'a country of organised disorganisation – of every man for himself'.[2]

---

[2] *Guardian International*, 25 June, 1995, p. 15.

Anything which belonged to the community was regarded as the property of the individual. The result is that taps on public water fountains, water pipes and other pieces of equipment tend to disappear as soon as they are installed. As one observer put it, 'Albania is enjoying a boom – but without any moral principles or collective conscience.'[3] Despite all this, however, the devastated economy has shown signs of recovery. After falling by almost half, GNP slowly rose again and the average monthly wage had risen, by 1996, to around $100. The inflation rate, which soared in 1992, has dropped below 10 per cent. The government deficit has diminished and the national bank has accumulated reserves of hard currency. Nevertheless, although goods are available for those with the money to buy them, the capacity of markets to solve Albania's problems may be reaching its natural limits. Major financial support from the outside world, such as the $500 million debt restructuring negotiated in July 1995, meant little to the poverty-stricken majority.[4] Agricultural mechanisation is still almost non-existent. Previously the co-operatives used the big old caterpillar tractors in centralised tractor stations, but by 1990 most were worn out and few survived the transition period in working order. Even if they had survived, they would have been far too big for the new very small plot sizes. The government attempted to remedy the problem by importing 2,000 small Chinese tractors, but this number barely meets the needs even of the Tirana environs alone.

The more the sleight of hand has been used in terms of international public relations, led by people in some foreign ministries and international organisations who can only be described as fanatical supporters of Berisha, the more domestic reality intruded. The May 1996 election was the culmination of this process. Shanty towns of displaced people are growing up around Tirana in which sanitary and living conditions are appalling.[5] In an attempt to escape poverty and increasing blood feuds over land ownership, thousands of northerners are migrating south to Tirana, leaving many mountain communities all but abandoned. Despite all this,

---

[3] Ibid.

[4] *Financial Times*, 27 July 1995.

[5] See report by Miranda Vickers in *The Times Higher Education Supplement*, 9 February 1996, p. 13. See also *Neue Zürcher Zeitung*, 10 November 1995.

Albania is still seen by some in the international community as an island of propriety. Government claims of high economic growth have also been received uncritically by the world financial institutions; however, the statistical bases used have been extrapolated from the 'Years of Anarchy' in 1990-1 to flatter recent achievements and are thus untrustworthy. If the statistical base used had been that of, say, 1985 when a commodity like cereal grain was produced in much larger quantities than in the mid-1990s or production levels were higher in the extractive industries, the Berisha economic miracle would appear much less impressive. It is arguable that the whole structure of International Monetary Fund and World Bank support for Albania in 1992-6 rested on manipulated economic statistics.

This contradiction between international political support and domestic unpopularity continued to dominate political life in 1995. The beginning of the year saw the DP in disarray, with the President's increasing unpopularity causing widening divisions within his own Party. The key defection was that of the Party Chairman, Eduard Selami. This affable, intelligent philosopher in his thirties came from the heart of the Tirana élite (it has often been rumoured that he is Enver Hoxha's natural son). He played a key role in party management for Berisha in 1993 and 1994, particularly at the difficult 1994 Congress when the President was already becoming increasingly isolated after the continual haemorrhage of support from the right wing of the DP in the preceding year. Selami was a key figure in the relationship with the United States, as well as with DP activists internally, and Berisha trusted him as a loyalist. After a year when the President had seen Selami more or less every day, he broke all links with him and, on the three or four occasions when they did meet, over a period of ten months, Berisha became extremely emotional and accused him of personal betrayal.[6]

An important and insufficiently regarded consequence of the endless series of breaks with former associates was the ossification of Parliament as a legislative body. The President soon had so few people of real ability able to conduct political business competently that when he was absent much of its work ground to a halt. This problem was accentuated throughout the year by a

[6] Interview by James Pettifer with Eduard Selami, 17 September 1995.

series of opposition boycotts, resulting in the ruling council of the Democratic Party becoming more and more the *de facto* legislature, as was shown when its initial proposals for the new electoral law were almost universally regarded as the actual legislation. In a similar vein, Berisha purged the head of the Supreme Court, Zef Brozi, in September by a decree which the opposition claimed to be illegal. After his dismissal had been ratified by the Berisha-controlled Constitutional Court, Brozi said: 'The mechanisms of the present state power have for months sought to put me in prison. But I believe that Albanians will understand that if I am jailed today, then tomorrow the same destiny may befall any Albanian who opposes the policy of those in power and the convictions of the despot, and is against the interests of some of the dishonest mechanisms of the present state power.'[7]

Brozi was dismissed on Berisha's recommendation partly because he openly criticised the Interior Ministry over human rights issues. He also criticised the way in which judges were dismissed, with no legal justification, simply because they differed politically from the ruling party. He also argued against the censoring of journalists merely because they were critical of the government. But where Brozi really angered the President was in resisting his efforts to influence the Supreme Court in the trial of five members of the Greek minority in order to keep them in prison. Brozi would not accept the sentencing of innocent citizens to eight years in prison for political reasons. But what finally sealed his fate was a decision to review the case of the imprisoned SP leader, Fatos Nano. Berisha, afraid that the Court might find Nano innocent, had to eliminate Brozi from the political scene. In this he succeeded, and the judge left Albania for exile and political asylum in the United States.

As in 1994, attacks on the independent media continued in a climate where the Mafia had become increasingly influential and were widely rumoured to work with agents of the Interior Ministry. The most serious incident was the near-fatal bomb attack on the leading newspaper publisher, Nikolle Lesi, at his home in Lezha in November. A massive explosion ripped through the apartment block where he lived on the north side of the town. Lesi accused the authorities of attempting to influence the independent press:

[7] *Albanian Daily News*, 23 September 1995.

'The offers take different forms; sometimes it's money, sometimes pressure from the ruling party, and sometimes those who won't accept get dynamited instead.'[8] As happens throughout the world, an increasing level of material corruption in politics led to rising public concern. Financial scandals have been common in Albania since the beginning of liberalisation, but many Albanians feel that corruption has now moved to the heart of the state machine and that, as in Ottoman times, political favours can be bought and sold more or less openly, particularly in matters such as development applications and foreign visas and passports. In response to the reaction from the public, Berisha announced a crackdown on corruption but to little obvious effect. In November 1995 a British television programme focused on corrupt business practice and political chicanery in the handling of British foreign aid programmes at the Albanian end. The revelations damaged the Berisha government's hitherto close relations with the Conservative government in London.[9] The British Ambassador to Italy, Sir Patrick Fairweather, whose responsibility included Albania, had to fly to Tirana to watch the programme with Berisha and calm his protests. This occurred after the Albanian government tried to persuade the British government to halt the transmission of the programme – an indication of the former's attitude to press freedom.

While political culture has become more corrupt, social life is more open and vibrant. The new habit of dining out in the plethora of recently-opened restaurants and the now fully-fledged café society have brought Tirana into line with other Balkan capitals. The old élite society that flourished in the capital before the Second World War was in many ways also a café society, and its restoration is one of the most positive features of recent years. But an extremely negative aspect of the transition has been a flood of hard-core pornography into Albania. The material has come mainly from Italy and Greece, and all news-stands now display a mass of such publications, almost all entitled 'Eros' or 'Erotica'. There are no age restrictions for viewing pornography in cinemas. There has also been an explosive growth of prostitution,

---

[8] Alex Standish, 'Albania's Dark Forces terrorise the Press', *The European*, 16 November 1995.

[9] ITV 'Cook Report', 28 November 1995. See *Koha Jone*, 30 November 1995.

some of it involving minors. In Tirana, Durres and Vlora, many women from Romania and Russia now work in the sex industry. However, in some centres where religion has more influence, particularly the traditional Islamic towns, a reaction has set in; in February 1995 Elbasan became the first town in Albania to place a total ban on the showing of pornographic films in its two cinemas.

Throughout 1995 pressure on the government to curb the growth of Tirana's shanty suburbs steadily increased. The coming to power of the DP in March 1992 persuaded many north-eastern highlanders that they would be given favourable treatment if they trekked to Tirana. At that time the authorities offered the Tropoja people land for settlement on the flanks of the Dajti mountain to the east of the capital, but the north-easterners spurned the offer, preferring Kamza, on the north side of the city and nearer to the centre. Some northerners have succeeded in the anarchic small-time trading that prevails around the capital and have used their earnings to build houses there, but the majority have grown increasingly poor. Large families are often crammed into tiny wooden shacks in Kamza with tar-paper roofs, without running water or sewerage, or at best with shallow, ineffective cesspits, which makes the risk of cholera and other infectious diseases ever-present.[10] In June 1995 police began clearing the Kamza shanty town , where an estimated 30,000 people live. Their attempts to move the inhabitants led to three days of violence in which the main north-south road was blockaded and several dozen people were injured. Up to 80 per cent of Kamza's population are from the north, particularly the President's home district of Tropoja. Intense competition for land, resentment by Tirana's population at Kamza's very existence and a growing health risk have turned the shanty town into a political time-bomb.

Under communist rule, state-subsidised collective farms in the north-east provided work and income for the highlanders. Rigorously enforced restrictions on movement within the country and the inability of Albanians to travel abroad prevented the dis-enchanted youth from migrating to the cities. The collapse of communism and the lure of potentially high earnings in Tirana and further afield, notably in Greece, led to a mass movement

---

[10] *East European Newsletter*, vol. 9, no. 13, 21 June 1995.

of youth out of the highlands. In many areas of the north-east there is a shortage of productive land, although in general the 2-3 hectares available to most families are enough for subsistence farming – unlike in the central highlands of Mirdita where the land is much poorer, if not totally barren and denuded. Whereas people from Tropoja district mostly went to Kamza, from Mirdita they went to the plains of Lezha south of Shkoder. More recently the Mirdita highlanders have set up a shanty town on the outskirts of Durres. As in other areas of Albanian life, land and the questions of legality surrounding it are central to understanding many of the present social conflicts. This was implicitly recognised by Berisha's appeal in September 1995 for people to move from the north to recolonise the largely deserted coastal areas. In asking Albanians to 'turn their faces to the sea', he hoped that the considerable number of right-wing opponents to the new land laws passed in the previous three years would forget their former property in a drive to develop tourist sites on the coastal strip.

One benefit that would result from a general northern exodus to the lowland plains would be a reduction in blood-feud killings related to arguments over redistribution of land. In January 1996, one village near Bajram Curri had fourteen males, all vendetta targets, in hiding in their farmhouse and only their womenfolk could safely go out to work on the farm – a situation which naturally caused considerable economic hardship to the family. By the beginning of 1996, according to research by the American Peace Corps, there were an estimated 60,000 people actively involved in blood-feuds throughout northern Albania. Another ambitious projection of Albania's future is the production of a plan by the Tirana municipality for the development of a 1,000,000-inhabitant conurbation along the Durres-Tirana corridor, and stretching south towards the towns of Kavaja and Rrogozhina. In many ways this may be less of a plan than the rationalisation of contemporary reality if current population movements persist. The salient point is that without massive and immediate investment in the infrastructure, roads and facilities for water supply and sewage disposal, the central and northern regions will come near to collapse. The government can do little to stem the migration of northerners to Tirana and the resulting development of the shanty towns into permanent suburbs. This in turn will exacerbate the already deep divisions between the indigenous inhabitants of

Tirana and the northern newcomers. North-south antagonism based on resentment over internal migration is increasing. An Albanian from Fier, echoing a growing sentiment, told one of the authors that he believed there should be a border post at the Shkumbi river and that no northerners should be allowed south without a passport.

But, as always in Albania, settling accounts with the past plays a large part in the reality of the present. On 7 July, 1995, the former PLA leader Ramiz Alia was released from prison in a gesture of reconciliation presumably designed to project an improved human rights image to the outside world. On 11 September the Vienna-based International Helsinki Federation for Human Rights claimed that the jailed opposition leader Fatos Nano and the son of Enver Hoxha had been convicted in politically-motivated trials and called for their immediate release before their appeal was heard by the Supreme Court. Nano, sentenced to twelve years in prison on charges of embezzlement and falsifying documents, accused President Berisha of perverting the course of justice in an attempt to eliminate his as a political opponent. The younger Hoxha was imprisoned for one year for criticising the country's leaders.

Ten years after his death, the name of Enver Hoxha still lingered on a few remote mountainsides. At the end of August 1995, an Albanian army unit attempted to destroy one of his last remaining monuments near Berat, 75 miles south of Tirana, by dropping napalm on the 450-foot-long tribute to him after attempts to blow it up had failed. The napalm blackened the white letters, making the stones indistinguishable from the surrounding Shpiragu mountain and invisible from the nearby town. While grandiose plans for the development of Tirana's infrastructure are afoot, the rest of the country quietly decays. The northerners are bitter about the worsening dilapidation of their roads – their only link to the outside world. The narrow mountain roads, like that which snakes between Peshkopija and Kukes and on to Bajram Curri, were built either by communist youth brigades in 1947 or by the Italians in the 1930s and have had little repair or general maintenance since 1990. The winters there are harsh and when the snow melts in the spring thaw, great boulders crash down the mountainsides creating potholes and causing further landslides. Widespread deforestation has caused faster run-off and more powerful floods, which are continually damaging the unmaintained rural road network. Overgrazing caused by the new private herds adds to the already longstanding erosion problems and the silting up of rivers.

Albania is buffeted not only by the ravages of nature but also by the tides of war. Along the road north of Shkoder dozens of newly-built petrol stations supplied the demand for smuggled fuel in Montenegro, in defiance of UN sanctions against the former Yugoslavia. Within Albania the American security guarantee – if it can really be said to exist – also brings difficult responsibilities. In July 1995, US transport planes carried equipment to Gjader airbase north of Tirana in preparation for unmanned Predator spy-plane missions to go out over Bosnia gathering intelligence on the location of troops and weapons to be passed on to NATO and the UN command for use in peacekeeping and air support missions. The mission marked the most significant US military deployment there had ever been in Albania.

Normally Gjader is a quiet spot. Shoeless peasants ride horses bareback over the weed-infested airstrip, sharing it with the occasional MiG-21. The 1958-vintage Soviet fighters, the mainstay of the Albanian air force, rarely fly because there is little money for training or spare parts. Like the Russians and the Chinese before them, the new superpower patron has begun to create little enclaves for its people within Albania. In an eastern suburb of Tirana the US government has built an American village with fenced-off houses under permanent guard. Once again, the difficulty of evolving political bodies and a functioning political culture in a modern European form was shown, in that leading committees of the DP were and are playing a legislative role much as the old Party of Labour internal committees did in these sensitive security matters.

The campaign for the general election scheduled for May 1996 began in earnest during the summer of 1995 with the Democratic Party devising a number of new and radical laws, in the hope that it would guarantee a second victory and in the process effectively re-establish a one-party state. The Genocide Law, narrowly passed by parliament at the end of September 1995, was central to these objectives. It was designed to deplete the ranks of the opposition parties by prohibiting anyone who had held a position of power before 31 March 1991, i.e. under the communist regime, from holding any parliamentary, judicial or governmental office. According to the DP, the aim of the Law was to 'prevent those who caused the economic, physical and psychological ruin of the country from ever having a chance to repeat those acts'. However, there was no need for such a law since Articles 73 and 74 of the existing penal code already allowed for the arrest and prosecution of those who had held high office under the old regime – men such as Gramoz Ruci, former leader of the *Sigurimi* and ex-Minister of the Interior, who was foremost in venting anger at the new law. The Genocide Law effectively banned not only the leaders of the two main opposition parties, Skender Gjinushi of the Social Democrats and the already imprisoned Fatos Nano of the Socialist Party, but also more than a quarter of the Socialist parliamentarians. As a by-product the Genocide Law delivered a severe blow to national unity by reactivating old wartime antagonisms which have never been laid to rest. Veterans of both the partisan National Liberation Movement and the nationalist Balli Kombetar have denounced people alleged to have committed atrocities against the other side during the war. An opinion poll taken by an Italian newspaper in early October showed that nearly 60 percent of the electorate planned to vote Socialist, a fact which alarmed foreign observers. The SP, knowing that it would inherit the country's chronic ills, openly admitted that it wanted to avoid winning a landslide victory, preferring to join in a coalition of all the opposition parties. The DP therefore carefully scrutinised the existing electoral law under which 4 per cent of the total votes cast would ensure representation in parliament. To eliminate the weaker parties it wanted the figure raised to 10 per cent, but both the European Commission and the United States strongly opposed such a move. Following strong pressure from the Americans, a 7 per cent threshold was agreed at the end of September. The Democratic Alliance then formed an electoral alliance with the small Social Democratic Party to ensure the political survival of the latter and present the electorate with a centrist alternative. Another major move designed to ensure government control over the voting procedure was the creation of a new administrative division, the 'prefecture', which would include a number of districts. The prefects then appointed were all DP supporters who, in the classic communist manner, owed their jobs directly to the Party. In the local elections held in July 1992 the SP had won more than 53 per cent, and the prefecture system was introduced by the DP after this shock defeat with the aim of 'liquidating local power'. Since then the limited power of the local administrators has been on paper only.

Before 1993 the local leaders of each district used to prepare the electoral lists at the polling stations. Then after the election the polling station commission would count the votes under the supervision of the local authorities. The police who supervised the whole operation were also under these local authorities. In 1996, however, the prefectures were nominated by the Minister of the Interior, so that the prefect had absolute control over the local administrator whom he could remove at his discretion. Therefore, the final results of the elections were controlled by the Interior Ministry because all the papers and documents had to be passed immediately to the zone commission and then straight to Tirana. Thus the whole process was easily open to manipulation.

Against this background there was widespread intimidation of the opposition, with many journalists having to flee the country in fear of arrest. However, European Union foreign ministries remained indifferent to the looming crisis. Opposition leaders stressed the importance of getting the Council of Europe to challenge Berisha over the attacks on the judicial system and the press, and tried to find support from traditionally supportive Greece, but in the power vacuum during the last days of the Papandreou government little was achieved. The President, who has the legal right to postpone the general election for forty days beyond the date originally scheduled, sought to delay the final election date as late into spring as possible. There is always a problem in Albania with general winter discontent; the lack of essentials such as electric power, hot water, fuel and fresh food add to the misery of damp homes and potholed streets turned into quagmires of mud. But the tensions and frustrations which reach their height in the winter months abate somewhat with the warmer weather and the relatively easier conditions of late spring. There were strong signs now that the Americans were becoming less keen to continue bolstering the beleaguered DP regime; human rights concerns provided a major stumbling-block for Berisha's visit to the United States in September, despite the success of the visit in military terms. It was assumed by Albanian observers and journalists that the US State Department was incensed that Berisha chose to issue the

Genocide Law, dismiss Zef Brozi, and introduce a law disfranchising small parties just on his return from Washington, in order to suggest to the Albanian public that these moves had the blessing of the US government. Nevertheless, the Dayton, Ohio, peace agreement was a minor boost for Berisha in these weeks, since it seemed to validate his pro-American foreign policy for the Balkans.

At the beginning of October, the Socialist Party launched its parliamentary election campaign with a big rally in Durres stadium, thus beginning its six-month battle with the smaller opposition parties to win the disaffected voters. The campaign was led by the SP vice-chairman Namik Dokle, the acting leader while Fatos Nano remained in prison. In contrast to the disarray of the DP, the SP was trying to project itself as united. However, the electorate was aware of increasing divisions in the Socialist camp between the young 'Eurosocialist' followers of Fatos Nano and the older more conservative ex-communists led by Xervat Pellumbi. Although Nano had aligned himself with the progressive Eurosocialists, the majority of the reformists rightly claimed to be untarnished by association with the former communist regime. Nevertheless, the traditionalist Marxists could assert that they were the more experienced politicians. The Eurosocialists pressed for more representation on the SP executive, which they criticised for prolonging the life of Marxist doctrine. There were attempts by both the DP and the SP to rid themselves of members and officials who were on record as having cooperated with the former *Sigurimi*, or who even worked as its agents. The Genocide Law did not automatically affect these people because there is no easily verifiable record of their clandestine activity. The old *Sigurimi* had a preference for recruiting agents with a 'bad' biography in communist terms – with close family members as dissidents or parents who had been shot by the regime. The DP in particular became something of a repository for former agents who wanted to escape their past – a fact well known to the SP from its time in government before the DP won the March 1992 election. The DP was therefore reluctant, except very selectively, to open up the *Sigurimi* files, which would clearly have caused it enormous damage. Instead it conducted a silent purge during the autumn of 1995 of its members whom it considered to have an unsavory past. The purge started in the lower echelons and worked its way upwards. Some 90 per cent of DP provincial and district leaders were replaced, and about half of the Party's national membership was placed under a ban.[11]

The May 1996 general election

Thus it was in an atmosphere of profound division and contradiction that Albania faced its first parliamentary election to be held under President Berisha's government. Both the Socialist Party and the Democratic Alliance brought charges that they were routinely denied access to the state-controlled media and that their meetings were illegally disrupted or broken up by police or SHIK agents. This indicates the atmosphere of general harassment and stress the country had been under for the previous four years; so much seemed to be at stake, with a new political and national identity still in the process of formation and the country always beset by its geographical position in a Balkan peninsula rent by the uncertainties of war and economic collapse. An Albanian writer summed up the general mood of the country: 'There exists within the nation's cultural ethos a very simplistic message – *sa mbaj mua, une do te baj tya* – what you do to me, I will do to you. The force of tradition, having combined with Albania's authoritarian and totalitarian past, had served to produce fissures in the democratic governance process with its system of checks and balances'.[12]

In the weeks leading up to the election the DP seemed to be seized by a sense of panic about the possibility that it would be defeated. Its agents were seen running around Athens buying up copies of the opposition newspapers *Koha Jone* and *Zeri-i-Popullit.* The opposition parties were prohibited from holding their rallies in prominent places such as Skenderbeg Square and the centres of other major towns. Instead they were forced to gather in remote places or indoors, which was often difficult due to the lack of buildings of adequate size in Albania. The Socialist Party's campaign was particularly low-profiled because of a severe lack of funding. According to the SP's chief financial administrator,

---

[11] See Sean Boyne, 'Albania's Communists paying for the Past', *Janes Intelligence Review,* October 1996, p. 438, for a comprehensive analysis of the growth of Berisha's security apparatus.

[12] N.J. Costa, *Albania: A European Enigma,* New York: Columbia University Press, 1995, p . 5.

Farudin Arapi, the state was bound to give the largest opposition party only $150,000 from the fund from which all opposition parties were entitled to draw under the electoral law. A deeply worried Arapi claimed that 'the minimum sum we need to conduct the campaign is $400,000'.[13] The party eventually got by with donations from the SP membership and several small and medium-sized businesses, and with the help of unpaid party workers who complained that their major expense was buying petrol for the vast distances they had to travel through the country, while DP activists merely tapped into the state's gasoline supplies. Earlier in the year, the DP had launched a major smear campaign against the Socialist Party, accusing it of being financed by Belgrade.[14] Barely one week before the election, the Democratic Alliance had still not received any money from the government to assist with its campaign costs. Many DA candidates had to pay for their own local campaign materials. In marked contrast, the DP's electoral finances were comfortably dependent on its numerous provincial potentates and fixers, many of whom had made small fortunes during the previous three years. Since commerce was thoroughly mixed up with local politics, the DP had access to a sizeable campaign fund. Some émigré money was also available to it, though probably much less than in 1992. Kosovars, in particular, tended to support the Republican Party, not the DP as it had done then.

Just one week before the election there were no opposition campaign posters or slogans to be seen anywhere, yet throughout Albania almost every wall in every village was decorated with the words '*rrofte PD*' or similar pro-DP slogans. Windows everywhere were plastered with DP posters, showing only the President. In this latter context the DP relied heavily on foreign advisers, particularly from the Konrad Adenauer Foundation in Germany who strongly recommended to the DP leadership in December 1995 that their campaign should be focused on Berisha. This was borne out in his campaign speeches, which concentrated heavily on the possibility of chaos if he was not re-elected. As

---

[13] *Koha Jone,* 22 February 1996, p. 3.

[14] *Albania* and *Rilindja Demokratike* on 24 January published articles alleging that the Serbian secret service finances the Albanian Socialist Party and the *Koha Jone* newspaper. For reports on this see ATA news agency, Tirana, in English, 1940 gmt, 24 January, *SWB,* EE/2520, 25 January 1996, p.1.

in communist times, the survival of the Party was equated directly with the survival and welfare of the state and nation.

A total of 140 seats were being contested with twenty-five at stake in a proportional vote the following week. Polling began early in the morning of 26 May, and before noon there were already several allegations of armed guards intimidating voters at polling booths and stuffing ballot boxes with fraudulent votes. By 6 p.m. the manipulation and intimidation had become so acute that the Socialist Party and several of the smaller opposition parties, including the Social Democrats and the Democratic Alliance announced that they were withdrawing from the elections and called for a boycott of the balloting just hours before it ended. Despite frenetic appeals by Berisha to ditch their boycott and take part in the second round of voting due the following Sunday, the opposition flatly refused to participate further in the process, claiming intimidation and vote-rigging by the DP. European countries put pressure on Berisha to organise a partial re-run of the election because of doubts over its fairness, but he vowed to press ahead with a second round of voting. Albania's Central Electoral Commission acknowledged that some voting irregularities had occurred and therefore ordered a repeat vote in thirteen constituencies. But the opposition also boycotted this re-run, which took place on 16 June, demanding a completely fresh election. The Democratic Alliance leader Neritan Ceka called the election a *coup d'état,* adding that the opposition had to resist such a fraudulent result. 'The day after tomorrow will be too late if we do not defend the free vote,' he claimed.[15] Nevertheless, the DP claimed a sweeping victory. Berisha conceded that there had been irregularities but said that they had not come close to influencing the results of the vote. Of the 115 seats contested in the first round, the DP won 95, or 67.8 per cent of the vote, while the Socialist Party won five. The Human Rights Party, which represented the ethnic Greek minority, won two seats, and a further ten parties faced a run-off. Opposition leaders warned that a parliament controlled by a single party would create 'a new dictatorship' and increase social and political tensions.

There was a mixed reaction from the large team of international monitors who had attended the elections. However the over-

[15] Reuter, 27 May 1995.

whelming majority agreed with the preliminary report of the Vienna-based Organisation for Security and Cooperation in Europe (OSCE), based on the findings of its observers who monitored about 300 polling stations in the first round. The report criticised 'serious irregularities' in the polling process, and a call was made for new elections in some parts of the country in a communiqué from the president of the OSCE, Swiss Foreign Minister Flavio Cotti. Some specific irregularities were cited. At a polling station in Gjirokaster, votes for an opposition party were counted for the ruling party. In another, votes for the SP were added to those for the DP, giving the latter a clear majority. In Berat one polling station recorded a turnout of 105 per cent, and in Kucova observers noted that when the ballot-box was emptied it contained pre-filled ballots, all for the Democratic Party. Similar abuses appeared to be widespread. The OSCE confirmed that the conduct of the elections had contravened international standards and had violated thirty-two out of seventy-nine articles in the Albanian electoral law.[16] In its communiqué the OSCE called on political parties to 'examine, for the sake of democratic stability, all measures including the possibility of partial repetition of elections, in order to resolve the dispute', and warned that the current situation might jeopardise the country's prospects for democratic development.

On 29 May the DP was declared the clear victor in the general election with results showing that its deputies had won a majority of more than two-thirds in the 140-seat parliament. The Socialist Party, which had thirty-eight seats in the previous parliament, refused to take up the five seats which the Central Electoral Commission said it had won in the first round. The Social Democrat leader Skender Gjinushi said: 'The elections were completely prefabricated, held under the threats of the police and SHIK, and were heavily manipulated.' He added: 'The manipulation was organised at the highest level and it is up to the people not to accept the results of these false elections.'[17] Two days after the election, opposition leaders, together with local and foreign journalists, were beaten up and temporarily detained by police when

[16] Office for Democratic Institutions and Human Rights of the Organisation for Security and Cooperation in Europe, Observation on the Parliamentary Elections held in the Republic of Albania, 26, May and 2 June 1996, ODIHR OSCE, Warsaw, 11 July 1996.

[17] Reuter, 30 May, 1996.

they tried to stage a rally to protest against the alleged manipulations and demand a fresh ballot. Phone lines to the headquarters and homes of opposition parties boycotting the elections were cut. Despite police warnings to people to stay off the streets, protest rallies were held in Tepelena, Patos, Fier and Permet, and several people were seriously wounded in scuffles with riot police. Even some foreigners were reluctant to seek hospital treatment in case their names were revealed to SHIK agents.

There were, of course, a few foreign observers who failed to see what all the fuss was about, and claimed that the election had passed off with the minimum of fraud and intimidation. One such, Anthony Daniels, felt that the OSCE had actually sent its monitors to Albania with the clear intention of accusing Berisha's administration and the DP apparatus of manipulating the elections regardless of the actual events. In a scathing article he wrote: 'Having gone to Albania as members of the British Helsinki Human Rights Group to observe the recent elections, my companions and I soon realized that the OSCE observers were determined from the very outset to condemn the government of Sali Berisha for election fraud: an *a priori* condemnation in which most of the observers were only too happy to join.'[18] Daniels alleged that many of the election observers were sympathisers of the former regime and that a Danish observer had been an active member of the Danish-Albanian friendship society in the 1970s, while the German delegation consisted of a correspondent of Deutsche Welle, the German equivalent of Voice of America, long suspected by Albanians of ideological bias in favour of the previous regime and two female Albanologists who trained at a time when a keen interest in Albania almost invariably denoted ideological sympathy with the Hoxha regime. Daniels reserved his strongest condemnation for the Norwegian observers, 'the largest and most powerful of the delegations'. He claimed to have seen the letter sent on their behalf to the Socialist Party of Albania 'by an organisation called Worker's International Solidarity, in which the delegation was referred to as "the comrades" (the letter was signed "Yours in Solidarity"), and which asked the Socialist Party to arrange cars and interpreters for the delegation. It was not altogether

---

[18] Anthony Daniels, *National Review*, July 1996, p. 43. See also the report of the British Helsinki Human Rights Group, Oxford, July 1996, for a highly controversial defence of the election.

surprising that their impressions were highly unfavourable to the government'.[19] However, even Daniels had to admit the government's monopoly of television air time: 'It was quite clear that President Berisha's ruling party awarded vastly more television coverage to itself than to any of the opposition parties.'[20] The DP echoed his view that the majority of foreign observers were left-wing and largely sympathetic to the previous regime. However, the international journalists present were virtually unanimous in their condemnation of the events.

The Meksi government Mark Two

The Democratic Party emerged from the elections with control of 122 out of 140 seats. On 1 July President Berisha, who adamantly refused to hold new elections, said in an address to the opening session of the new parliament: 'The new Albanian parliament which emerged from the free and fair elections on 26 May will continue to follow with devotion the road on which the previous parliament embarked.[...] This parliament will give the country the laws it lacks and will perfect new laws, so that Albania will enter the year 2000 with a complete and more perfect framework of a state ruled by law, including its institutions and laws.' Towards the end of his speech, Berisha revealed his fury over the opposition boycott of the election: 'I would like to avail myself of this occasion to invite the deputies of the left-wing opposition to abandon their red boycott and not become accomplices in one of the ugliest acts in the entire history of world democracy, an act which was carefully prepared somewhere to destabilise Albanian democracy and trample Albania's sovereignty underfoot.' Berisha's speech echoed his belief in the conspiracy of the 'red pashas' and their willingness to do deals with the 'enemies of Albania' (almost certainly a reference to the Serbs and the Greeks). The falsity of this view is demonstrated by the active support the weak Simitis government in Athens gave to the Berisha campaign.

The second round of voting on 2 June passed off without incident and without the participation of the opposition. But the scenes of police violence in Skenderbeg Square when the elections

[19] Anthony Daniels, op. cit., p. 44
[20] Ibid.

were over led to widespread international criticism, with the Council of Europe suggesting that the elections should be annulled and new ones held within eighteen months. The Americans, in particular, voiced strong dissatisfaction with the entire electoral procedure and urged Berisha to 'go back to the drawing board' to resolve what was considered by all concerned to be a very unsatisfactory situation.[21] As a result, US diplomats stayed away from the opening session of Albania's new parliament to make clear that the United States did not believe that the electoral disputes were over. Despite having backed Sali Berisha over a long period, the Americans claimed that the government's attempts to solve the political crisis resulting from the way the election was conducted were wholly inadequate. 'The United States does not want to give the impression that we consider this matter closed and it would not be appropriate under the circumstances to attend this ceremonial event,' said Charles Walsh, press attaché at the US embassy in Tirana. However, most of Tirana's diplomatic corps attended the ceremony in a demonstration of continuing European Union acquiescence in the Berisha regime.

Following the announcement of the list of ministers in the newly-appointed government, there was much talk in Tirana of the considerably weakened power of the Premier, Alexander Meksi, balanced by his deputy premier Tritan Shehu. An article in *Zeri-i-Popullit* summed up the gossip in the capital:

Former deputy Prime Minister Dashamir Shehi, former Interior Minister Agron Musaraj and former Foreign Minister Alfred Serreqi, all well known as Meksi's men, will no longer sit round Meksi at the oval table. In their places, Meksi will face Tritan Shehu as Foreign Minister, Halit Shamata as Interior Minister, and Kristofor Peci as Justice Minister. This triumphant trio in the struggle of the clans completes Berisha's domain in the government circle, which also includes Safet Zhulali, Albert Brojka, Besnik Gjongecaj, Dylber Vrioni and Maksim Cikuli, all high-ranking combatants in the 'cold war' between the Berisha clan and the Meksi clan in the Democratic Party. Alexander Meksi, formerly one of the DP's most important people, is thus left entirely isolated in a list of appointments that cynically bears his name. The bargain appears to have

---

[21] Reuter, Vienna, 20 June 1996.

been a tough one, and it cost Meksi's group dear. Four important government seats, in which for three years his people sat and did a great deal to defend him, have been sold at a high price to pay for the premier's chair. Tritan Shehu is the greatest victor in all these movements. The DP chairman, deputy Prime Minister and Foreign Minister is the real prime minister of the Meksi government Mark Two.[22]

The new administration swiftly promised that it would deliver on campaign promises to kick-start economic growth by reducing taxes for farmers and business and stepping up badly-needed infrastructural investment.

The SP said that it would continue to work as a constructive opposition force outside parliament, despite being in the midst of open turmoil and crisis. The split in the SP, which had become public the previous autumn, was partly responsible for derailing its election chances. Luan Hajdaraga, the SP deputy chairman, explained: 'We are conscious that the time has come to make changes in the main party's documents, programme, statute and leadership. The SP is in a continuous reformation process which has now become more imperative. It is impossible for a large party with a great influence with the Albanian electorate like the SP not to undergo such a restructuring process.'[23] In a letter to party headquarters written from his remote prison near Tepelena, Fatos Nano put forward a motion for reforming the SP. He advised bidding farewell to Marx by 'cutting him out of the party's programme'. However, the SP's headquarters received Nano's plea with little enthusiasm. Objections were immediately raised to many points in his proposed motion, which for the first time caused a major clash between the party Presidium and the Socialist leader himself, on whom the SP had relied for its policies for the last few years and during the recent election campaign. Up to the time of writing Berisha has resisted calls from human rights groups, including Amnesty International, to free Nano from prison.

It is a fitting epitaph for the first Berisha administration that the 1996 election represented such a major backwards step from the fair elections of 1992. Berisha now had firm control over

---

[22] *Zeri-i-Popullit*, 12 July 1996.

[23] ATA news agency, 3 July 1996.

parliament, the police, the judiciary and the media. The international community began to reappraise its relationship with Albania, with the EU halting any further development of a trade and cooperation agreement agreed earlier in the year. Why should Berisha have feared new elections if, as he said, so many Albanians supported him? He had also won international support because he represented a bastion of stability in an otherwise unstable region. However, in the light of the 1996 election his role had to be reviewed since he now appeared not to be able to maintain stability or democracy in his own country and had therefore become a dangerously unpredictable element. Albania's slow drive towards democracy had been put sharply into reverse. As Hoxha's bunkers became gradually covered over by grass and foliage, it was clear that his political heritage would be less easy to erase.

In the aftermath of this disastrous election, the DP government had to face many new difficulties. The first of these was the severe damage to the public relations success it had scored in the previous three years, projecting an image of Albania as a progressive and increasingly democratic country. The old stereotypes of violence and social disorder associated with the 'Years of Anarchy' in 1990–2 had recurred in the international press coverage of the election, and no amount of argument about the exact degree of manipulation and political chicanery could alter that. As the violence was clearly instigated by the police and paramilitary apparatus, and played out before the very eyes of diplomats and foreign reporters and observers, the usual claims by the DP administration that ex-secret policemen from the old regime were the instigators of all political disorder had no credibility.[24] The same applied to the electoral malpractices themselves, where the electoral process enabled previously uncommitted and non-specialist observers to see the reality of the Berisha political machine.

It is difficult to imagine favourable views of Albania being maintained within international organisations such as the Council of Europe. Possibly military organisations such as NATO will conduct 'business as usual' with Albania, but elsewhere this could prove difficult. Governmental and European Union aid flows may well decrease, and the country will be seen as a higher risk by

[24] See article by James Pettifer, *The World Today*, July 1996, pp. 180–1.

many foreign investors. Assassinations of public figures associated with the regime began to occur, as some elements in opposition resorted to violence. On 15 July 1996, the chief of the police commissariat of Pogradec, Agron Gjyrezi, was shot dead while sitting outside a café.[25] Events such as this must add to the overall impression of instability.

The inevitable pattern of criticism from international organisations and human rights groups is likely to accentuate Albanian isolationist trends which, once activated, are always a potent element in the national psychology. This will reduce the influence of Albania as a factor for stability in the region and, at the same time, the influence of foreign powers over Albanian foreign policy positions. In view of the deepening crisis in Kosova, this may be the most potent and difficult legacy of the May 1996 election. The diplomats and politicians who argued for the preservation of the DP regime at all costs in this election may have created a poisoned chalice.

It is also likely that the proponents of support for the DP administration in terms of 'stability' may find that their efforts have been fruitless. The corruption of the state involves not only politics and the manipulation of the general election but also the economy. The period between 1992 and the time of going to press (early 1997) has seen the emergence of financial conglomerates in Tirana offering to pay very high rates of interest on savings based on the model of 'Pyramid' banks elsewhere in Eastern Europe. The old phrase 'Albanian Pyramid', which originally referred to the archaic political structures of the country, has now taken on a new meaning. There are ample links between organised crime and at least some of these organisations, and signs that Albania may become a classic example of the development of what in Eastern Europe has come to be called 'anarchocapitalism'. The state will, in practice, be very weak and unable to discharge many of the normal functions of government for its citizens. Most available resources will be devoted to the security apparatus, which is designed to keep President Berisha in power indefinitely. There will be an absence of foreign investment and a return to many aspects of traditional 'Balkan' society of the pre–First World

[25] BBC, *SWB*, EE/2667 B/2, 18 July 1996. Also, a leading official in charge of prisons was assassinated a week later by unknown gunmen.

War era, with local satraps of the President exercising almost unlimited power in their regions. The international community will be expected to finance the crippled central state – also indifinitely. No serious political opposition to the government will be tolerated. If this turns out to be Albania's destiny, it will be a poor reward for those who risked their lives for democracy in the years of hope after 1990.

The collapse of many 'pyramid' schemes in December 1996 and early 1997, and the social disorder that accompanied it, makes this disappointing future more likely. Tens of thousands of Albanians lost their entire savings, and protest demonstrations were attacked by riot police. It appears that as much as $1 billion had accumulated in the 'pyramids' over the previous five years, and their total collapse would have wiped out a large proportion of the national capital.

The ultra-free market ideology of the government thus entered a stage of profound crisis, with the probability of far-reaching political consequences. The opposition attempted to develop a united democratic coalition, but the widespread and random arrests of politicians from both right and left demonstrated the fragile nature of democracy under the Berisha government, and forced the international community to recognise the reality of Albanian society in the Balkan crisis.[26]

---

[26] For accounts of the 'pyramid' crisis, see articles by James Pettifer, *Wall Street Journal*, 28 January 1997; Miranda Vickers, *The Independent*, 7 January 1997; and Richard Owen, *The Times*, 27-29 January 1997. For a report of the International Monetary Fund's warning to the Albanian government, see *Albanian Daily News*, 11 October 1996.

APPENDIXES

A

THE FIFTIETH ANNIVERSARY OF LIBERATION

Sir Reginald Hibbert gave the following account in April 1995 of the significance of this event in a communication to the authors:

Albania's Independence Day Celebrations on 28 November 1994 were given a novel colouring. The 50th anniversary of Albania's Liberation from Nazi-fascist occupation was celebrated on the same day. Previously 29 November was Liberation Day. As it used to be a principal festival in Enver Hoxha's time, it fell from favour after the fall of communism. Now the government adopted the day but altered the date. Old Partisans grumbled at being deprived of their date; those on the opposite wing, old Ballists, Zogists and 'nationalists', and more especially the émigré communities in America and Britain, were shocked to be asked to celebrate 'Liberation' as well as Independence. As far as they were concerned, Albania was enslaved in 1944, not liberated. Now, as during the war, resistance to communism was more important to them than resistance to German occupation.

During the celebrations in Tirana it became clear that the government was making a deliberate effort to fit the National Liberation War into respectable Albanian history while continuing to anathematise Enver Hoxha and communism. The banners of the wartime Brigades of the Albanian National Liberation Army (ANLA) were carried at the head of the military parade, followed by a phalanx of Partisan veterans. Various leaders of the wartime Levizja Nacional Clirimtare (LNC, the National Liberation Movement) were given decorations, some posthumously, some in person. They included several undoubted communists, of whom two had the great rarity value of being founder members of the Albanian Communist Party in 1941 and one the equal rarity value of being Moscow- and Comintern-trained. The common characteristic of all those who were honoured, whether by decorations or by being mentioned in the Prime Minister's keynote speech, was that they opposed or broke with Enver Hoxha soon after the war or were pushed aside or persecuted or liquidated by him.

In his speech before the gala concert on the eve of Independence and Liberation Day, Mr Aleksander Meksi, the Prime Minister, gave an explicit re-definition of Albania's wartime history. His central theme was the need for national unity. He saw the Peza Conference in 1942, where the LNC was formed, as a step in the right direction, but an insufficient step because it was communist-dominated and the nationalists stayed away and formed the Balli Kombetar. As a result, the Mukje conference in August 1943, at which the LNC and Balli Kombetar tried to get together, became the make or break point. According to Mr Meksi, it nearly suc-ceeded in bringing about the much-needed national unity, but this was dashed by Enver Hoxha, who would not share power and served the interests of the Yugoslavs.

At this point Kosova comes into the argument, because the Mukje discussions envisaged an ethnic Albania, with Kosova being allowed self-determination at the end of the war. It was this that the Yugoslavs could not stomach. Tito's emissary Vukmanovic Tempo happened to be visiting the Albanian comrades at the time and demanded that Hoxha should denounce the agreement. From this point onwards, although the LNC and the ANLA fought patriotically against the Germans, divided Albania spiralled downwards into the Hoxha dictatorship.

Mr Meksi's thesis was unity, and in the first place internal unity. This seemed natural enough for a government which had recently lost the referendum on a new constitution. It was time to try to recover some centre ground. Judicious rehabilitation of the LNC and ANLA point in that direction. While there are few families in Albania which did not suffer in some way under Enver Hoxha, there are also few which did not have some con-nection with the LNC and ANLA. The Albanian government has to govern a real Albania and not an imaginary Albania committed perpetually to a witch-hunt against vanished communism such as émigré circles tend to cherish.

Nevertheless, Mr Meksi's emphasis on Mukje carries implications for foreign policy. It implies a link between internal unity and the cause of ethnic unity, the aspiration for national unity with the Albanians of Kosova and Macedonia. It was notable that

'President Rugova' and 'Prime Minister' Bukoshi of Kosova were at President Berisha's side as the most honoured guests throughout the celebrations. The crisis in Kosova makes the process of re-writing Albania's wartime history an uneasy one, open to misunderstandings. It is one thing to denounce Enver Hoxha for denouncing Mukje: it is quite another to give the impression that the aim of an ethnic Albania which was altogether unrealistic in 1943 might be realistic today and might indeed be an essential component of the unity theme.

The Liberation Day celebrations in Tirana were made the occasion of finally correcting the record as regards Britain's wartime connection with Albania. The government invited as many of the wartime British Liaison Officers as they could find. Unfortunately, we are a dwindling band and only Colonel David Smiley and I were able to go. I was very glad I went, as it meant that those who served with the LNC and ANLA, i.e. with the Partisans, were represented as well as those who committed themselves unreservedly to Kupi and the 'nationalists'. Both Colonel Smiley and I were awarded the Order of Liberty, First Class. Honours were even, as they should always have been.

I was also able to stand beside Colonel Smiley and step up with him to lay wreaths at the inauguration on 27 November of the new British Commonwealth war cemetery in Tirana Park. The original cemetery was destroyed during Enver Hoxha's reign. The new cemetery has been laid out with headstones from the Commonwealth War Graves Commission near the monument to the Frasheri brothers, where the remains of the dead servicemen were consigned to an unmarked common burial by Hoxha. The new cemetery is pleasingly sited by a grove of trees. A central stela erected by the Albanian government commemorates the fallen in both languages. The inaugural service, conducted by an Anglican chaplain from Naples, was accompanied by full military honours by the Albanian army in the presence of the Albanian Minister of Defence, other high Albanian officials, the British ambassador, several Allied ambassadors, Service attachés including the Russians, and a large gathering of Albanian friends and sympathisers, including many old Partisans. I was very glad to be able, reciprocally, to lay a wreath next day at the Albanian national memorial at the ceremony led by President Berisha to commemorate those who fell in the Resistance, in effect the Partisans.

Much was re-written during the weekend of the celebrations. Much still remains to be re-written. For example, Mehmet Shehu's pre-eminent role in the war is ignored. His name is not mentioned, presumably because he stayed with Hoxha nearly to the end. One day he and others like him will also have to be re-incorporated into Albania's history. But that is a matter for the Albanians.

In conclusion, I would say that the commemoration ceremonies for the 50th anniversary of the Liberation were made the occasion for rehabilitating some of the Partisan leaders who took part in the National Liberation Movement and for reviving, as something to be honoured, the memory of the Partisan Brigades. Those who were rehabilitated were men whom Enver Hoxha had cast aside, persecuted or liquidated; but that was the fate which overtook most of his war-time colleagues. The effect has therefore been to give the National Liberation Movement a respectable place in Albanian history although it was communist-led, while maintaining the anathema on Enver Hoxha and all his works.

This deliberate extension of the national embrace to include the Partisan tradition was accompanied by a parallel gesture towards the British who played the principal Allied role in relation to Albania during the war. The post-communist government of Sali Berisha had hitherto reserved its respect and favours for the British officers who had worked with the Zogists in 1944 – Lord Amery, Colonel David Smiley and their companions. Those who had worked with the LNC and Partisans were treated coolly, if they came to attention at all. My history of SOE's activities in Albania and of the support given to the Partisans was sharply criticised in the government newspaper *Rilindja Demokratike* in 1992. At the commemoration of the Liberation in 1994, invitations were open to all surviving British liaison officers of 1943-5. Only Smiley and I were able to be there. We were accorded equal honours. In these ways the Partisan movement was restored to the national bosom, and the government adapted its stance in such a way as to appear more comprehensively national.[1]

---

[1] Some of the ex-SOE officers who were in Albania in the Second World War formed an important pro-Berisha lobby in London after April 1992. Although wartime protagonists like Lord (Julian) Amery were on the whole too old for active politics, their cause was taken up by other Conservatives. In 1993-5 their influence inhibited serious analysis in Conservative circles of the complications of the Albanian situation which the one-sided Berisha government was failing to deal with. See also Sir Reginald Hibbert, 'The War in Albania and the Conspiracy Theory', *Albania Life*, vol. 1, 1995.

B

ALBANIA: BASIC INFORMATION

Area	28,748 sq. km
Agricultural land (1992)	11,585 sq. km
GNP per capita (1993)	$422
Population (1992)	3,400,000
Urban population as proportion of total (1992)	36%
Projected population in year 2000	3,900,000
Population density (1992)	118 per sq. km
Population density of agricultural land (1990)	463 per sq. km
Population growth rate (1991)	2%
Urban population growth rate (1987-92)	2.7%
Life expectancy at birth (1992)	73 years
Crude death rate (1990)	5.6 per 1,000
Infant mortality (1992)	32 per 1,000 live births
Population per physician (1990)	731
Hospital beds per 1,000 inhabitants (1990)	5.8
Secondary school enrolment (1992)	45% of relevant age cohort
Illiteracy rate of population over age 10 (1989)	7.9%
Newspaper circulation (1990)	42 per 1,000 population
Labour force (1992)	1,700,000
Female share of labour force	52%

Sources: Albania, Directorate of Statistics; World Bank and IMF staff estimates, 1994-5.

Note. A number of these figures are probably under-estimates, particularly the rate of growth of urban population, illiteracy and GNP *per capita.*

C

THE LAST COMMUNIST GOVERNMENT OF ALBANIA, SEPTEMBER 1990

STATE

Presidium of the People's Assembly

Chairman (nominal head of state)	Ramiz Alia
Deputy Chairmen	Xhafer Spahiu
	Emine Guri
Secretary	Sihat Tozaj

GOVERNMENT

Council of Ministers

Prime Minister	Adil Çarcani
Deputy Prime Ministers	Hekuran Isai
	Pali Miska

Ministers

Agriculture	Pali Miska
Construction	Ismail Ahmeti
Education	Skender Gjinushi
Energy	Besnik Bekteshi
Finance	Andrea Nako
Food Industry	Ylli Bufi
Foreign Affairs	Reiz Malile
Foreign Trade	Shane Korbeci
Industry and Mining	Besnik Bekteshi
Internal Affairs	Hekuran Isai
Internal Trade	Pajtim Ajazi
Justice	Enver Halili
Light Industry	Bashkim Sykaj
People's Defense	Kiço Mustaqi
Public Health	Ahmet Kamberi
Transportation	Hajredin Çeliku

Minister to the Presidium of the Council of Ministers	Farudin Hoxha

296

Minister Secretary-General of the Council of Ministers	Niko Gjyzari
State Planning Commission	
Chairman	Bujar Kolaneci
State Control Commission	
Chairman	Simon Stefani

THE ALBANIAN WORKERS' PARTY (PLA) LEADERSHIP

Politburo

Members	Ramiz Alia
	Muho Asllani
	Besnik Bekteshi
	Foto Çami
	Adil Çarcani
	Hajredin Çeliku
	Vangjel Çerava
	Ms Lenka Çuko
	Xhelil Gjonj
	Hekuran Isai
	Pali Miska
	Kiço Mustaqi
	Simon Stefani
Candidate members	Xhemal Dymylja
	Llambi Gegprifti
	Niko Gjyzari
	Pirro Kondi
	Qirjako Mihali

Central Committee Secretariat

First Secretary	Ramiz Alia
Secretaries	Foto Çami
	Xhelil Gjoni
	Abdyl Backa

Party Control Commission

Chairman	Pilo Peristeri

D

THE 1991 ELECTIONS IN ALBANIA
REPRESENTATION OF PARTIES IN PEOPLE'S ASSEMBLY

Districts	Total	Party of Labour	Democratic Party	Omonia	Committee of Veterans
Berat	14	13	1	–	–
Diber	12	11	–	–	1
Durres	19	6	13	–	–
Elbasan	19	13	6	–	–
Fier	19	19	–	–	–
Gramsh	3	3	–	–	–
Gjirokaster	6	4	–	2	–
Kolonja	2	2	–	–	–
Kruja	8	4	4	–	–
Kukes	8	8	–	–	–
Lezha	5	3	2	–	–
Librazhd	5	5	–	–	–
Lushnja	11	9	2	–	–
Mat	6	6	–	–	–
Mirdita	4	4	–	–	–
Permet	3	3	–	–	–
Pogradec	5	5	–	–	–
Puka	4	4	–	–	–
Saranda	7	4	–	3	–
Skrapar	4	4	–	–	–
Shkoder	19	3	16	–	–
Tepelena	4	4	–	–	–
Tirana	29	10	19	–	–
Tropoja	3	3	–	–	–
Vlora	14	7	7	–	–
Total	250	169	75	5	1
%	100	67.6	30	2	0.4

Source: Statistical Yearbook of Albania, 1991.

E

THE 1992 GENERAL ELECTION AND ALBANIAN POLITICAL PARTIES UNDER DEMOCRACY

The elections in March 1992 were the first fully democratic elections in Albania's history, and for this reason they merit separate analysis. Eleven political parties participated. The electoral system used was a combination of majority voting in constituencies (100 seats) and proportional representation from national lists (40 seats). Eleven parties fielded candidates in the constituencies. Five were qualified to put forward lists, by having candidates in more than one-third of the constituencies. These were the Democratic, Socialist, Social Democratic, Republican and Agrarian parties.

Democratic Party

The first of the opposition parties to be formed remains the largest and is now the dominant party in Albania. Its leader was *Dr Sali Berisha*, now President of the Republic. Following his election to the Presidency he was replaced as Party leader by *Eduard Selami*, formerly the Party's general secretary. Its vice-chairmen, elected at its conference in September 1991, were *Neritan Ceka* (leader of the Parliamentary group), *Azem Hajdari* (student leader) and *Arben Imami*. Ceka has since resigned. Other leading members in its early days were *Gramoz Pashko* (Minister of Economics, June-November 1991) and *Genc Ruli* (Minister of Finance, June-November 1991). The Party was founded in December 1990, born out of the student revolt against the Albanian government and the PLA, and legalised on 19 December. It has a newspaper, *Rilindja Demokratike*.

In the 1992 campaign the Democratic Party put up candidates in 97 of the 100 constituencies and also had a list for the additional seats to be apportioned under the PR system. In February the Party said that it would be prepared to go into coalition with the Republican and Social Democratic Parties.

In the election the Democratic Party received over 60% of the vote and had 92 seats. It formed the government under Prime Minister *Aleksander Meksi*, with the Republican and Social Democratic Parties each having one portfolio. There were also two independents in the government.

Socialist Party

The PLA held its 10th Party Congress in June 1991 and emerged as the Socialist Party, having purged much of the old leadership and elected one of a more reformist character. *Fatos Nano*, previously Prime Minister and then Minister for Foreign Economic Relations, became the party leader. Its deputy chairmen were *Ismail Lleshi*, an academic lawyer, brought into the higher echelons of the Party in December 1990; *Spiro Dede,* a previous Party secretary; and *Xervet Pellumbi*. *Dritero Agolli*, formerly President of the Writers' Union, was probably the most outspoken critic of the previous policy during the Congress. It ended with a statement dissociating itself from much of its past activities and policies.

It is the only party to have contested all 100 constituencies in the election, and it put forward a list for the proportional element. It had 38 members in the National Assembly. However, it only managed to get six candidates elected through the constituencies and had to rely on the proportional element. *Fatos Nano* was one of the six. A number of former Ministers, including the ex-Prime Minister *Ylli Bufi*, were among those elected.

Republican Party

The Republican Party was the second opposition party to be formed after December 1990 and was legalised in early January 1991. Its chairman is *Sabri Godo*. It has a twice-weekly newspaper, *Republika*. The Party participated in the March 1991 elections, but it did not have the momentum of the Democratic Party; it was squeezed by the electoral system (50%+1) and had no representation in the Assembly, having only received 2% of the vote. In its early days before the 1991 elections it was also criticised by the DP for saying that President Alia was the only person who could 'maintain equilibrium'.

Social Democratic Party

The Social Democratic Party was legalised in April 1991. Its chairman is *Skender Gjinushi*, a professor and former Minister of Education (from 1987 to early 1991). The vice-chairmen, elected at its congress held in January 1992, were *Teodor Laco* and *Haxhi Aliko*. The General Secretary *Lisen Bshkurti* was previously secretary of the youth movement. The party, which claims to have about 25,000 members, received 4.3% of the votes in the election and has seven members of the National Assembly. Gjinushi was the only one elected from a constituency (he was not opposed by the DP)

Union for Human Rights

In the 1991 election the Greek minority supported a party called *Omonia* and three candidates were elected. Subsequently the government decided that this could not be a party because it was ethnically based, and its candidates were barred from the 1992 election. A new party was then created, in February 1992, called the Union for Human Rights, with ethnic Albanian as well as Greek members. The party contested the election, putting up 29 candidates, and received 2.9% of the votes, which gave it two members of the National Assembly. It is now known as Omonia.

Other parties

The Agrarian Party, which was legalised in February 1991, put up 46 candidates in the 1992 election and received 0.63% of the vote. In March 1991 it established a weekly newspaper, *Progresi Agrar*. The party claims to be of the centre, but appealing above all to the peasantry.

The Communist Party was formed at the beginning of 1992. Its chairman was *Hysni Milloshi*. It put up 31 candidates at the election but did not qualify to have a list. It received 0.4% of the vote.

The Christian Democratic Party had 11 candidates in the election and received 0.35% of the vote. Its chairman was *Gjergj Ndojaj* and its general secretary, *Vangjel Buli*.

The Ecology Party was one of the earliest parties to be formed, immediately after the foundation of the Democratic Party, and was legalised in January 1991. The chairman is *Namik Hoti*. It has a newspaper entitled *Albania*. It had 7 candidates in the 1992 election, but only received 0.04% of the vote.

The National Unity Party was established in March 1991. Its chairman is *Idajet Beqiri,* who was elected at its national conference held in July 1991. There is a party paper, *Kombi* (The Nation).

Minor parties

Democratic Alliance (September 1991)
Universal Party (January 1992)
National Democratic Party (August 1991; chairman *Fatmir Cekani*; pro-monarchist)
Independent-Centre Party (August 1991)
Albanian People's League (September 1991; chairman, *Sejdi Kondi*; general secretary, *Hasan Hasani*)
Political Association of Macedonians in Albania (September 1991)
Party of Democratic Prosperity (October 1991)
Legality Movement (February 1992)
Right National Alliance (February 1992)
Social Workers' Party (March 1992).
National Democratic Covenant Party (March 1992)
Right-Wing Republican Party (March 1992)
Social Reformist Party (May 1992)

Source: FCO/RAD.

F

THE DEMOCRATIC PARTY GOVERNMENT FORMED AFTER THE 1996 GENERAL ELECTION

Prime Minister	Aleksander Meksi
Deputy Prime Minister and Minister of Foreign Affairs	Tritan Shehu (also chairman of the Democratic Party)
Interior Minister	Halit Shamata
Finance Minister	Ridvan Bode
Defence Minister	Safet Zhulali
Justice Minister	Kristofor Peci
Minister of Industry Transport and Trade	Suzana Panariti
Minister of Mining and Energy Resources	Abdyl Xhaja
Minister of Public Works, Land Use and Tourism	Albert Brojka
Minister of Health and the Environment	Maksim Cikuli
Minister of Agriculture and Food	Bamir Topi
Minister of Education and Sports	Edmond Lutja
Minister of Higher Education and Scientific Research	Besnik Gjongecaj
Minister of Culture Youth and Women	Teodor Laco
Minister of Labour and Social Issues	Arlinda Keci
Minister of Privatization	Dylber Vrioni
Minister without Portfolio	Hasan Halili
General Secretary to Council of Ministers	Arjan Madhi
Secretary of State for Economic Relations at the Ministry of Foreign Affairs	Selim Belortajka
Secretary of State for Tourism at the Ministry of Public Works, Land Use and Tourism	Robert Ceku
Secretary of State for Local Government at the Interior Ministry	Njazi Kosovrasti
Secretary of State at the Defence Ministry	Leonard Demi
Secretary of State at the Ministry of Mining Resources and Energy	Sokol Bejteri

303

Secretary of State for Transport at the Ministry of Industry, Transport and Trade	Arben Babamero
Secretary of State for Sport at the Ministry of Education and Sports	Marjeta Pronjari
Secretary of State for Youth and Women at the Ministry of Culture, Youth and Women	Roza Pati

Source: Rilindja Demokratike, Tirana, 12 July 96.

G

EUROPEAN UNION PROGRAMMES IN ALBANIA
FUNDS ALLOCATED BY SECTOR EACH YEAR (*millions of ECU*)

	1991	1992	1993	1994	1995	1996-9 estimates
'Phare'	10	110	75	29	70	140
Heading B 7.500 (aid for economic restructuring of Central and East European countries), of which						
—Humanitarian aid	10	50	10	7	—	—
—Balance of payments support	—	35	35	—	35	—
Heading B 75020 (Cross-border cooperation)	—	—	—	20	18	72
Food aid	—	80	—	—	—	—
EIB loans	—	—	—	—	34	—
Other cooperation						
– on energy Heading B 4.1041 (Synergy)	—	—	0.27	0.7	0.77	—
– on the environment Heading B 7.8100 (Life)	—	0.255	0.33	0.8	0.346	—

H

ALBANIA'S PARLIAMENTARY ELECTIONS, 1996

	Votes[*]	% of votes	Seats	% of seats
Democratic Party	914,218	55.5	122	87.0
Socialist Party	335,40	20.4	10	7.0
Republican Party	94,567	5.7	3	2.0
National Front	81,822	5.0	2	1.5
Union for Human Rights	66,529	4.0	3	2.0
Legaliteti	34,019	2.1	—	—
Social Democratic Union	32,430	2.0	—	—
Democratic Alliance	25,679	1.5	—	—
Social Democratic Party	25,019	1.5	—	—
Christian Democratic Party	21,068	1.3	—	—
Democratic Union Party	11,789	0.7	—	—
National Unity Party	3,939	0.2	—	—
Total	1,344,619		140	
(Voter turnout 89%)				

[*] First round of voting, 26 May 1996

Sources: Rilindja Demokratike, 22 June 1996, p. 2, and 3 July 1996, p. 2; and International Republican Institute, *IRI Observation Report on the Albanian Parliamentary Elections of May 26, 1996* (Washington, DC, 1996), p. 32.

SELECT BIBLIOGRAPHY ON CONTEMPORARY ALBANIA

Albania (World Bibliographical Series, vol. 9), ed. Antonia Young, Oxford: Clio Press, 1997.

Alia, Ramiz, *Report to the 9th Congress of the Party of Labour of Albania*, Tirana, 1986.

——, *Our Enver*, Tirana, 1987.

——, *Une, Ramiz Alia*, Tirana: Dituria, 1993.

Biberaj, Elez, *Albania, A Socialist Maverick*, Boulder, CO: Westview Press, 1990.

——, 'Albania at the Crossroads', *Problems of Communism*, Sept.-Oct. 1991.

——, *Albania in Transition*, Boulder, CO: Westview Press, 1999.

Danaj, Koço, *Totalitarizmi në Marrëdhëniet Ndërkombëtare*, Tirana 1996.

Drakuli, Slavenka, *Café Europa*, London: Abacus, 1996.

Elsie, Robert, *Kosovo – In the Heart of the Powder-Keg*, Boulder, CO: East European Monographs, 1999.

Hadji-Ristic, Peter, 'Shaking Albania's Torpor', *Index on Censorship*, 1/1991.

Hibbert, Reginald, *Albania's National Liberation: the Bitter Victory*, London, 1991.

History of the Albanian Party of Labour, Tirana, 1976.

Horvat, Branko, *Kosovsko Pitanje*, Zagreb, 1989.

Hoxha, Enver, *Selected Works*, Tirana, 1989.

——, *The Khrushchevites*, Tirana, 1980.

——, *The Titoites*, Tirana, 1982.

——, *The Anglo-American Threat to Albania*, Tirana, 1982.

——, *Laying the Foundation of the New Albania*, Tirana, 1984.

——, *Vepra* (Works), 71 vols, Tirana, 1968-85.

Kadare, Ismail, *Doruntine*, London: Saki, 1992.

——, *Albanian Spring*, London: Saki, 1995.

Krasniqi, R., 'Persecution of Religion in Communist Albania', *ACEN News*, no. 128 (March/April 1967).

Marori, Miodrag, *Balkanski Dzoker-Albanija i Albanci*, Bar (Montenegro), 1995.

Pettifer, James, *The Blue Guide to Albania*, London, 1994.

—— (ed.), *The New Macedonian Question*, London: Macmillan, 1999.

Pipa, Arshi, *The Politics of Language in Socialist Albania*, New York, 1989.

——, *Albanian Stalinism*, New York, 1990.

Pipa, Arshi, and Sami Repishti, *Studies on Kosova*, New York, 1984.

Prifti, Peter R., *Socialist Albania since 1944*, Cambridge, MA, 1978.

Shehu, Bashkim, *L'automne de la peur*, Paris: Fayard, 1993.

Shnytzer, Adi, *Stalinist Economic Strategy in Practice: The Case of Albania*, Oxford, 1982.

Ushtria Çlirimtare e Kosovës. Dokumente dhe Artikuj (Documents of the Kosovo Liberation Army), Aarau (Switzerland), 1998.

Vickers, Miranda, *The Albanians – A Modern History*, London, 1995.

——, 'The Status of Kosova in Socialist Yugoslavia', *Bradford Studies on South Eastern Europe* (University of Bradford), 1994.

——, *Between Serb and Albanian: A History of Kosovo*, London, 1998.

Winnifrith, Tom (ed.), *Perspectives on Albania*, Basingstoke: Macmillan, 1992.

Newspapers, Periodicals and Documents

Radio Free Europe Reports, 1981-9.

Republic of Albania Public Investment Programme, 1996-1998, Tirana, 1996.

Tanjug (official Yugoslav news agency), Belgrade.

Oxfam Report on Albania, Oxford 1992.

Greek Helsinki Committee for Human Rights, 'Report on the Parliamentary Elections of 22 March 1992 and the Political Rights of the Greek Minority', *Balkan Studies*, vol. 34, no.1 (1993).

The Contract of the Democratic Party with Albania, Tirana, 1995.

Koha Jone, Tirana, 1993-6.

Zeri-i-Popullit, Tirana, 1989-96.

Rilindja Demokratia, Tirana, 1990-6.

Koha, Pristina, 1994-6.

Koha Ditore, Pristina, 1997-9.

Flaka, Skopje, 1991-6.

Kosova 'Infofax', New York, 1992.

Illyria, New York 1991-6.

The World Today, London, 1989-96.

The Times, London, 1989-99.

The Guardian, London, 1989-99.

The Independent, London, 1989-99.

The Financial Times, London, 1989-99.

Ta Nea, Athens, 1988-95.

Kathimerini, Athens 1989-95.

Neue Zürcher Zeitung, Zurich, 1989-95.

East European Newsletter, London, 1992-5.

Albanian Observer, Tirana, 1994-5.

Albanian Economic Tribune, Tirana, 1993-5.

BBC Summary of World Broadcasts, London, 1988-95.

Foreign Affairs, Washington, DC, May 1995.

Albanian Telegraphic Agency, Tirana, 1988-95.

INDEX

abortion, 140

Academy of Sciences, 122, 153

Adriatic coast, 209, 213, 215

Adriatic Sea, 1, 25, 51, 219

Agence France Presse (AFP), 91, 93

Agolli, Dritero, 69, 301

Agrarian Party, 55, 56, 67, 300, 302

agriculture, 5, 25, 84

Ahmed Mohammed Ali, 104

Ahmeti, Ismail, 297

Ahmeti, Vilson, 75, 240, 241

Ajazi, Pajtim, 297

Albania, 303

Albania: 'Balkan Gulag', 3; economy,
3, 6, 7, 14, 130, 241, 269- 70; history, 8; atheist state, 12; flight from,
29; isolation ended, 40; name
change, 63; demise of industry, 66;
seen as Islamic, 104; state and religion, 107-8; Catholics, 109; religious
tolerance, 110; Orthodox, 111-13;
Evangelicals, 113-16; Christians,
114; BBC broadcasts, 127; crime,
128-31; food-aid, 135-7; macho
mentality, 139; population growth,
140; and Kosova, 142-65; and
Macedonia, 166-80; and Montenegro, 180-5; ethnic minorities,
186-208; and Islamic world, 218;
freedom of speech, 239; foreign
debt, 240; basic information, 296

Albanian(s): migrants, 4; political life,
9; pyramid, 10, 289; society 10, 289;
society, 10; industry, 14; gold reserves, 29; government, 42; politics,
50; life, 76; Islamic community,
103; Americans, 109, 151, 159;
average age, 116; folk art, 119;

roads, 126; drug traders, 135; national identity, 142, 211; army, 154;
in FYROM, 166, 167, 171, 172,
173, 174, 175, 176, 177, 178, 179,
180, 183, 221; in Balkans, 169; in
Montenegro, 180-5; expelled from
Greece; emigration to Greece, 200;
foreign policy, 209; gold, 224; electorate, 287; political parties, 300-3

Albanian Communist Party, 77, 78, 85

Albanian-American Civic League, 60,
151

Albanian League of Youth, 21

Albanian National Liberation Army
(ANLA), 291, 292, 293

Albanian Orthodox Church, 111, 112,
113, 151, 198

Albanian Party of Labour: *see* PLA

Albanian People's League, 303

Albanian Union of Writers and Artists,
69

Albanian Workers' Party, 83

Albanianism, 96

Albanological studies, 222

Albfilm, 124

Albturist, 119

Alia, Ramiz: 4, 5, 11, 12-13, 14, 15,
17, 19, 20, 21, 22, 23, 24, 25, 28,
30, 31, 32, 35, 36, 37, 39, 42, 44,
46, 47-8, 49, 50, 51, 52, 53, 54,
56, 60, 62, 63, 64-5, 67, 69, 75,
77, 92, 102, 114, 129, 147, 148,
149, 168, 190, 191, 214, 222, 223,
228, 233, 246, 258, 263, 275, 297,
298, 301; loses seat, 58; decides to
resign, 81; under arrest, 91; sentenced to jail, 257; released, 267

Alieanca, 250

311